THE INVISIBLE HAND

BUSINESS, SUCCESS & SPIRITUALITY

DAVID GREEN

I did not seek change. Change came to me.
I did not seek spirituality. Spirituality came to me.
I did seek material success. Material success came to me.

None of this could have been achieved without the Invisible Hand.
This book is dedicated to the warriors and the worriers
on the road to material and spiritual success.

The author is donating 50% of his profits from the book to charity with the main aim to inspire and help people who are less fortunate than ourselves.

Publisher: Masters & Son Limited, St Peter Port, Guernsey, Channel Islands
www.mastersandson.co.uk

Cover, book design & typesetting: Matt Swann Creative

Cover concepts: Michelle Fine & Silke Steber-Martin

ISBN 978-0-9926487-0-1

CONTENTS

INTRODUCTION

Eighteen years ago I was an ambitious, focussed entrepreneur enjoying life. After starting to train for a charity trek, a bad back injury, which had previously prevented me from sitting down for a year, returned with a vengeance. That night I received a life-changing healing experience. When I woke up the next morning, I was able to stand up straight again, free of pain, free of injury. This stunned me. I was taken aback and lost for words – I could find no rational explanation. A dormant energy had been awakened within. What had happened? It was beyond all of my experience and knowledge. As if struck by invisible lightning, my life changed in an instant. Overnight, without desire, logic, preparation or thought, the spiritual path had opened up to me.

Before this monumental event, my married life consisted of excessive work mixed with travel, good food and wine. I was incredibly busy and had no time or interest for spirituality, yet when this awakening arrived, unannounced in the midst of my working life, it even accelerated the material success that eventually came to me. Through amazing grace, incredible good fortune and sheer hard work I was able to retire at the age of 42.

My experience shows that even busy people are perfect candidates for meditation. So how did I find the time to meditate? I concluded logically that if I could find the time to be stressed and restless, then I could find at least fifteen minutes each day to meditate to be calm and contented. Meditation also helped me to become more efficient and focussed when I worked extreme hours. So is it worth meditating for a short period? The sage *Vasishta* in *Yoga Vasishta*, an ancient text, states that thirteen seconds of meditation has the same auspiciousness as giving away a valuable possession to charity; 101 seconds of meditation gives the same merit as performing a sacred rite and twelve minutes of meditation multiplies the merit 1,000 fold.

As I became more in tune with this invisible power within, my worldly success was enhanced by my spiritual practice and my spiritual practice was enhanced by my experience in the material world. On both paths the common theme is to continue when difficulties arise and to proceed even when the eventual result is not apparent.

I fully respect that following and practising religion in the traditional sense is important for some, yet I empathise with the non-religious reader for whom the words "God" and "religion" may be off-putting. I have never been religious. For the first thirty years of my life I was agnostic with no interest at all in religion, yoga or spirituality. "My God" who I often refer to as the Invisible Hand, God or the Divine, represents a hidden, loving and guiding force that gives love to everybody and not just to the exclusive few who practise – and preach about – religion. My God is beyond religion and does not discriminate. My God encourages love and generosity, not fear and greed.

The portrayal of a heaven and hell scenario with the threat of a vengeful God for those who do not conform or toe the line never attracted me. The "religion" that I have adopted is to be a better person, to be kind, loving and forgiving to others and myself. When I fail dismally I try again. I have become aware that the Invisible Hand is guiding, loving and protecting me even when I am immersed in day-to-day life. Surely this same hand is helping everybody.

I am reminded of a beautiful story. If a person carries out 99 good deeds and makes one mistake, other people will remember the one bad deed and not the 99 good ones. If a person makes 99 mistakes and carries out one good deed, *my* God will remember the one good deed and forgive the 99 mistakes.

In this book I share my experiences of business, success and spirituality. I describe strange, mystical experiences in Egypt, how I meet different spiritual masters, learn about meditation and how at the same time I establish and build a business until it is sold, setting me up for life. I share my observations regarding the different people I have met in business and spirituality that have shaped and inspired me. Finally I expand on some of the spiritual teachings and practices taught to me by two realised masters from India over the last 15 years. These teachings, many of which are not widely known in the West – or even in the East, have helped me to find more balance and contentment.

The reader may find some of my experiences extraordinary – just as I did, yet those who know me will tell you that I am rational, methodical and logical. These life-changing events have overtaken any preconceptions that I had, are authentic, requiring no embellishment. I have discovered that the material and spiritual paths run parallel to each other. Both paths require courage, endeavour and discipline to overcome the obstacles, difficulties and aggression that arise along the way.

I am grateful to all of those who have helped me proceed on the jagged edge of life.

CHAPTER 1

IN AT THE DEEP END

I asked the Great Master: "What is the purpose of life?"

He replied: "You are only born for Self-realisation.
You are only born to find the truth of life.
Every action in this world is for that purpose."

"Speak!" The 91-year-old Great Master stared at me through his round, silver-rimmed glasses with a huge grin. His beard was white and his face wrinkle-free. As an entrepreneur I was used to meeting different people but not spiritual masters! This was my first personal *darshan* with him. *Darshan* means receiving a blessing or literally "the vision". I remained calm inside but it was sweltering in his small room and my pulse was racing much faster than usual. The central heating was on yet the outside temperature was 28 degrees! It was as if he knew my every thought and all the questions I wanted to ask. As he spoke, his hands danced elegantly with slow, gentle movements. I had the uncanny feeling of being with someone who knew me already although we had never met. In his presence, for the first time in my life I felt total peace, joy and calmness. As we talked, he nodded encouragingly in a knowing and loving way.

"Hari is the destroyer," he said, "and also the sun! It is hot, is it not?"

I was sweating, yet he was as dry as the desert!

I had come to Florida from London a few days before for one reason only. I wanted to meet the Great Master.

My close friend Dan had arrived here some months earlier. Dan had travelled around India for a year searching for his guru. One day he arrived at an ashram near Calcutta and the senior monk told him that his guru was in America. He could not quite believe that a guru was sitting in an ashram in Florida but, following some kind of gut instinct, he took this advice and, after meeting the Great Master, had stayed with him ever since. I on the other hand had no desire to find a guru or to learn yoga or meditation. My image of yoga was one of people stretching their beautiful, supple bodies into various contortions, followed by a pungent concoction of carrot juice, wheatgrass and spinach, all the time talking about the universe and how we are all one! This was just not me at all. However, when Dan told me it was possible to have a private audience with the Great Master, I was somehow intrigued and wanted to meet him.

The white angels (his devotees) fluttered around him, not really sure how to behave or how to please him. Some walked about in silence, avoiding eye contact, while others took the role of self-appointed guards of the Great Master. They worked tirelessly in the gardens, tending the banana and mango trees and the hundreds of rosebushes that had been lovingly planted around the grounds. In the stifling, humid heat, no matter how many hours they devoted to weeding the lush garden, more weeds would emerge the next day. As I entered the ashram gates for the first time, I caught my first glimpse of the Great Master who was in the garden instructing and directing his devotees on how to graft mango trees together. He acknowledged me, smiled and touched my face, but said nothing. His skin was very fair yet his demeanour was distinctly Indian. He had only just stopped travelling around the world teaching yoga. He had left India to teach in the West at the age of 67 and had finally stopped travelling when he was 90.

The next day in the afternoon, fifteen of us were sitting in front of the Great Master under the inviting shade of the veranda. To begin with he was talking generally but in time he focussed his gaze straight into my eyes. He pointed towards me with his long forefinger and said, "I will tell you about foggy London!" It was the first time that he had spoken to me. He proceeded to tell me how he had visited London in 1973 without a visa. He had arrived from Belgium by boat and carefully chose which line to join, sensing which customs officer would be his "visa" for entry to the United Kingdom. The visa officer was intrigued that anyone would risk coming by boat without a visa.

"You are my visa," he told the officer with a smile.

As he cleared Customs, some people became curious and began to follow him. Having taken the train to London, he taught them Kriya Yoga, an ancient non-sectarian yoga and meditation technique. He also recounted how he had spoken at Speakers Corner in Hyde Park. After he finished his story, he said to me reassuringly, "We will teach you, we will teach you." I was trying to keep control of my thoughts in front of him, particularly the negative ones.

The day before my private meeting with him, I had received initiation into Kriya Yoga. There are many different yogas taught in the world which give the recipient mainly physical benefits. Kriya Yoga differs as it is a complete meditation technique giving all round mental, physical and emotional benefits. I would later discover that Mahatma Gandhi and Mother Teresa took initiation into

Kriya Yoga and it is the only yoga mentioned by the sage Patanjali, in his *yoga sutras*, often referred to as the 'bible of yoga'. This ancient practice should only be taught by the guru or through his appointed, experienced teachers. The whole technique, including some simple physical positions (asanas), is carried out with eyes closed and attention kept on the breath. Luckily for me, flexibility is not necessary and the technique can be practised on the floor, cross-legged, lying down or sitting in a chair depending on one's physical ability. It can be practised anywhere in normal clothes without breaking sweat.

Initiation in the spiritual context is a ceremony where the teacher or master purifies the seven main *chakras* (which are energy centres) located around the spine and the head. The word initiation is derived from the Latin word "initium" meaning beginning. Initiation marks a new beginning in the person's life and is not some strange ceremony where you hand over all of your possessions or where you are blindfolded or brainwashed! For me it was a beautiful ceremony where the teacher placed his hands over my *chakras* and chanted prayers in Sanskrit. I felt such purity that the experience brought tears to my eyes. I felt an incredible sense of inner focus and profound love. It was as if some part hidden deep inside was suddenly, finally revealing itself to me, all this in stark contrast to my uncomfortable stiff body as I attempted to sit cross-legged on the floor. A natural-born yogi I certainly was not. My last memory of sitting on the floor was being force-fed warm milk at kindergarten! This was far more nourishing.

During the initiation process, the initiate is able to perceive the divine sound otherwise known as the AUM or OM sound. AUM is chanted by many people who go to yoga classes. However, the AUM sound can be heard continuously without chanting. It is likely that many people around the world are actually already hearing the AUM sound but they and their doctors think they are suffering from tinnitus – which is something quite different. The AUM sound is pleasant and comforting once the recipient knows how to focus on it. Apparently there are fifty different sounds deriving from AUM that people can perceive. It can manifest as anything from a flute sound or a high-pitched whistle to a low rumbling sound and many others in between.

Apart from the divine sound, the initiate can perceive two other main inner manifestations during the process of initiation. These are divine light and divine vibration. I had already experienced divine sound and vibration before my initiation, but only experienced inner light a few times. The teacher who initiated me was a monk who was dressed in bright orange clothes. He asked me whether I could feel the vibration. My whole body was vibrating as if an electric current was passing through me.

"Can you hear the sound?"

Yes, I could. It was a distinct rumbling sound.

"Can you see the light?"

No, I could not. Inwardly I thought, *let's see if he can bring the light.* I could only see darkness with my eyes firmly shut. I was almost betting that nothing would come. The monk touched the back of my head. Suddenly I jolted backwards involuntarily. A light switch had been flicked on inside my head. I was in warp mode, *Star Trek*-style! A moving tunnel of light with black and white specks appeared from nowhere as if I was travelling through a void at great speed. I could not believe it. This was not my imagination! Even I was impressed.

Why am i here?

In my first private audience with the Great Master the day after initiation, I asked him many questions about life and spirituality. He answered each of my questions, smiling patiently. Then a question came to me:

"What is the purpose of life?"

He replied, "You are only born for Self-realisation. You are only born to find the truth of life. Every action in this world is for that purpose."

I was taken aback. *What is he talking about?* I thought to myself. I was 34 years old and nobody had ever told me this before. I had been taught by my father, a self-made man, that the purpose of life was to be successful in the world.

My spiritual and religious upbringing had consisted of being raised in a non-observant Jewish family who went to synagogue three times a year. God and religion were never discussed. I intensely disliked being dragged along to synagogue on religious holidays as I found the whole process hypocritical and boring. I witnessed how the men talked about football or business, while the women discussed fashion or relationships. Meanwhile I was sent to a traditional Church of England boarding school from the age of eight which meant that I had to attend church every day until I was eighteen. At least these services had rather more sincerity to them and I do remember quite a few hymns although I did decline an invitation to become a chorister after thirty minutes singing in the choir.

Because of my upbringing, I had no interest at all in religion. On reflection, I was probably more of a believer than a non-believer but I was nevertheless agnostic. I did not pray and never contemplated for a moment whether or not there was a God. This lack of interest in religion and spirituality continued. When I finished school at eighteen having decided not to go to university, I doggedly pursued a career in finance.

My main goal and ambition was to be successful and to enjoy the fruits of my labour. My father's message was simple: I could have what I wanted if I worked hard. Through this conditioning, I thought that making money and enjoying the trappings that came with financial success was the key to happiness. I worked hard and played hard like many others with the aim to retire early. Only later would I truly realise that money cannot buy love, calmness, good health and peace of mind. I would also understand further that the skills and disciplines required to make money were in my case an essential form of spiritual training which would lead me to see how spiritual consciousness and fulfilment were the real key to joy and success.

Boarding school education had helped me develop from a shy quiet child, who had come from a difficult family environment, into an independent, confident person with well-honed survival instincts. The school had brought the best out of me. I was no more than average academically, but an inner belief and confidence developed. I saw that hard work put me on a par with my more intelligent peers. Although I enjoyed competition in sports and academic pursuits, if others were more talented, I was rarely envious or disappointed if they beat me or finished above me in class. Instead their ability showed me what I could achieve with more practice and hard work.

These early imprints helped me realise at the start of my career that doing any job well was hugely satisfying. In turn my efforts were recognised in the form of financial reward and client satisfaction. This motivated me. To earn money unfairly was of no interest. Doing a job ethically and striving for excellence were vital to me.

In conclusion, my first religion was ambition. In due course this would help me recognise that gaining materially is nothing more than a manifestation of spiritual freedom.

So how did a non-religious, cynical, material-seeking person find himself in front of an Indian guru?

IT'S A KINDA MAGIC

One night, having dinner with my family, I picked up a newspaper that I rarely read. Inside was an advertisement for a trek to raise money for a children's charity. I thought it sounded like a good idea and cut it out. I went home and announced to my wife Joy that we should do the trek. She asked me how I intended to do a trek when I would not even walk to the local supermarket. Joy had a point as, after suffering a series of back injuries, my squash days were well and truly over. The next day I began training for the first time in five years. A run would be a good start, I thought. At the time I was 31. My mind told me I was young and fit again, but my legs and lungs objected and followed only reluctantly. On the third day I slipped a disc in my lower back and was bent over, twisted and in agony. This old injury had returned with a vengeance. It was as bad as it had been when I first suffered it many years earlier. The last time this had happened I could barely sit down and needed physio three times a week for a year while having to stand up at work. I was cursing.

By chance Dan was coming over for dinner that night. On seeing my agony he asked if I wanted him to do some healing on me. In recent years he had become disillusioned with his work in commercial property and had been experimenting in the New Age world. In spite of our close friendship he had never discussed it with me. I did not believe in healing at all, but was in such pain that I agreed. I had nothing to lose. He stood behind me and put his hands near my back. I could feel an intense heat in my lower back even though he did not touch me. He continued this for ten minutes. I thought nothing further of it and after dinner went to bed early.

The next day the pain had disappeared. I was able to stand up straight. I could not believe it. This was not my imagination. Something extraordinary had happened. On waking up that morning, I felt a strange, wholly unfamiliar energy in my body and in particular in my hands. This tingling sensation, with its mix of heat and vibration, varied in intensity from gentle to more powerful electric shockwaves. It was as if I had been plugged into an invisible grid. I was experiencing something indescribable and intangible. My back pain had left me. Before getting out of bed, I stopped for a few seconds and contemplated what had happened to me. Then the thought arrived: *I bet I can do that.* This experience was the catalyst that, in an instant and forever, changed my life.

Mystical egypt

As I continued to ask questions of the Great Master, I remembered a mysterious, but inexplicable experience that happened shortly after my healing epiphany. I asked him, "What was Egypt all about?"

I could picture myself in Egypt again.........

After my healing experience I began to explore more about energy and meditation, so when I was invited by Dan to join a spiritual group to the Pyramids I decided to go. So here I was, a straight-laced businessman, en route to the Great Pyramid in the dead of night in a rickety bus with a psychic, a white witch and others who practised other dubious New Age professions! Happily I was not wearing my habitual uniform of a suit and tie – that way I would have stood out more starkly and felt even more awkward than I did already.

The silence was intense as the group headed away from the hotel in our minibus towards the Great Pyramid. This was not the time to be afraid. Eighteen of us had arrived in Egypt ten days before. Some, including myself, were uncertain why we had joined the trip. When we compared notes, it seemed that there was no real rhyme or reason for why we had come, yet there was a collective sense among us that we were somehow destined to be together and that one way or another our lives would never be the same again. Dan was the group leader. He told us he was taking us to the important Egyptian "energy" centres to receive codings that would supposedly be of paramount importance to our futures and to pray for more Light in the world. This was all hocus-pocus to me, but it sounded intriguing so I went with the flow. During the trip, coincidences kept occurring, confirming our visit was far from ordinary. As we travelled along the Nile, each time we stopped unannounced at a temple, priests in white would appear from nowhere to welcome us and take us to restricted areas of the temples where they performed ceremonies. It felt as if I had been transported directly from my sober business world into a bizarre sci-fi movie in which I had a starring, but unscripted role.

The last day of our visit to Egypt was timed to conclude with an evening inside the Great Pyramid on the full moon on the day of Buddha's birthday. As I was later to discover it was also the birthday of the Great Master. The atmosphere in the hotel lobby even hours before we left for the Great Pyramid was electric. Another group had also planned their visit for the same day. They were in the hotel lobby awaiting their bus, dressed in long, elaborately decorated robes. I sensed a dark, chilling energy around them. Was I being paranoid or was my sixth sense correct? Who were they? Later I would learn that they belonged to a group known as the Acharnin which is the Aramaic word for "the Others". They were unhappy that our group had secured exclusive access to the Pyramid for midnight on that auspicious evening while they had to settle for carrying out their own ceremonies in the early evening.

When I recall these experiences and thoughts, even as I write this, I still wonder how a down to earth, unimaginative entrepreneur found himself in such a surreal set of circumstances. This was not a dream. Yet here I was, and this is what happened......

It soon emerged that some of the Acharnin unconnected to the other group had signed up to be part of our trip. They had carefully worked their way around us since arriving in Egypt, interested to find out about our individual fears, subtly probing for weaknesses. It was as if they were hoping to spread doubt and fear among us in order to destabilise our focus on the Light. They had offered "healing sessions" to several members of the group who then suffered from various illnesses, fatigue and some had endured terrifying dreams. These illnesses and nightmares that had spread amongst the group had not been a coincidence. As this hidden picture unfolded I somehow knew that we were here to learn who we were and that whatever faith we possessed in the forces of good was going to be sorely tested.

My previous experience, only a few days before our last night in the Great Pyramid, near the ancient city of Saqqara, had been profound. On that day we had descended 200 metres underground into a catacomb. I was at the front of the group and felt some invisible but unmistakeable force within driving me to proceed ever faster down the narrow rusty spiral metal staircase. I was being pulled inexorably onwards down the stairs as if being drawn in by a powerful magnet. The air within this mysterious place became thick with arid dust which soon coated the lining of my throat. When we reached the bottom of the stairs we were met by the keeper of the tomb. He gestured for us to follow him, wanting to take us to the opening on the right, but intuitively I wanted, needed to go straight ahead. He beckoned three times but I was not going to be told otherwise. Something was telling me to go that way.

Eventually the tomb-keeper yielded and led the way. We approached the opening in front of us, illuminated only by a row of bare electric light-bulbs. As I entered, I noticed at once that in the ground was an open tomb made of white rock. The chamber was small. Only five of us could fit through the opening. I felt focussed only on what was ahead of me and had forgotten the rest of the group who were behind me and wanted to know why we had stopped. I saw one of the Acharnin from our group yet somehow her presence felt insignificant to me. Then suddenly and without warning my body began to convulse uncontrollably. My mind was void of all thought and I felt neither pain nor fear and yet I found myself sobbing – tears streaming down my face. It was as if I had stumbled upon a long-hidden memory buried deep in my subconscious – no words could explain my experience. I had been plugged directly into a distant memory socket. My friend Michelle comforted me, rubbing my back gently and, touched as I was by this gesture of tenderness and warmth, I felt no need for reassurance. There was nothing wrong with me at all. It was more of a release, a glorious awakening. It felt like coming home only this time I was arriving at a home that I had never consciously visited before. Gradually my spasms subsided and I retreated from the cave opening and proceeded back into the corridor to the left, where the tomb-keeper had initially wanted to lead us. Walking through a portal at the end of this corridor, I entered an exquisitely beautiful room, one that looked as if it had remained untouched for thousands of years. The ceiling was adorned with images of the moon and the stars which had been lovingly and carefully hand-painted in gold and Aztec blue. The walls were painted with images depicting a series of tales of a young boy and his life, accompanied by ancient Egyptian hieroglyphic text. Somehow I felt inextricably linked with this boy. These images had been created several millennia ago and yet it felt uncannily as if I was looking at myself as a young child in a different life.

My tears were now long gone having dissolved into a sense of profound inner joy. I felt elated, cleansed – purity was pouring through me. An invisible switch had been turned on fully and my body was vibrating and connected to a pure infinite life-force of love and divinity. My companions Lionel, Françoise and Elisha joined me to share the moment. I was – and remain – a logical person. What on earth had just happened to me and why? I was a straightforward, level-headed individual who relied on his unshakeable rationality. In that split second I just knew that I could no longer rely on sensible, careful analysis or my tried and tested beliefs. For in that place, at that moment I could not escape the sense, the profound intuitive knowledge that I had returned home. This was the place of my ancestors.

The experience had overwhelmed me. It swept away any preconceived feelings and thoughts, but left me utterly calm and composed. The Light engulfed my body. Invisible jump leads had been connected to my head, hands and feet. I was alive, pulsating and full of energy which I wanted to share with the world! In less than one hour I had been given a wholly unexpected and unimaginable experience. I felt huge release and lightness in my body.

Once we returned to the bus the rest of the group was eager to share in my experience and find out what had happened to me. I was happy to share my feelings and emotions. Words tumbled out of my mouth almost meaninglessly as I tried to relay eloquently the event which had just taken place. It was impossible to put into words – I was attempting to express the inexpressible. Sensing this, Dan pulled me quietly to one side and suggested that I be still for a while and calm myself down. He knew that nobody would really be able to relate to my experience.

As the sun set behind the Sphinx, we headed back to the hotel in preparation for our first night in the Great Pyramid. We lazed around in the lobby area. One of the Acharnin who had avoided me for most of the trip, approached me and invited me to share my experience with her. I would later discover she was the leader of the Acharnin. She was obviously fascinated but at the same time seemed cold to my joy. Just as I was starting to talk, Dan came down the stairs and asked if I could spare him a moment. We found a quiet corner as he told me, "All I want to say is that some of us are here for different reasons and I just wanted to bring this to your attention."

My eyes had been opened. He did not need to say any more. Everything was suddenly clear. I had felt all along that something was wrong but had not been able to put my finger on it. As I reflected back on Dan's warning and to all the illnesses and nightmares that were being experienced I could now see that the Acharnin had an ulterior motive – to spread darkness and convert some of us to their cause. Joy, my wife at the time, later told me how she had been asked to speak about her own fears. Meanwhile two of the Acharnin had performed a "healing" ritual on Louise at the Valley of the Queens. Afterwards she was violently ill with a high fever and panic. They were, it seems, trying to take her over to the dark side. She was deeply shaken and really frightened.

Before the balanced, grounded reader takes me for a madman, please be assured that the cynical, dogmatic businessman was still very intact. I went into Louise's room to see if I could assist her in any way. When I entered she looked like she had seen a ghost and was suffering from fear, nausea and extreme discomfort. Dan was already guiding her through a visualisation process to free her from the discomfort and discordant energy which was clinging to her. I sat quietly on the bed facing her as she sat in the chair with her eyes closed unaware that I had entered the room. Calm began to fill the room as Louise was being purified and released from the darkness which had been infused into her body. I focussed on the Light pouring through her and prayed for her. Suddenly, as if a dark force had been wrenched from inside of her, Louise became radiant and peaceful, smiling and laughing with her usual *joie de vivre*. Had she been possessed? In front of my own eyes I had witnessed a complete transformation occur. She had found her way back into the Light. I made my way back to my room and reflected quietly on the events of the day. The zenith was yet to come.

The Great Pyramid awaited us. My thoughts then returned back to being in the serene presence of the Great Master. He smiled at me and pointed to his forehead and growled: "Egypt is in here. Everything is inside".

Chapter 2

WORK IS WORSHIP

City life

I was kicking my heels at the station. It was 6.09 am. The bloody train was late. Five minutes passed. Still nothing – the platform was eerily, unnaturally quiet. There was nobody else around. Only then did it dawn on me that it was Saturday! I returned to my apartment just across the road from the station, cursing under my breath. As I stared into the mirror my white face shone back at me, contrasting starkly with my red tie. Saturday was usually smoked salmon and bagel day. Not today. The deli would not be open yet. It would have to be the traditional English fried breakfast. It was early and I was hungry. Tomorrow would have to be deli day. My weekend routine had been broken.

I had joined the frenetic world of the bond markets after working in the staid, gentlemanly environment of corporate asset finance and merchant banking. Being a bond trader was quite different to sitting in front of the finance director of a company, selling finance over a civilised cup of tea and biscuits!

A year earlier, I had found myself sitting next to John on an aeroplane on the way back from a holiday in the Algarve. He was working as a senior bond trader for Merrill Lynch. We exchanged telephone numbers and had lunch a few times whenever I was in the City (the Square Mile). One day out of the blue, I received a call from him telling me that there was a position available on the corporate retail desk in the trading room of a large US securities house which he had just joined.

The Invisible Hand was, it seems, already at work without my knowledge, in much the same way that a parent helps a child, silently, behind the scenes. This opportunity would later give me the chance to become either a Eurobond salesman or a trader depending on which area suited my talents. At 21, I was considered almost too old to join these markets. If offered the position, I would need to decide whether to keep my job in corporate asset finance or take the plunge into the markets. I went for the interview with the head of trading and the head of the retail desk. The next day, they called and offered me the job. My present salary would rise by 30% even though I had no experience in these markets. The problem for me was that the package did not include a car. I had always had a company car and wanted to hang on to this perk. Nobody else had a car on the retail desk but this did not stop me from telling my prospective employers that I wanted a car as part of the deal. Job opportunities in these markets were like gold dust, but I confidently stuck to my guns anyway. The head of retail called me back. "You can have the car but you need to keep shtum about it or it will cause us problems with the other staff." Not being afraid to ask, even though the stakes at the time for such a rare job were relatively high, had paid off. Confidence breeds confidence and I was certainly not afraid to ask, a theme that has paid off time and time again in my life.

When I turned up for work on my first day, I was invited to a champagne lunch. I was also given the keys to my company car which to my surprise was a sports car, a significant upgrade to the workhorse company cars to which I had become accustomed. In the evening, there was another drinks celebration for a trader who had been promoted. Everyone I met seemed to be a president, a vice president or an assistant vice president! I had no idea who was important and who was not. Lunches in my previous jobs had entailed a sandwich in the car between meetings with clients. It seemed obvious that eating and drinking were requisite parts of my new job, at which I soon became an expert!

TRADING PLACES

"⅜ths, ⅞ths – what do you wanna do? These bonds trade like my wife cooks, not very well and not very often!" John's joke was met with laughter from the male-dominated floor. We were in the trading room – over 200 people spread out in different teams according to currencies or new issues desks.

"103 choice price," cried out another dealer.

"Geezer, geezer!" applauded the traders around him in unison on the floor.

A choice price is where a trader is so confident in his ability to trade a particular bond, that he quotes the same price for buying or selling that bond. He was foregoing the normal requirement of a half-point spread between the buying price and the selling price. I had never been in such an aggressive environment. Highly charged egos all competing with each other. How would I cope?

Not long after I started the job, a trader was removed and I was promoted into his position. My new business cards were printed and an expense account opened. My phone lines were flashing on the board. I picked up line one. Another trader from a rival bank wanted a price. There were no screens telling me the price to make or what the market price was either. It was my call to make the price according to my view of market conditions.

"Where are the World Bank '07s?" I was asked.

"6371," I replied.

That meant £96 ¾ was the "bid" price I was willing to buy bonds and £97 ¼ was the "offer" price I was willing to sell them. The term "willing" meant that I was obligated to follow market etiquette to either buy or sell at the price quoted by me to another party up to a figure of £1million even if I did not want to do so. Traders would ask each other for quotes on different bonds alternately. In a normal call each trader would be expected to make three or four prices. Every time I quoted a price my stomach would flutter, fearing that I had made a wrong price. The pressure was immense but exhilarating.

If the offer price I quoted was too low, the other trader would short me (i.e. buy what I did not have). If this happened then I would have to rush around the market to cover my short position. If the bid price I quoted was too high, I might be forced to buy bonds from the seller that I did not want. If I had a position already, and wanted to sell bonds to make a profit, I would make the offer price more attractive to encourage the caller to buy from me.

A trader has many enemies. The main enemy is the unknown. Any major world event or crisis could trigger an increase or decrease in prices in a split second. Meanwhile, the other banks and securities houses that called for a price always had an agenda either to dump unwanted positions or to cover their short positions. The third enemy was our own salespeople not only in our office but from other offices around the world. They were on commission and constantly tried to catch out the trader hoping to elicit a wrong price so they could make more money. There were two sales people to be wary of: Jean-Luc based in Lugano in Switzerland and Paul in London. If the former asked for a price and then subsequently bought or sold on behalf of clients, I knew instinctively that a runner was about to take place or that I had set the wrong price. A runner is where the seller is offloading bonds to different market-makers simultaneously without the other traders knowing. This creates a sharp drop in the price as supply becomes far greater than demand. As for Paul, although gregarious and pleasant in social environments, he would push and shout if he did not get the price he wanted. He was a big earner and was ruthless in satisfying his clients' and his own desire to make money. Sometimes an argument would erupt between a trader and a salesperson, especially when the salesperson came back twenty minutes after the price had been quoted and the market had already moved. The sales person would want the old price while the trader would insist on making a new price. Prices moved constantly but still the salesperson would do anything to maximise their commission. My boss, John, would bellow at them and say, "These are not door numbers you know, they keep moving."

"950 to go," said the dealer at the other end of the phone.

He had sold me £950,000 of bonds I did not want. The lights on the telephone board were now flashing all at once, winking at me, daring me to pick up another call. These were not friendly callers. A chorus of lights was a sure sign that we were on the end of a runner. We would find out through our friends in the market what the runner was and then pick up the phone and face them head-on. I had been asked the "burning question" as John would so eloquently put it. Everyone was scurrying to offload a new unwanted position to another trader. After the excitement died down, by the end of the day, depending on other market factors, the prices normally stabilised to where they had started before the runner had begun. Activity in trading creates profits for some and losses for others.

I had joined the Eurobond market in 1986 before Big Bang which marked the deregulation of the financial markets in the UK. Nevertheless nobody's position was secure even when employers were making money. One Monday morning, a month after I joined the company, the Head of Trading who had interviewed me did not come to work. His desk was cleared; not much comment was made and his replacement was announced. It was business as usual. People were removed or transferred routinely without notice.

Then in October 1987 the crash came. The aftermath saw banks retreat and lay off staff ruthlessly. Even John, who was the senior trading manager, was removed from his position and left the company the same day. Remarkably I did not lose any money during the crash but before I knew it, I too was one of the casualties. Layoffs took place in the thousands. The party was over and in my case it had hardly begun. Although I had passed my SEC "US Securities" regulatory exams, and my salary had more than doubled in a short space of time, the reality is that had I joined earlier, before the end of the bull market, I would have earned potentially twenty times more. However, now that the bear market had arrived, these types of opportunities quickly became few and far between. I did have offers to become a FX (foreign exchange) trader or broker but decided not to take them up.

I learnt four important business and life teachings particularly from John and my trading experiences. Firstly, the successful traders took the least risk. They virtually removed out of the equation the main enemy: the unknown. These traders rarely kept large positions of bonds overnight therefore minimalising their risk. They would only hold large positions a few times a year when they were confident in their judgement of the market direction. Secondly, it is never wrong to take a profit. Taking small profits on more than one transaction generates large profits in the long run. Thirdly, always leave a profit for the next person. Do not be greedy. Lastly the first cut is always the cheapest. In other words, when a loss arises, it is better to sell at a small loss early on rather than let the loss increase over time.

The above principles have stood me in good stead in life: successful people stack the odds in their favour and are not greedy.

Ultimately I was happy to leave an environment which was overly aggressive and often puerile, but it was a good learning experience. I knew inside that this career path would not have suited me in the long term and that my conditioning through observation of my father building a business was really the natural path for me to follow. It was time to have a go myself – to be more in charge of my own destiny.

EARLY OFFICE EXPERIENCE

From a very young age, during school holidays, my sister and I worked for my father stuffing mailshots in envelopes. Although a mundane task, we enjoyed competing to see who could finish first. This meant we earned more than just pocket money and gained a sense of value.

My father was a publisher. Even when I was just nine years old I loved to see how many spelling mistakes I could find in his magazines. This was well before the age of the spell-checker and office computers. I usually managed to find a mistake, much to his annoyance, and often after the magazine had been printed. He soon gave me the part-time job of editing during the holidays even after other people had checked the copy.

I also had lots of fun in his office. I mastered the art of surreptitiously putting mustard sweets in his staff's coffee and the odd cigarette-exploder in their cigarettes. I can still vividly recall the picture of his fellow director Ben, lighting up in front of me, while sitting back rocking in his chair and chatting to a client on the phone when the cigarette exploded. He dropped the phone and nearly fell off his chair.

Looking back, I can see how important these early experiences were in shaping my attitude and desire. Every interaction in an office environment, taught me about communication, getting things done and having fun!

DARKNESS

I remember going to work with my father as a child in the 1970s when the "three day week" was introduced. What was the "three-day week"? Essentially, there was not enough power in the country due to strikes so offices only had power for three days instead of five. Businesses then had to operate by candle-light! These memories instilled in me the need to be flexible and proactive in business regardless of the obstacles.

I also observed the vital importance of loyalty between employer and employee. My father had some very loyal staff and I saw how this was an essential ingredient to success. In addition, he was an expert salesman who could persuade anyone to part with their cash. I witnessed how he could even persuade clients on the phone to double their advertising space in his magazine when at the start of the call they were doubtful whether even to subscribe for the next issue!

His hard work for many years, often against a backdrop of economic adversity, slowly paid off thanks to his ambition, drive and self-belief. He was confident that he would succeed, had a huge capacity to work long hours and a business sense that enabled him to spot an opportunity and go for it. My father went from being a youngster with no education who was always in trouble at school to a self-made man. He found a way to channel his fighting spirit and his burning desire to achieve financial success. From an early age his ambition had been to own a Rolls Royce. It worked for him as his "driver" – he used this goal as a target – and did not give up until he achieved his desire. However, as the only child whose parent turned up to the school gates with a Rolls Royce, I found it a bit embarrassing, to say the least.

Spiritual aspirants may shun his ambition as shallow, but having a target is important in both spirituality and business. Wandering aimlessly does not help spiritual or material seekers. After some success or experience is gained, the target may diminish or change. The experience of success always counts. The Great Master pointed out often that work is worship if carried out consciously.

INVINCIBILITY AND VULNERABILITY

My initial focus on success was to do well at school (at least most of the time) both academically and at sports but I always had the aim to be successful materially. My father instilled in me the work ethic to earn money and never to rely on handouts. He told me many times that if I worked hard I could have whatever I wanted in life. I believed him. However, I have also observed in others that success does not necessarily continue indefinitely.

Success for a given person at one time in their life does not mean that the same individual has some kind of divine right to be successful again and again. The Midas touch does not last forever. Many people are successful in one business and then become involved in a string of loss-making ventures. They abandon their good, sharp business sense often through ego and end up diminishing their capital over time. This has taught me to quit when I am ahead and that over-confidence and reliance on past success can lead to lost focus and poor decision-making. The buffer of having money to invest after being successful in business can make one numb to loss. Putting good money after bad with the false promise of bigger and better profits becomes the paradise of fools. Good fortune rarely continues forever. The past does not determine how the future will turn out.

This common mistake among successful business people is built upon the misguided belief that they can replicate success in a business that they know nothing about, having spent years working in a business that they know everything about! Take the case of Martin, a market trader. After thirty years of working his pitch at the local market selling fruit and vegetables, he could semi-retire. However he went into a courier business with a friend. Within a year most of his hard-earned savings had gone. He ended up losing his money and his friend. He had to go back to working in the market.

I have learnt from the successes and failures of others and know that I am by no means invincible. In fact each day I am more aware of the vulnerability of my life – but I feel strong and no longer afraid in that vulnerability. This is the opposite to my observation of the dog-eat-dog world of boarding school and indeed large office environments. Can it be right that many are scared to admit to their shortcomings or ask for help from their peers or superiors because of fear that others will use their weakness against them? As I am now less defensive and more open as a person since retiring and meditating more, I know that the positive benefits of being open outweigh the negative effects and I am attempting to become more loving and tolerant of those around me.

EARLY CAREER

Apart from working in my father's office, I had a wide variety of holiday jobs. When I was sixteen, I worked in telephone sales for an external wall-coating company in the summer holidays. The job required me to cold-call people straight from the telephone directory in the evening. In three hours I would make 100 calls. When I became good at the job I was able to make on average six appointments per session and was paid commission for each appointment. What I learnt was that it was important to follow a pre-written script. I did not believe this at first but after making it up as I went along on a few calls without success, I reverted back to the script which worked. This did not mean that I could not add my own personality to the call. The nature of the job helped me to learn quite quickly to take rejection. I also developed the inner sense of when it was necessary to fight my corner. I remember phoning one man who was clearly very angry. He asked me why I was calling him when he was in a meeting. I politely replied that had I known he was in a meeting, I would not have called him. He was lost for words!

This job helped me to begin to learn what to say and what not to say, how to say it and how not to and saying what I mean and meaning what I say! Speaking slowly with constant eye contact is also a sign of confidence. The Great Master told me how Mahatma Gandhi advised him to speak slowly, clearly, loudly and distinctly.

Asking for what I want using the very same words will yield different results depending on my tone, energy, body language and confidence. These are vital lessons in life which I am still mastering. If all else fails I laugh and smile.

I also worked in a menswear shop in the summer holidays. I remember helping a man buy his first suit for a family wedding. Having never worn a suit, he was really uncomfortable and hunched his shoulders all the time. I encouraged him to relax. He was unsure whether to buy it or not. He wanted to go to some other shops to see what else was available but he was worried someone would take the suit he had tried on. I assured him that I would hold it back for him and when he returned after trying it on again, he decided to buy it. He also gave me a £5 tip. I had not expected this at all. I felt good not just because of the money but more because he appreciated the service. In both business and spirituality, reward seems to come unexpectedly if one's attitude is caring and positive.

I had another holiday job in a second-hand jewellery shop. After a few weeks there, a large, well-dressed man came into the shop with his girlfriend. He was very enthusiastic and asked to see different rings. I placed several rings on the glass top for him to view. After some time, he left the shop without buying anything. A few hours later we realised that he had stolen one of the rings. My boss was not too happy and told me in future to take one ring out at a time and to put it back before offering another one. I learned two important lessons from that experience: not to be too trusting of a smiling, enthusiastic person and, on another level, when selling, sell one thing at a time. I was happy to learn lessons from my mistakes, but am still practising the art of not repeating the same mistakes again and again.

Another time I helped an elderly man paint his flat. The advert asked for someone with painting experience. I was fifteen and bluffed my way into the job. He asked if I had painted before and I told him that I had. I did not lie as I had attended art classes at school! In the end, it took two months to paint his flat. We got on very well and he worked alongside me throughout the job. Every day his wife would make us a hot meal with dessert. We chatted about the meaning of life. After two weeks he asked me to be honest with him and tell him if I had ever painted before. I told him that I had not. He smiled and told me that he was impressed with my guts and also my work.

From the age of twelve I was a paperboy and in my early teens also worked in a solicitor's office and an accountant's office. The cumulative effect of these holiday jobs was that by the time I was eighteen, I already had very broad work experience before even securing my first full-time position. All of these jobs taught me how to deal with people. A smile and a little common sense have taken me a long way in life. This gave me a distinct advantage over others of my age – I already had limited practical experience of how businesses actually operated rather than relying on imagination or theory.

In addition, I was pleased to discover that as if by magic once the pound signs appeared in front of the numbers I became quite an adept mathematician!

FIRST FULL-TIME JOB

Despite the fact that my grandmother had earmarked me to become a budding lawyer, after nine years at boarding school I simply had no desire to go to university. I did not want to wait years to qualify and to do still more studying. Therefore fresh out of school, I began applying for jobs in the City. I had two interviews, one with an international bank, the other a merchant bank. Before attending the interview at the latter, I obtained a brochure about the bank from a friend's father. Dressed in my grey pin-striped suit and squeaky new shoes, I waited in the reception area and was then summoned to meet Brian the manager. I was confident but still had butterflies in my stomach. His first question was, "What is merchant banking?" I started to reel off the headings of what the bank did from the brochure that I had read. The phone rang. He excused himself and left to take the call. When he came back into the room, he told me I had forgotten one area. Before he could finish the sentence, I replied, "Gold bullion dealing." As I write this, I have no idea how I can remember this detail so specifically. Not the sort of thing that one thinks about every day. From that moment I could see that I had begun to win Brian's confidence as he began to chat with me more informally. The job was already half-mine. He informed me that most candidates came to interviews without knowing what a merchant bank actually did. Apparently there had been fifty applicants for two job vacancies. Of these, thirty had made spelling mistakes on their CVs, so he discarded them immediately and eventually just saw eight people. Thirty years later, even with spell-checkers on computers, I doubt that the statistic is much different for spelling errors in job applications. He told me that if people could not be bothered to check their own CVs then he could not trust them to check their work. This statement was not lost on me. I was asked back for a second interview, followed by lunch with himself and his assistant manager which was a little nerve-racking. I must have managed to eat without spilling food on my tie as two days later I received the offer letter. I was offered the job at the princely salary of £4,300 per annum. I accepted and turned down the international bank which had offered £5,100.

My preparation for the interview gave me an edge over other candidates and helped me to increase my chances of success. This is no different for any business meeting. Good business people know what they are talking about and prepare properly as do spiritual teachers.

I began in the merchant bank as a loans administrator in the domestic banking department. My job was to fix loan rates for large corporations requiring me to liaise between the dealers and the finance directors. I joined in the summer of 1982. I met Eddie who worked there and who later came to work for me when I set up my business. Eddie stayed for seven years in spite of telling me on my first day that he was leaving soon.

The merchant bank employed a mix of public school boys, Oxbridge graduates and a few others. Out of several hundred employees, there was hardly a manager over forty – in fact the only one that was, turned out to be a fraudster! There were twenty directors and all of them bar one were over six-feet tall. They were all graduates except for the "small" one who had worked his way up through the bank from his first job in the post room. He was our director. He may have been shorter than the others but his mind was as sharp as a razor. I was always amazed when presenting a letter to him for signature that had already been double-checked how he could instantly see any errors. Luckily it did not happen too often. Although the directors or managers were not of entrepreneurial blood, some really bright people worked there. One colleague could do *the Times* newspaper crossword in around three minutes.

In this job, time was of the essence. Interest rate fixings were at 11.00am. Not at 11.01 or 11.10am. Banks stick rigidly to time. When banking closes at 3.30pm, it closes promptly. They do not wait for latecomers or listen to excuses. This principle is sometimes applied in spiritual life when the master wants to show the importance of punctuality to the student. He will lock the door to the meditation room at the exact time of the class so latecomers cannot enter.

An interesting part of the job was training Oxbridge graduates. They were highly intellectual, well spoken young men with posh accents. One or two of them were condescending. As bright as they were at passing examinations, it amused me that they had difficulty sending a fax to the right number or managing to do a fixing at the right time. No discipline!

Overall I received excellent training from this top merchant bank. My father had advised me to work for a leading bank as he said that I would not only learn how to do things properly, but also learn how not to do things. He was absolutely right.

The bank had some wonderful traditions and perks like giving a huge turkey and ham as a Christmas present along with a bottle of whisky and lunch in the staff restaurant. After six months in the job I became a second signatory, authorising me and another employee to release funds. It was an incredible sign of trust for a bank to give this level of responsibility to an eighteen-year-old. In those days "My word is my bond" was the motto. In addition, I learnt how to analyse financial accounts and helped present credit committee transactions to the board of directors.

Although this was not an environment that encouraged proactivity, when I discovered that the bank had twice the exposure to one client than the directors thought, I was allowed to work out a way to stop this from happening again. I suggested to my manager that I visit the director of each department to collate the department's exposure to every corporate client and to keep it updated monthly. This was before the days of computers. These lists became known as the "Green lists". The name was still in use at least ten years after I left although by that time presumably nobody knew why.

After twelve months I had the desire to progress and increase my pay. Salaries did not increase very much and the bank began to lose one or two people. As my discontent remained unaddressed, I was offered an opportunity in gold bullion-dealing within the group but I did not want this job. I started to apply for different external jobs. One money-broker invited me to become the second person in the City to work as a European Currency Unit or ecu trader. The ecu was the forerunner of the Euro. I declined the job.

By chance, my colleague Eddie saw a job advertised for people who were over 23 years old, to be a finance representative for a large subsidiary of a major bank. He had been given an interview with the recruitment consultant and suggested I come along. I was nineteen and Eddie was twenty. Lesley, the recruitment consultant and I got on well. He told me that in spite of my age he wanted to put me forward for the interview. I would be by far the youngest applicant ever. Eddie was told that he was too young for the job.

There were three positions available selling finance to small and large corporates. When the big day came for the interview in St James's Street, I met Sid, the regional director and Celine, the personnel manager. When I went inside they joked that I looked a bit like a member of the royal family. I retorted that I was a bit surprised but asked if they could arrange for his beautiful princess to be my wife! We all laughed. The ice was broken. From that moment the job was mine! It is really true that the first few minutes and even seconds of a meeting or an interview set the tone and the likely outcome. After that the interview was like chatting with friends about finance. Luckily they liked me and wanted me to have the job. Humour and self-deprecation are helpful assets to have. I certainly enjoy life more when I display them. My starting salary was £6,200 and I was given a company car. At nineteen this was a really good perk. However on a bright summer's day it was a bit unfortunate when I had to report to my manager that my car had been written off! My eye had wandered away from the road towards the beautiful moving female scenery on the pavement. I had hit the back of a Volvo which didn't even have a scratch. Luckily my replacement car was far better.

When I resigned from the merchant bank after accepting the new job, the management were really unhappy. I was even invited up for tea on the hallowed eighth floor where only directors had offices. I discussed my new job with a senior director while sipping tea and eating cakes. He could not persuade me to stay and did not offer the money

I wanted. At the end of the meeting he wished me luck and said that perhaps one day I would return as their asset finance manager. I replied 'perhaps as your asset finance director' and walked out! He was lost for words.

IF YOU PAY PEANUTS YOU GET MONKEYS

Only after I left did the directors of the merchant bank realise that their pay structure needed to be reviewed. Then they gave the remaining employees the salary increase that I had been seeking. Even at nineteen I realised that waiting for the best people to leave was not the smartest approach to managing a business. The cost of recruiting and training replacements who may be worse than the person who has just left is not an intelligent or proactive way to run a business of any size. I have found that both large and small companies often manage reactively as their cumbersome and restrictive structures may not allow proactive approaches by local managers or directors. Reactive management instead of proactive management is not the way to keep good staff.

When running my company, I learnt that it was sensible to pay the really good employees more than they would earn working for the competitors. It would make them think twice about leaving.

SECOND JOB

In my new job, I had my first encounter with external consultants. The finance house I joined had recently been through a merger of two rival companies. Post-merger, the air was rife with old prejudices. Of the two companies that merged, one had been highly aggressive and the other

47

highly conservative. The aggressive company had fared better in the merger and had pretty well taken over the whole operation of the new merged entity which had over 100 offices around the country. My office was one of only two where the regional management had survived from the more conservative company. The directors had appointed a huge, well-known firm of consultants to oversee and advise on the merger. I met a man, a laid-back cigar-smoker, who was one of the few remnants in my regional office. He told me that when an external consultant was appointed it always meant job cuts and redundancies. He was right and was eventually made redundant himself. Laid Back Cigar Man would later prove to be an important person in my business life.

I strongly believe that too often consultants are employed simply because of management cowardice. Good management should be brave and canny enough to deal with problems and find solutions. Over-reliance on outside consultants can illustrate management ineptitude or the lack of courage to make decisions. No doubt management in large public entities overuse consultants because it is not their own hard-earned cash paying the fees. Surely they would think twice if they owned the business.

In the regional office, I came across one particular trudger called Tim – uninspiring and unambitious. He was one year away from retirement and made credit decisions from behind his pipe and glasses. One day I needed his sanction on a particular transaction. He refused to do the deal. I was unhappy because the deal was, in my opinion, of good quality. I therefore went over his head and sought out his boss, Sid, who had hired me, who sanctioned the deal.

Tim went potty. He was furious and scolded me for standing up for what I believed in. It made no difference to me. I told him that since the deal did not need his signature there was no need for him to be so concerned. I could never tolerate people, regardless of their position, who were afraid to make decisions and would just take their monthly wages. Of course he was unhappy because someone of my young age had directly challenged his seniority. Nevertheless, the deal was done. If I was old enough to meet finance directors of large companies then I was old enough to push a deal through that I believed in. Just because he was far more senior than me did not deter me.

Going to the highest authority has never fazed me in business and in spirituality. In fact I have found in most cases it's the fastest way to gain the desired solution. In this job I often dealt directly with the head of credit for the whole company. I just picked up the phone and asked for him and he spoke to me. Colleagues around me were amazed. They would not dare phone the head of credit. If I needed a decision quickly in order to do my job it was logical for me to go to the top person. I built up a good relationship with him and this helped when I wanted something done in a hurry. I was careful not to call unless an urgent need arose. I think that he also quite liked talking to someone in the field who was at the cutting edge of the business. Sometimes, colleagues would ask me for a favour to obtain a quick decision for them. Meanwhile in spirituality I have never been afraid to ask a question directly of a master – I believe it is always best to go straight to the source.

This natural directness was the positive conditioning I inherited from my father. I used it to my advantage which ultimately was to the advantage of my employers. If I want something then most of the time I find the way. I am not deterred easily if intuitively I feel a goal is achievable.

The word entrepreneur derives from the French verb "entreprendre" meaning to begin something. Broken down, "entre" means "between" and "prendre" means "to take". So the successful entrepreneur takes the real opportunity which others cannot see. A good entrepreneur always finds a way to get his or her own way. However this does not mean that to be successful one should treat people badly or walk all over them. In fact the opposite is true. It helps to be enthusiastic, amiable and charming to others and there is always a creative and legitimate way of doing business. Dishonesty is not necessary. Results arrive through honest determination. The cream always rises to the top. If I was ever unhappy with someone I was working with I would find a solution to avoid too much contact with them so that my performance was not affected. Alternatively I would confront the situation even if it ruffled a few feathers.

Such characteristics are also helpful for those who are treading the spiritual path. The Bhagavad Gita, one of India's holiest scriptures broadly means "to fight". If we cannot stand up for what we believe in then what chance do we have to face difficulties?

I learned very quickly that trusting my own inner judgement was far more reliable than trusting the negative response of someone else. This was the beginning of my full-time career.

CHAPTER 3

DOWN TO BUSINESS

OUT OF DARKNESS COMES LIGHT

While I was working in the City, my father decided to sell his business. He had found a buyer and the price had been agreed. Due diligence, which takes place when the buyer and its advisers review the financial information of the seller, had begun. I found myself on a cold, stormy night at my father's office with his external accountant trying to reconcile some figures which had been questioned by the buyer.

My father had expanded his business successfully from publishing to organising trade exhibitions. Because of the success of his main exhibition company, exhibitors often paid advance deposits one year ahead of the next show to guarantee their place. Although the accounting for the business was straightforward somehow the figures did not add up. He had employed Des, some years before as his internal accountant. Des had a sad story. His daughter had suffered from a brain tumour and this meant that he sometimes had to work irregular hours to visit her in hospital.

As the night went on, we tried to contact Des about the discrepancies but could not get hold of him. He did not return the calls the next day either. Something was wrong. We thought that his daughter must be seriously ill. A few days later the police called. He had turned himself in. Des had been defrauding my father for years. The takeover was called off. When the forensic accountants followed the trail of his fraud, they discovered how he had "tested" the system initially by defrauding small amounts to see if he would be caught. He had set up a bank account in my father's name and forged his signature, paying cheques into the account. The bank manager admitted later he had seen the cheques but never thought to query them.

Over a period of two years, he had stolen nearly £250,000. Later we discovered that Des did not even have a daughter and had defrauded the local political party in a previous job and had already been to prison.

The buyer retreated, the deal was off and my father was left staring at a massive cash hole. His world had been shattered. However, out of darkness comes light. Fortunately, two positive events followed. Firstly, after many years of legal wrangling, my father's auditors' insurers eventually compensated him for the lost money. Secondly the business continued to grow.

One year later, my father was contacted by another potential buyer. I was at home with him and the rest of the family were on holiday.

We went to the offices of the prospective buyer at night to meet Leopold, the CEO and Leon, the Chairman. Leopold was tall, boisterous and hyperactive. Leon was the opposite. Short, reserved, smiling and silent – holding his cards close to his chest. We sat around a small table in a warehouse. They told us that they wanted to buy my father's business and they wanted to do the deal that night. After the preamble and an exchange of pleasantries they started to talk figures in terms of P/E (Price/Earnings) ratios. This is the ratio which indicates the value of a business derived by multiplying a number against profits. Leopold started to talk numbers, quite literally. He started with "three". No reaction. He went to "four" and then "five". My father and I looked at them silently across the table. Were they talking millions or P/E, I asked myself. When we spoke later my father was thinking exactly the same. We showed no reaction even though we were both confused by what was being offered. Leopold continued to increase the offer each time looking at Leon for approval. Finally he stopped at a number and then said million. My father and I stayed cool. It was already double the amount that he had been offered by the previous buyer that had pulled out before he had discovered the internal fraud. Now things were getting interesting. My father and Leopold started to discuss possible terms of a deal and I wrote the "heads of terms" which represented the basis of an agreement on the back of a white A4 envelope. All parties signed the terms as the basis for a future agreement. My father and I spoke in private. I suggested that we should walk away and let them sweat a bit. When we returned, they reiterated that they wanted to do the deal that night. My father told them that he would think about it. We calmly went to the car and left. My father was excited. On the way home, we discussed whether they might offer some shares in the buyer's business as a sweetener. He called them back an hour later once we had pulled into the driveway at home. Still sitting in the car, my father told them he would accept the deal if they added a sweetener of 100,000 shares. They agreed. As a 21-year-old, it was fascinating to be part of takeover negotiations. I became involved in the process and attended meetings with lawyers and accountants. Leopold and Leon became really very successful and my father's business was referred to as "the jewel in the Crown" in a newspaper. Amazingly they did not retain my father at all, not even for a day. They chose to let go of all of the senior contacts who had been essential for the company's growth to date.

In fact, more than forty years after the main exhibition

was founded, it is still going and still sells 75% of its exhibition stands at the end of one year's show for the next year in advance. Good businesses always survive.

The moral of the story is that even in the darkest hour good can still come. In this case the good was far better than ever anticipated or imagined. Due to Des's "success" in fraud, my father sold his business for double the price.

Regardless of our belief at the time, disasters and difficulties in life can soon become blessings.

LET BUSINESS COMMENCE

For those who are setting up a business or even those pursuing the path of spirituality the following pages detail some of the minutiae and thought that went into setting up my business. Success emanates from the 1% of minute detail which subtly affects the other 99%. This 1% is the difference between success and failure – as fine as the breadth of a hair. The entrepreneur who pays attention to detail has a greater chance of succeeding. Meanwhile, the spiritual seeker who pays attention to the inner 1% of habits or thoughts which they want to change will surely progress on a firmer footing.

LIFE IS ABOUT TIMING

I was made redundant from my trading position shortly after the sale of my father's business. Prior to that we had discussed the idea of setting up a finance house. When my redundancy came through, he offered to invest the initial capital to start the company. Even though I was only 23, I was wary of being in charge of any type of family business and I insisted on being the decision-maker. This left my father as a passive third-party investor and non-executive chairman. It was strictly business. I had to be very strong bearing in mind his hands-on nature and overpowering personality. I disliked intensely any hint of nepotism and made it clear I needed *carte blanche* to run the company. He respected this, even when he sometimes disagreed with the ongoing strategy or my stubbornness in doing things my own way. The business would be run as I wanted. Recently he told me that he would have had no qualms in withdrawing his investment if I had not shown the ability to do the job. Quite quickly, I pretty well ignored and forgot that the initial investment had come from a member of my family. It allowed me to grow the business without pressure, but became miniscule in time, bearing in mind that after eighteen years the business had £125 million of banking facilities at its disposal. I am very grateful for the faith my father put in me. His reward was to receive back his investment many times over, while I was able to secure my own financial future.

A patient investor who has confidence in the management is vital to give a business the chance to succeed. I was fortunate to have an understanding and patient investor who also acted as a good sounding board.

RECESSION

When the business (Key) was set up in the late 1980s, the UK entered one of its worst recessions where interest rates rose to 15%. This meant that it was far harder to raise funds from the market, but on the other hand, there was clearly a demand for our lending facilities. The business concept was to lend to the legal profession to help smooth their cash flow for mandatory overheads such as professional indemnity premiums, tax payments and other capital items. Legal practices are very profitable but their cash flow is irregular due to the time it takes to bill clients and then wait to be paid. Another reason I targeted law firms is because they were low risk and each partner was automatically personally liable for any debt. My theory was that unless every partner we dealt with was getting divorced, gambled or drank their money away, we would probably be safe as there was always one partner that could clear our debt at any one time. Although large banks fought aggressively to do business with law firms, I was convinced that there was a space in the market for a niche player like us. I knew instinctively and from experience that banks never really understood their clients' requirements. One could argue that banks have a monopoly on lending so to compete we had to become experts and offer well-developed financial products tailored to their actual needs. We saved clients a lot of time and money and reduced their need to have never-ending discussions with their banks that were slow and cumbersome in their decision making processes.

On reflection, I probably could not have chosen a more competitive market to enter into by pitting myself against the multi-billion pound resources of huge banking operations. Rather than compete head to head, our finance products sat alongside a client's existing bank facilities. While we had a far smaller range of products than the banks, we never attracted clients who the banks did not want. We were successful because we created products based around essential annual requirements giving us repeat business.

It took me nine months to set up and plan the business. I retained only one client from my second job and employed a secretary. We required different bespoke documentation to comply with legal financial regulations as well as systems to collect money from clients. In effect, Key had to have the credibility and robustness of a well managed bank without the bureaucracy. This meant setting up tight controls, credit-sanctioning processes and systems that cross-checked and followed the path of money all the way from our lenders to our clients or the suppliers of our clients. It was vital to set up this type of structure in order to persuade financial institutions to lend money to us. Years later our auditors told me they had never seen such tight controls and procedures and double checks both manual and computerised.

Lending to a high quality client base has very low margins. Our net profits were only 1% of loans advanced, so to make a profit, we needed to borrow and then lend substantial amounts. Like all businesses we needed to reach a critical level of turnover before we could start making good profits. However as lenders we were always at risk during the transaction period. As lending increased the skill was to grow without loosening our credit-sanctioning policy. This policy remained as robust from the day I started the business up until the day I left. Bad debts destroy profits. We hardly had any. I did not want to build a business based on high turnover and poor quality clients. Turnover for turnover's sake is foolishness exemplified.

This may all seem very detailed to the spiritual seeker or budding entrepreneur but preparing a solid foundation is vital for sustainable growth whether it be material or spiritual. In Kriya Yoga, the sequence of techniques is carefully laid out and structured by the masters to give the aspirant the maximum advantage and experience. However if the techniques are not followed correctly or in order, normally due to mental laziness, then the best result will not be achieved. Meanwhile if an entrepreneur takes a lackadaisical approach instead of carefully building every aspect of the business, then achieving success will be tough, and failure more likely.

STEADY GROWTH

After one year Laid Back Cigar Man joined me. I had known him since my second job. He was a deep thinker with a dry sense of humour and a cool head. Our personalities were different but our styles complemented each other well. Some clients preferred to deal with Laid Back Cigar Man and others with me. The business could not have been successful without him. Slowly, clients, staff numbers and bank facilities grew from our first credit line of £500,000. It was important for us to be trusted by both our funders and our clients. My values and ethics remained even as the business expanded. Although a strong, dogmatic person in many ways, I could be quite flexible when it came to winning business. However I was never flexible on my principle of doing business in the right manner. We always met our obligations. We never did a deal we were not happy with even if we were passing the credit risk to a third party. Funders always remember the deals that go wrong and who introduced them. As we gained the trust of more lenders, we were able to borrow more. It took much longer for us to grow than I would have liked. I was impatient as the growth and success of the business was restricted by the credit lines available to us. I do not see impatience as a bad quality in business or spirituality as long as it does not lead to poor decision-making or recklessness. It is easy for me to look back in hindsight and say that everything happens at the right moment in both business and spirituality. Although I believe this to be true, when desire is strong and the result does not come it is easy to forget this truth.

Discernment and discrimination

I enjoyed the challenge of doing business with people from different backgrounds and learned how to deal with a myriad of personalities. One of the more flamboyant and colourful characters in the market was Bob. He ran a large finance company and he certainly knew how to wine and dine the City institutions who loved him. Bob would boast that he had no bad debts and huge credit lines in place – more than fifty times their capital base. Laid Back Cigar Man and I were doubtful. We used Bob for large corporate transactions where the profit margins were too low for us to write ourselves. Instead we were paid commission for introductions. We employed Eddie who I knew from my first job to generate this business which was separate from our main operation of dealing with lawyers. Bob's hunger for business grew but so did his involvement in riskier deals.

When the day came for him to deliver on £5 million of "blue chip" business that we had introduced to him, a problem arose. Bob's underling, Steve, shuffled nervously. "We don't have the money", he told me. I was livid. We were not able to deliver what we had promised to our clients and we had to reimburse them out of our own commission. Thereafter we preferred not to deal with Bob, however we had a couple of deals outstanding, including a large transaction for a firm of solicitors. All was going to plan. We had smashed the competition on price and had spent significant amounts of time preparing the documentation. Suddenly the client who had been in a hurry to conclude the deal went quiet on us. Something smelt wrong here. Eventually and rather abruptly we were told that they had gone elsewhere. My instinct told me that Bob's company had cut us out of the transaction. Had they been unethical and forgotten the old adage of never biting the hand that feeds you? If so I would never deal with them again. I was unhappy but how could I prove it? On the next transaction where we were owed commission, I also prepared an invoice for the introductory fee for the above solicitors that we should have earned. Laid Back Cigar Man and I went together to their offices. I kept a straight face and casually presented the "additional" invoice to Steve, Bob's sidekick. I told him that we knew that they had done the deal through another broker but they still needed to honour our fee as we had been the original introducer. Steve was taken aback. How could we have known? His gaze shifted and he muttered under his breath that another introducer had gained a far higher return on the deal for them. As for the solicitors, they thought that they had been clever by going through someone else but ended up paying more because of the way the deal had been restructured. Steve wrote out a cheque for the £12,000 fee and Laid Back Cigar Man and I went out for a long lunch. The Invisible Hand ensured that Steve buckled and that we were compensated.

Karma in action in the business world! Divine justice is active even in the shark-infested waters of commerce. Bob's business eventually went bust in spectacular fashion owing tens of millions to their bankers. Bob and a fellow director ended up in prison.

KEY BEGINNINGS

When I started Key, I took great care in choosing logos, creating letterheads and brochures. This process was time-consuming, costly and often emotionally fraught. It is easy to lose oneself in pride or delusions of grandeur, but while image is important, none of this actually generates any income.

In terms of staff-numbers, we were always small. When

the business was sold we employed fourteen people some of whom were part-time. An important staff member was Fiona who originally joined us on a temporary appointment as a PA. Her skills spread into the administration of the business and she was highly trustworthy.

After our main product and market was identified, Laid Back Cigar Man and I painstakingly set out to build the company. We followed the old-fashioned method of writing to potential clients and then calling them a few days later for an appointment. We normally followed up a canvassing letter by phone on a Tuesday, Wednesday or a Thursday but avoided Friday afternoons or Monday mornings. Our logic was that on Monday mornings staff are catching up with work that they had not completed on Friday afternoon. We found that good calling times were 10am–12.30pm and 2–4.30pm. This method, after some trial and error, increased our chances of speaking to the person we wanted. Of course we needed a thick skin and a smile to carry out this often soul-destroying process.

To seek out new clients in such a systematic way required dedication and discipline. Distractions often arose when we were cold-calling potential clients and I was easily diverted from the task by day-to-day events which could really have waited.

For those practising meditation, distractions can come in the same way. The mind can easily look for a way to interrupt even after a few minutes of meditation. The temptation to pick up a ringing phone or reply to an email or text seems to arrive uncannily just after beginning to meditate. These interruptions can always wait but somehow the sense of priority and discipline to meditate is forgotten. Why do I sometimes choose to do something which is unnecessary and unproductive, especially when it can wait, instead of something which is beneficial for me? Nothing is ever that urgent. A friend of mine Ed who is 65 recently started to meditate after I showed him some simple techniques. One day I rang him and there was no reply which was unusual. When I asked why the phone had rung out he told me because he was meditating and I had instructed him not to pick up the phone as everything could wait!

The question is whether my life is being run by others or myself? If I can manage to watch a TV programme and not pick up the phone then I can manage to meditate. If I practise simple disciplines in my daily life and ignore mundane distractions then I can develop self-control of my mind. Meditation helps develop these qualities.

When developing our client base how did we know who to call or write to in the first place? We decided to build our own database from scratch rather than paying to use the database of a marketing company which may or may not have been accurate or up to date. We built a powerful database which we updated annually. A marketing letter has no value if it goes to the wrong person. In the long run we found that the database helped us speak to more potential clients. This painstaking process made a big difference and although labour intensive, the results made it worthwhile.

Even the preparation of a one-page marketing letter would often take us ten drafts just to agree the wording. When I explained this to my brother who is in recruitment in the City, he could not believe that anybody would employ this method rather than just making contact on the phone straight away. He could not grasp that writing a letter, especially now in the age of emails, greatly increases the chance of it being read because it physically lands on the addressee's desk. The follow-up phone call is then more likely to result in the would-be client agreeing to a meeting.

I believe that meeting a client is the best way to cement a relationship. It always gave us the edge to win business.

Wherever your attention is there you are!

Securing an appointment is one thing, but knowing what to say and asking the right questions when in a meeting is quite another. It is no different to sitting in front of a spiritual master. Many seek a guru but how do they use the time when the meeting finally occurs? The Great Master tells the story of a student sitting in his room for a short time to meditate. The student told the Great Master about his family and how little spiritual progress he was making. After a while he began to get up to leave for an urgent meeting. At that moment two attractive female devotees came to sit down. The student's attention turned to the women and away from the Great Master. He stayed for another hour! The Great Master asked him how he had suddenly found the time to stay when he had such an urgent meeting.

Another revered master from India, Ramakrishna Paramahamsa, was asked by a spiritual seeker why he had not made spiritual progress. The master replied "Women and gold". No doubt the answer of "men and gold" would also apply to women. Masters have an uncanny way of expressing the truth in a few words!

At Key, our practical knowledge grew as we gained more clients. It is fascinating how many clients or potential clients believed initially that we could not help them only to realise after meeting us that we could. This made the job satisfying and rewarding. I always enjoyed winning business where the client believed that we could not assist them.

Whether the focus is on business or spirituality, good experience can easily wipe away initial negative thoughts and beliefs.

Once our client numbers exceeded the two hundred mark we never looked back. We really knew what we were talking about compared to a local bank manager who had two or three legal practices as clients. By the time we had over 1,300 firms on our books, I doubt that any other bank or finance house in the country could have matched our expertise. One of the major banks even approached me and asked if we could introduce business to them! I politely declined. I did not want to risk a bank upsetting our clients. After all the main reason we were successful in business was because we were not a bank. In addition, our advantage (until the business was sold) was being independent. I rarely met any client, large or small, who was happy with their bank. In fact clients loved to moan to us about their banks, the poor service they received and the amount of errors the banks made.

After many years of experience with legal practices, we knew all of the quirks and nuances of these firms according to their type of work and the size and location of the firm. Our business excelled because we gained real expertise and useful information for our clients which was not available elsewhere. It was satisfying when clients openly told us how they enjoyed dealing with us, and how simple we made their lives. Hard work pays off in both business and spirituality, making the long and often painful hours of preparation worthwhile.

Keep it simple

My approach, whether in daily life or when I was in business, has always been to look for the simplest way to solve a problem. Logically I believe and trust that there is always an answer; it just may take time to arrive, either from my own contemplation or the input of someone else. Seeing a problem as a challenge to solve rather than simply a difficulty helps me. I have also adopted a similar approach to spirituality. I did not take the attitude that meditation was difficult or easy, just different because it was new to me.

The Great Master said that if we remain "on the top" by keeping our attention on the crown *chakra* and watch our breath, then there is nothing else to do. However, this simple teaching is lost as most meditators watch the mind and not the breath. The restless mind cannot comprehend that such a clear and concise teaching can lead to the truth. Instead many spiritual seekers search for more teachings through books and different techniques. This can be helpful and inspirational if not overdone but if it results in confusion then it can hinder spiritual growth. The Great Master recommended that we read a few lines from a spiritual book or scripture each day and then contemplate its meaning. I am not searching for more spiritual information so my mind is comfortable to follow what my gurus have and continue to show me. I read only occasionally but always see the same message: the answer is inside! Luckily I have been shown a way to look inside so I just need to practise and enjoy the journey.

My mind enjoys a simple approach. Does yours? A pragmatic approach conserves mental energy. I endeavour to avoid confusion at all costs. Simplicity is more helpful than confusion.

CLIENT RETENTION

Once a client started doing business with us, they usually stayed. I remember the old adage that it takes five years to win the business of a really large client and another five years to lose them. This point is not lost on me. It takes time, patience and endeavour to cultivate new clients. However, once we had them I never wanted to lose them and fortunately they did not want to lose us.

Another idea I had was to offer our existing clients "priority" on our funds ahead of new clients to reward loyalty. Most banks do the opposite. I took the logical approach to build long-term relationships with existing clients, treating them well and not taking them for granted. We even managed to attract firms that did not borrow from their banks. Maximising an opportunity with an existing client already on our doorstep was obvious to me, yet how many businesses bother? The most satisfying transactions were signing up clients who shared a building with a bank or a competitor.

Perhaps there is a spiritual angle to consider from this business experience regarding sticking to the task. In business, the more knowledge and expertise we gained helped us to perfect the product and service the client required. Once we found the magic formula we did not change our products unnecessarily but refined them subtly. The proof was the high client retention.

In spirituality I have mirrored this experience. After meeting the Great Master I have practised Kriya Yoga every day without fail because I knew regular practice would build up my practical knowledge and expertise. I have gained by sticking to one technique and have learned more from in-depth practice. Kriya Yoga is the carefully prepared magic formula for calmness. Through diligent practice my meditation has expanded in a slow, revealing, evolutionary way leading to more contentment.

The Great Master told me that after one minute's Kriya practice extreme calmness comes. When he told me this at the time I did not believe that this could be possible. After fourteen years of practice, I am beginning to see that what he told me so long ago was true. I can close my eyes, focus on my breath and often feel instant peace.

Spiritual seekers who constantly jump from one technique or from one master to another cannot possibly learn the subtle intricacies and the effect of practising a specific technique. I found a technique that works and is changing me for the good, so I stuck to it. Entrepreneurs who cannot transform one idea into a finished product to sell but jump from idea to idea will not succeed either. Completing 80% of any task is of little value unless the final 20% is finished. Absolute focus, sincere endeavour and practice cannot be avoided if one wishes to achieve success in business or spirituality. I have found that as positive experiences accumulate, the endeavour dissolves into more joy and contentment as the efforts bear fruit.

In business and in spirituality, the careful investment of time is rewarded many times over. Once the high point of the curve is reached and overcome, every action becomes more natural and what seemed difficult at the start becomes easier.

LUCKY BREAK

At Key, it took four years for our "lucky" break to come when we were appointed by the main insurance broker in the legal market to offer finance to their clients. Laid Back Cigar Man had called them to find out who they recommended. By "chance", the call was perfectly timed because they were unhappy with their existing finance arrangements. We were invited to a meeting with Peter, the CEO. He was straightforward and to the point. He knew who we were and that we had a good reputation. He agreed to use us for a trial period to finance a specific scheme. If they were happy, they would give us an exclusive deal for all of their lawyers' business. We picked up 150 new clients in the first month. Once we were seen to be allied to the market leader, this led us to being recommended by other insurance brokers.

What determined that Laid Back Cigar Man had called at the right moment? Luck? Intuition? Destiny?

No business deal works unless there is mutual benefit. We maintained confidentiality and fairness with all brokers, both large and small who recommended us. We built up longstanding relationships even though many brokers merged and demerged. Change leads to uncertainty in business but somehow we managed to jump through the hoops by satisfying new owners or directors of the merged broker. If our "friends" were the least dominant party in a merger, then there was a high risk we might lose the business.

I enjoyed my relationship with Peter as we were both straightforward. He was a man on a mission and absolutely honest. He supported us well and fortunately this relationship continued with his successor. The relationship worked because it was built on mutual trust.

Trust is an essential component in all healthy relationships in whatever path we are pursuing. I do not give trust blindly but it is a beautiful facet of life worth cultivating even if at times disappointment comes. If I am let down, I partially blame myself for not judging the other person correctly. I find it rewarding to see how trust grows between myself and others. Lending money is a high form of trust.

As soon as we handed over money to clients we lost all control. It was up to them to honour the contract and repay us. I enjoyed deciding who we should lend to and who we should decline. As the business grew we were writing over 1,000 transactions per annum. The art was to spot the handful of clients to avoid. As highly as I trust my own judgement, very occasionally we would be caught out.

The Great Master warned me to beware of the wolf in the sheep's clothing. I am not paranoid but watchful.

COMPETITION

It is said that imitation is the highest form of flattery, but when a main high street bank set up in direct competition with us, by investing in large offices and staff and offering cheap rates to all and sundry, times became tougher. Their personnel were trained to offer a lower rate whenever they knew they were competing against us. This made life really difficult over a four-year period. Fortunately the business plan dreamt up by their CEO did not work due to the huge overheads they incurred and a large bad debt. We maintained our clients by slightly cutting our margins. When we came across aggressive competition, we kept our nerve. Or perhaps more accurately Laid Back Cigar Man kept his nerve and I agitated on ways to beat them. At the start of a marketing campaign, I would sometimes quote a slightly higher rate and lose a small deal to a non-client when I knew that a competitor was quoting against us. This would lull the competitor into a false sense of security. As more competition entered our market place, this actually became advantageous because clients became sick of being bombarded by letters and emails from fifteen different lenders or finance brokers. Clients would just bin the information or check our quote with another company to ensure we were still competitive. If a firm was going to phone six different funders, then we would not waste our time quoting.

SHOULD I STAY OR SHOULD I GO?

After ten years of running Key, loans advanced reached £20 million per annum. As previously mentioned, funding had been more difficult to raise than I had anticipated. Although the business was doing well, I became dissatisfied. I wanted Key to grow more quickly. I wondered whether I should leave and set up as a healer for business people. Since my healing experience in 1995, I had begun to give healing to friends and family who came with different ailments. In time other people were also recommended to see me. I enjoyed helping them to be more relaxed and wondered if a career in healing would be more fulfilling. The Great Master gave me some advice. He told me to stay with my work. I had said nothing about my intention to leave Key.

From that point onwards, it was as if the floodgates had opened. Two years after meeting him, the amount we lent doubled to £40 million. Two years later to £80 million. The Kriya train had left the station and I was hanging on the back! Only a few years down the line the business was sold and we were lending £100 million per annum to the legal profession. We had reached the critical mass and profitability needed to attract a buyer. The story of the sale is described later in the book.

I had never interlinked spirituality and business together before, but I was certain then, and remain absolutely certain today, that the Great Master appearing in my life had a significant impact on my success in business as well as my spiritual life.

CHAPTER 4

EARLY SPIRITUAL EXPERIENCES

EXPERIENCE SURPASSES BELIEF

On the morning after my healing epiphany, I began to practise healing on myself and then on Joy. I felt a tingling sensation and heat in my hands. I was the same person as the day before, but I had experienced something extraordinary. It gave me a new sense of protection and comfort. So a serious injury became a life-changing moment. During the months ahead I became very sensitive to energy. If someone standing near me had a pain in their body, I could feel that pain in the corresponding part of my own body. I also felt an invigorating pulsating energy particularly around my forehead and the crown. When the day came for me to give healing to another person apart from Joy, my father volunteered. I was nervous. Would it work or would I look like a fool? I stood near him as he sat with his eyes closed. I placed my hands over different parts of his body and in particular above his head. After thirty minutes he opened his eyes. I asked him what he had experienced. He told me that it was as if a light switch had been turned on in his head! All he could see was light and his eyes were closed. I was amazed as I had no awareness of his experience.

As my sensitivity developed, Dan showed me how, if I called the name of an angel or a master, their presence could be felt in a subtle way. If I did this I felt extreme warmth in my body instantly, normally in the centre of my chest. I found it hard to believe yet this is what happened.

FIRST MEETING WITH A SPIRITUAL MASTER

In 1995 I met Hugging Mother. This was the first time I had met a guru. It was a brisk October night in London soon after my healing experience. I knew nothing about her but went along with Dan to see what it was all about. The hall in Battersea was packed. There were lots of different characters, more women than men, many wearing white which made it look like a cricketers' convention! To queue we sat on the floor and shuffled along waiting for several hours to receive a personal hug. I had no expectation, but as time passed by I became impatient. I was more interested in going to bed in preparation for work the next day as it was nearly midnight. Dan persuaded me to stay. As I approached nearer to her on my knees I felt an intense heat around me. Hugging Mother was sitting surrounded by her close devotees. She welcomed each person with open arms, pulled them to her shoulder and hugged them. Sometimes she would laugh and talk to those around her. Many devotees were singing to the beat of Indian music which made me feel a little uncomfortable and almost sneering inside. Was this the Beatles meets Maharishi all over again? Singing about love and devotion was not part of my day to day reality. *Didn't these people have jobs to go to or were they unpaid groupies on social security?* As I write about this visit I realise how easy it is to judge a book by its cover but nevertheless these were my thoughts. I was five people away from her now. I was beginning to sweat. The temperature rose significantly as I was being drawn closer. It was becoming hot and uncomfortable. Hugging Mother glanced up and looked at me for an instant whilst hugging someone else as if to see in advance who was coming her way. I shuffled closer and closer. I was given a tissue to wipe off the sweat and then I was thrust onto her shoulder. I could smell the strong aroma of vanilla essence as she was hugging me almost taking my full weight on her shoulder. She was whispering "Darling, darling, darling" into my ear! This was surreal. A total stranger was hugging me with so much love. My office colleagues or friends would have had a good chuckle and questioned my sanity. It was over in a flash. She laughed, threw flower petals over me and gave me a sweet. As I got up I felt a strange sensation in my body and the heat was still there. A deep heat remained inside my chest. I sat for a while with my eyes closed, a little shell-shocked and then we left for home. Then I began to laugh almost continuously in the car. It was as if someone had infused me with an invisible love drug! I was as high as a kite for hours and full of happiness. It was my first experience with a guru – my first *darshan*.

In spite of the unfamiliar surroundings, the experience was far greater than my inner prejudices and judgements before the hug. Hugging Mother is amazing. Although she looks no different to you or me, apart from the fact that she seems happy all of the time, she sits sometimes for more than twenty hours with only a short break. She does not move from her cushion, drink, eat or go to the toilet. She is in total control of her bodily functions. After sitting from nine in the morning until five in the afternoon she returns at seven at night and can be there until nine the next morning. When she is finished she has even been known to sweep the hall! Hugging Mother travels almost continuously, programme to programme, from country to country, hugging hundreds of thousands of people. How can that be possible?

It seems that the true gurus are the human prototypes of divinity sent by the Invisible Hand to be an example to others. Their life is not for themselves but for us. I experienced this at first hand. Having been lucky enough once to meet her privately, I got to know the secretary of her organisation. One year I was unable to attend and I told him. Hugging Mother told the secretary that she would give him *prasad* to send to me on the last night of *darshan*. *Prasad* is normally food or some token that the master blesses and gives to his or her devotee. It derives from the Sanskrit word *prasada* meaning kindness or grace. By the time he came up for his *darshan*, after thousands of others, it was early in the morning and he had forgotten all about it. She however had remembered and gave him a sweet, a flower and some sacred ash and said: "This is for David."

Hugging Mother and other masters display boundless love and energy, purely for others. For me this constant flow of love demonstrates that she is truly plugged into the divine source. Even the most eminent scientist would have trouble explaining her never-ending energy even on a basic physical level. I also know that the Great Master never slept much. Spiritual masters can go days without sleep even when they are working full tilt.

SILENT MOTHER

A few months later I went to see Silent Mother for *darshan*. Silent Mother is an Indian saint living in Germany in a region south of Frankfurt. A group of us went from London. I found myself in a small village near her home, waiting with 250 other people in a car park. Once the signal to go to *darshan* had been given, we walked through a deserted residential village and came to a house. The thought came to me that I would love to sit "in the lap" of Silent Mother for my first experience. As if my thoughts had been read by her, I was shown a chair less than ten feet away from where she would sit, smack bang in front of her. It was my lucky day. It was 6.10pm. *Darshan* would start at seven. I closed my eyes and began to meditate. I fell into a semi-conscious state fairly quickly. I was lucid but "spaced out". I felt high and infused by her energy – even though she was not yet in the room. The time passed quickly. At 7pm precisely she entered and we all stood up. Everyone was crammed into a large extended living room. Some put their hands together in the Indian way as she came in. She emanated a divine beauty but showed no facial expression or emotion at all. We sat down. *Darshan* began. People were already forming a queue on the floor. I watched, intrigued. I observed how her expression never changed and that her hand movements were precise. In the last eighteen years of visiting Silent Mother, her facial expression has always been the same and she displays a natural physical stillness, as if she is in total control of her body and emotions. She looks neither happy nor sad.

So how is *darshan* given by Silent Mother? Firstly it is given in total silence. A complete opposite to Hugging Mother where there is movement, music and laughter. It can take at least two hours for everyone to receive *darshan*. To sit totally still and silent for that period is not so easy especially if the bladder has other ideas. When it is your turn for *darshan* you kneel down in front of her and she puts her hands on your head. Sometimes she places her hands on the temples and other times on the top of the head applying gentle or firmer pressure. After ten to thirty seconds she removes her hands and you sit back and look into her eyes. When *darshan* is finished Silent Mother closes her eyes and you go back to your chair.

On my first visit, I was very interested as I had not witnessed until then a room full of silent people sitting patiently for hours. All types of people were there, men and women, old and young, some dressed smartly and some not. I observed her hands and her expression. Then it was my turn. Down I went on my knees. She placed her hands on my head. Thoughts were flying around inside. She removed her hands and then I looked into her eyes. Such beautiful eyes. Our eyes met, fixed invisibly together. My mind was suddenly still. After twenty seconds she closed her eyes. It was over. My heart skipped a beat. I felt deep heat inside my body but also a strong vibration as if I had been plugged into an electric grid. My body was charged with divine electricity and I had to control myself to stop it from shaking. I was rocking! Afterwards we went out for dinner and shared our different experiences. We went back the following few nights. It was equally fascinating and still is today whenever I go to see her.

When I am given *darshan* it is as if some of the burdens in my life are being removed and I am being charged with spiritual energy often referred to as *shakti* or *kundalini*. In general, the experience is calming but the mind is often restless. I have experienced some of my best meditations in Silent Mother's presence. In the valley where she lives the whole area is infused with her energy. In between *darshans* and during the day, I have often felt knocked out as if I had jet lag. The *darshan* process seems to begin from leaving my house until I arrive safely back home.

Meeting my orange brother:
smiling swami

Six months after meeting the Great Master, I went to a Kriya Yoga programme in Paris. His chosen successor, Smiling Swami, was guiding the programme. I went with a friend. As we entered the hall, he was sitting outside alone. I introduced myself briefly and we went inside and sat at the back. The lecture began. He spoke in English which was translated into French. My eyes were closed as I felt a little tired from the journey. Halfway through the lecture, ringing in my ear was the sweet sound of his voice. "Hey Mr London, why is a butterfly called a butterfly?" Was he talking to me? I opened my eyes. He smiled at me and repeated the question. I had no idea. Even I was interested to know the answer. He continued the lecture. At the end he took questions about Kriya Yoga and spirituality. The first question was asked. He then said that he would take all the questions and answer them one after the other. He had no pen and paper. He would need to remember the questions. I began to count them. There were over 100 people in the room. The questions came one after the other. Some about health; some about religion; others about yoga. This lasted for at least ten minutes. My friend and I looked at each other. How was it going to be possible to remember all of the questions? I had counted thirty. Smiling Swami thanked everyone for the questions and joked that he had forgotten them all. Systematically he proceeded to answer them one by one. However somehow he had shuffled the questions in his head according to the topic. We were impressed. He did not miss a question.

After the lecture we returned to our hotel. We had not

felt much spiritual vibration during the lecture. We arrived in our room and chilled out. At the same moment, we both felt an uplifting energy inside, gentle and subtle, which began to rise. We both began to laugh until we cried.

The weekend continued and during each talk or discussion somehow he would bring me into the conversation. He asked me why in the West people used a knife and fork. I instantly replied that it was easier than using chopsticks. Smiling Swami activated a different part of my brain with his questions and there was an instant connection between us, full of fun. My link with him was set from that first encounter.

When we said goodbye, he noticed that both myself and my friend were losing our hair. He commented that we were lucky because it was a sign of virility and wealth. He asked whether we wanted to be wealthy or virile. I replied, "Hopefully both!"

CALLING CARDS

I have noticed over the years that each master I have met has a different calling card for me to recognise them. When I see Hugging Mother or think about her I will often feel huge heat in the chest area. When I am going to Germany to see Silent Mother, I feel a gentle energy around me as if I am being guided to come to see her. These experiences are comforting and act as a reminder to keep going on the spiritual path. They are far healthier than alcohol, free of charge and good for me. In the presence of the Great Master I felt huge heat in my whole body and with all of the gurus I feel that the area around the top of my head is "opening up". When I am with Smiling Swami I feel a serene energy enveloping me but it feels different to what I experience with Silent Mother. When I have spent time with both of them, there are periods ranging from days to sometimes weeks where my breath hardly moves in my waking hours. It has happened after or during the time that I meet them. I am not able to replicate the experience using techniques or otherwise. These experiences reaffirm to me that there is something else of value in this world driving me apart from the pursuit of external pleasures. When the Invisible Hand becomes fully visible to me then I will be making progress.

I have met one or two other masters where I had good experiences and some other self-proclaimed gurus where I had little reaction and no connection at all. Although I cannot vouch for their authenticity or my reactions, I have found the most resonance with the masters I describe in this chapter.

I continue to visit Hugging Mother and Silent Mother and of course Smiling Swami. If I think of them as I meditate I can sometimes feel their "calling card". What they and the Great Master all have in common is the ability to create an uplifting inner feeling of joy inside of me which is totally different to joy from external worldly pleasures.

Sometimes I do not see them for a year or two and then I may see them several times in one year. There have been "coincidences" when I have learnt that one or other of them is in the same place where I am on holiday without my prior knowledge. A few years ago I was in Canada and discovered that Silent Mother was also visiting for the first time in more than twenty years. Once I had three days of *darshan* with Hugging Mother in London and was going to Paris the following day on holiday. I then discovered that she was also going to Paris so I received six days of *darshan* in a row! It is as if my itinerary is being invisibly managed. More cynical readers may call it sheer coincidence. For me coincidence is just a concept for events that I do not fully understand. In eighteen years I have probably had 150 *darshans* with Silent Mother and forty with Hugging Mother. I have spent the most private time with the Great Master and latterly with Smiling Swami. These two have given me practical advice and guidance in all aspects of my life on both spiritual and practical issues. My experience of *darshan* is an intense exposure to divine energy coming direct from the source through the guru. As I discovered early on, *darshan* works regardless of my beliefs.

In 1998, at the end of my first visit in Miami to see the Great Master, he encouraged me to come back to see him soon and regularly. I have already described my first meeting with him. My masters have given me the opportunity to have a close relationship with them. The Great Master took the role of loving friend and guide even on worldly matters. Smiling Swami does the same but is more like a brother. We relax, joke and laugh, share stories, opinions and experiences. Once I asked him if he had befriended the wrong person or whether I needed the most help! He joked that our relationship was a done deal. The contract had been signed.

THE COST OF SPIRITUALITY

Does it cost any money to see a guru? When attending a programme there are basic food and accommodation costs. When receiving Kriya Yoga initiation there is a cost of around £150 which covers attendance of a two-day programme. I have never once been asked to donate money by any of the gurus I have mentioned. In India it is a custom when having a private *darshan* with a guru to give a small donation. Most of the gurus I mention have their own charitable organisations ranging from education to health. When I believe in the cause and know that the money is being spent wisely I have contributed voluntarily. I am particularly keen on children's charities that promote education. The donor helps create the environment to learn but the child needs to put in the effort to study. I have had some involvement with a school set up by Smiling Swami in the name of the Great Master for poor children in Orissa, India.

My experience of these gurus is that they are very practical and very humble. They display one common trait: unconditional love for others. This is how I know when I am in the presence of a true master. Even though I am sure that they have different abilities to me, they act and behave in a human, loving and unassuming way. When people say that they are doing *seva* (selfless service) for the guru, I see it more the other way around. The guru is selflessly serving me.

I have observed at close quarters that my masters do not waste a second of their lives. When the Great Master looked after his own guruji, Swami Shriyukteshwarji, he asked him why he did not take care of his body properly or eat well. Shriyukteshwarji who would sit cross-legged for hours and hours on end in open eye meditation, replied that he did not even have time to blink as he was so absorbed in universal consciousness!

Even on his deathbed, the Great Master was still teaching his students until his last breath. His final words were "Peace, bliss, love, joy, divinity."

The underlying teaching of my masters is to be loving and joyful. This basic teaching on how to approach life seems to be missed by many around them. Their approach has deeply influenced me. I want to live in joy and die in joy.

MEANING OF GURU/WHAT IS SPIRITUALITY?

"What is spirituality?" I was asked recently. I replied that spirituality manifests through a person in the form of love and kindness with consciousness and awareness. But how do we manifest these qualities? By "becoming aware of the invisible behind the visible". This is in effect the meaning of the Sanskrit word *guru*. "Gu" means invisible and "ru" means visible. The spiritual guru makes the "invisible" visible. The true guru is the divine catalyst who helps the disciple to accelerate spiritual progress and the fulfilment of desires which leads to a state of desirelessness.

My parents, school teachers and work colleagues have in a sense also all been my gurus. Without them I would not have had the opportunity to grow and learn. A common misunderstanding of a spiritual guru in the West is "someone dressed in orange clothes who will take away all of my problems". Another misconception can come from the parents of the devotee who may believe that the guru is "someone who wears orange and wants my child's money, mind and possessions". True gurus will not lead anybody down this path. If you are fortunate as I have been, the guru will impart a practical technique like Kriya Yoga to help bring success in life. The guru will encourage inner growth, independence and not take possession of your mind or money. The Great Master often said that he wanted his students to be greater than him. What I have been given to practise by my masters is purely because of grace, yet the real grace is that I have been given the desire to practise.

BE WARY OF DECEPTION
DISGUISED AS PERCEPTION

What else have I learnt from meeting these masters? Firstly the people around the master are not the master. Secondly, nearly every master is criticised often by people who have never met them. In spiritual circles, the maxim of "my guru is greater than your guru" is common practice. Thirdly, true gurus are those who practise what they preach and give out love infinitely and continuously. In the case of the masters I have mentioned, witnessing their constant outpouring of love and the sacrifice that they make for others, dissolves my negatives and helps me become more loving to myself and others. They just show by example how to deal with life and the difficulties that arise. They have never criticised me. This teaching by example subtly shows me how to repair or improve on my weaknesses. The Great Master told me many times, "I do not need to tell you your negative qualities. You know them already. I will tell you about your positive qualities." He did this to an almost embarrassing extent. This was a refreshing approach. He also told me that I knew about the outer world but he would show me the inner world. He reiterated that there was no separation between spirituality and materialism. On the contrary he said: "Everything is spiritual".

Taking a prophet

In the same way that many have trouble in taking a profit in business, those on the spiritual path have trouble in taking a prophet as their spiritual guide! Is it the medicine or the doctor that is unpalatable? Chopping and changing is fine on the path of self-discovery, but if it continues it will just create more restlessness. It is crystal clear to me that the message from a true master is the same. Practise, practise, practise!

Conditioning

I once went to see a ninety-year-old *advaita* master in Mumbai called Ramesh Balsekar. *Advaita* is the path of "non duality" which means that God and man are not considered separate but are one. Ramesh was an ex-banker. He gave *darshan* in the form of questions and answers. I immediately noticed how restless the people were who came to see him in spite of the fact that many claimed to be meditators. Ramesh really listened carefully to each question. He then answered simply with love, care and understanding.

Ramesh challenged whether we could really be held responsible for our restlessness or even our good or bad habits. He pointed out that we have all been "conditioned" from the moment of birth influencing our lives, successes and failures. I have been like a sponge, absorbing good and bad from different environments and people, my education, my diet and my relationships. How can I increase the positives from that conditioning and reduce the bad effects?

Ramesh poignantly said that nobody can really be blamed for their actions which are due to their conditioning, starting with their genes. This approach resonated with me as it was logical but I find it harder to accept when related to the perpetration of a serious crime. Yet if a child is born into a family who for generations have been criminals, there is a good chance that the child will follow in the family's footsteps. The same applies for children born into other families, good or bad. In the past there may have been a family "industry" like a restaurant, butchers, bakers or other professions which the family ran. Sadly a more common pattern today is of generations of families being unemployed. I feel fortunate not to have been born into such an environment and it acts as a reminder to me to be forever grateful for the opportunities I have been given. On the surface, life is unfair and this appears to be the nature of life. But do I get what I deserve even if I do not understand why? Of course it is easier to be joyful in life when life has been good to me. But really how joyful am I even when materially I have so much more than others? Material success does not guarantee internal happiness even though those who seek material gain think it will make them happy. In fact the opposite is more likely to be true. Smiling Swami comments that rich people have something in common with poor people: they both spend their time worrying about money.

I NEVER MET A HAPPY ENVIOUS PERSON

So if conditioning determines almost everything, how can people with no education and poor parenting succeed over those who have good family backgrounds and good education? My father had little education and was self-made, yet he never complained that life was unfair. He just got on with it. Who decides the apparent unfairness and fairness which begins from birth? Do we judge what is fair or unfair according to circumstances alone and do we think life is unfair more when our desires are unfulfilled? Jealousy, envy or greed come when people are unhappy. The opposite qualities of satisfaction, kindness and generosity are present when we are happy. I am humbled by the incredible way others overcome their difficulties with a smile.

The Great Master commented, "Your food is your food, so do not look at the food that is on somebody else's plate." I like this beautiful but simple teaching. In my life I have identified what I wanted and have done my best to achieve that desire without concerning myself with the abilities or possessions of others. It never crossed my mind to be envious or view anyone as being more fortunate than me.

My approach to spirituality has been similar regarding the spiritual experiences others have compared to my own. I have never aimed to see light, feel vibration or hear sound. I have taken the attitude that if it comes it comes. Rather than aim to achieve something spiritually, I have allowed the process to unfold without using my inbuilt discipline to achieve an experience or manifest a spiritual desire.

WHAT IS SUCCESS AND HOW TO JUDGE IT?

In recent years, I have discovered that inner contentment is my true success. This deep realisation has come from experience and not theory. After years of being a worka-holic I mastered the art of restlessness! Luckily after leaving finance I found calmness because the desire to achieve something in the world had left me. If I had still been ambitious then the restlessness would have continued even when not working. As much as I enjoy the possessions that money can buy, they cannot bring me true inner happiness. What use is a big car or a big house if I am not truly happy inside? I was not brought up with this teaching. My conditioning was to make money, be successful to "have what I want" and happiness would follow. While material success has been extremely advantageous, the real inner joy has come through meditation. Material success was not and is not enough. Inner contentment was highlighted to me when I visited Tibet in 1999. A group of us travelled across hundreds of miles of beautiful landscape to Mount Kailash, sleeping overnight in tents in the wilderness in temperatures of minus fifteen degrees Celsius. The landscape was staggeringly beautiful but this would have soon faded if I had to live permanently in these conditions. When we pitched camp, out of this deserted, silent land, adults came from nowhere with their young children. They appeared as if by magic, all smiling and happy. They had an air of extreme peace and joyfulness although they were obviously really poor. They had not come to beg from us but just to meet us. I have no idea where they lived or how they survived but even when we gave them a plastic bottle of water they were genuinely happy and grateful.

So how can impoverished people like this be content? Firstly they do not have the expectations generated by the Western marketing machine. They are free from the conditioning of TV, movies, newspapers and adverts which affect our dreams and expectations, most of which are unrealistic and unachievable. Success and having what we want is presented as being so easy to attain by the media. Unless we achieve material success then buying what we want on borrowed money can only lead to a mountain of debt. Even extremely well paid people with families, second homes, three holidays per year and private education for their children, often end up spending more than they earn. Society does not encourage us to save any of our income and those that do generally end up paying for others who do not even if they can save. These external influences help to mould our belief systems, which once set are difficult to break.

Smiling Swami often says that, "Expectation leads to disappointment." He also says, "Hope for the best but prepare for the worst". This does not mean that pessimism is being promoted, but realism is vital. I have always found that the more preparation I make, the less surprises I receive. Running a business without preparation can only lead to failure, no matter how many orders are coming in. The lesson from these Tibetans that I met was "go back to basics". This is where real inner happiness resides.

THE REAL THING?

When this "new" world arrived on my doorstep, how did I know if the master I met was the real thing? What was my expectation or imagination of what a guru should be like? If I am truthful I cannot claim to know 100%. I follow the logic that I cannot know a master unless I am in a state of complete truth and consciousness. It is akin to the university professor teaching Nuclear Physics to a one month old child. Judging a guru can be further complicated by those who claim to be a guru or an advanced master when they are just fine actors. However, I do know a good footballer when I see one and I feel blessed by the masters that I have met. A good barometer is to experience peace or inner joy in the presence of a master.

I heard the story of Sri Anandamayi Ma, one of India's greatest saints, describing her visit to a town where she was told a great holy man sat for days on end without moving his body except to eat or drink. One night she went to see him when nobody else was there. She told him she knew he was restless inside and that he should not appear to others to be a holy man accepting their food and drink without working. He admitted he had mastered the skill to totally control his body and liked the adoration and being looked after by others. He admitted his wrongdoing and stopped this practice.

There are even those who judge which masters or gurus are advanced by what they read or hear from others without actually meeting them. It would be more appropriate if the accuser was put on the stand rather than the guru. However, I am sure that there are many false gurus that look, act and dress the part and I have met some monks who have the dreaded disease called "guru-itis". Looking the part and speaking authoritatively about the scriptures is not enough if in private they behave quite differently. In India, monks are given long unpronounceable names which often end in *ananda* which means "in bliss". So *caveat emptor* applies when choosing a spiritual guide or any professional adviser for that matter. In business, I have met plenty of qualified accountants or professionals who look and act the part, but are not as I would expect judging by the quality of their advice. I am also suspicious of those who have so many qualifications and who then mistakenly portray themselves as having superior standing or knowledge to others. I applaud higher education but the insincere ones can keep their Masters and I will keep my masters! It is no different to me thinking that I know someone only to discover later hidden aspects of their character that surprise or disappoint me. I just go along with my instincts and gut feel but I have no right to judge others although I find myself doing just that time and time again. I am making an effort to change this habit – after all what do I really know about anybody? The journey is to know myself and my own true nature.

If the experience of being with a guru is positive then I am inclined to seek their company more as I would with any other positive person. I did have to overcome some internal prejudices that arose due to the way that people dressed and behaved around the masters. To see everyone wearing white was a culture shock for me. Of course in a hot country like India, wearing white is practical. I keep my own individuality but hopefully remain respectful of others. This world that opened up to me, of strange music, incense and different customs was so outside of my conditioning. It was never like this at the deli in the East End when, in my earlier life we queued up for late-night bagels and smoked salmon.

ASHRAM EXPERIENCES

Ashram comes from the Sanskrit word *asrama* meaning "place of refuge" which in turn derives from the word *srama* meaning difficulties. By putting the "a" in front of *srama*, *asrama* represents the "removal" of trouble. There is also a Western meaning: "Free holiday accommodation with full board in a hot climate with a bit of housework or cooking to do!" An ashram is supposed to be a place to recharge the batteries and find time and peace away from the stressful world whilst increasing one's spiritual practice. At most ashrams there are meditation programmes to attend. In India it is a sign of respect to bow to someone who is older than you or to a monk. In addition, instead of shaking hands, the Indians put their two hands together to greet someone. The two hands together represent union: a joining of hearts of the giver and the receiver. It is an act of humility.

When I first came to the Great Master's ashram in the USA it was strange to see Westerners bowing and touching their foreheads on the feet of the Great Master even though it is standard practice in India. What does the bow signify? Have you watched people practising yoga? They often bend back their forefinger to touch the thumb. This is the bow in miniature form. It represents the bending of the ego. On the spiritual path "ego" is spoken of as if it is bad news! "All ego" some people pronounce when anybody expresses an opinion. At first I found the idea of bowing strange and demeaning. In fact even in churches people bend their knees to pray so it is really not that different. If offered sincerely it is a beautiful way of showing humility and respect and is as common as a handshake in the West. My advice to visitors going to ashrams is to be yourself and not to leave your brain outside of the gates of the ashram. I follow what feels right for me and do not follow the sheep. Visitors to an ashram are also expected to help keep the facilities maintained or to prepare food for the day. If done with a loving and prayerful attitude this is *seva*. Ashram residents certainly work hard for long hours and the visitors normally get the fine tasks such as cleaning the toilets, so be prepared! One close friend who I met in 1998 nearly ran from the ashram when she was given the toilets to clean. She asked me why when she visited these places she always was asked to clean the toilets! It can happen that the people giving out the jobs start to become mini masters or gurus. The guru has an uncanny knack of appointing those with hidden control tendencies to positions of supposed authority. Self-importance is opposite to the Great Master's teachings of selflessness yet it still can happen when people are given authority or become teachers.

I advise visitors to be comfortable in what they are doing but if you are going to stay free of charge at an ashram then you need to do your fair share to help keep the place going. It is not much different in this regard to staying at a kibbutz. As is the norm when in someone else's home, to follow the rules out of respect is fine but to follow blindly without discernment is not healthy either. So what type of people stay long term at an ashram? Often I see people who find it hard to survive in the world. An ashram allows residents to leave those responsibilities behind. This does not mean that it is not a tough environment. Meditating three times per day, observing silence as much as possible and doing tasks which may not be to your liking is not easy. In addition, like boarding school, living in close quarters with strangers soon brings up its own issues and tensions. People who visit ashrams are not always sweet and kind either! I really admire those who live in ashrams who genuinely are pursuing the goal of spiritual truth yet who do so in a humble and caring way. Being kind and humble to the guru and then being difficult and uncooperative with those around you misses the point and the teachings of a guru completely. Everybody should be treated in the same way with loving respect, but "shoulds" and "woulds" do not make the world go around. True spiritual seekers carry out *seva* daily with this attitude towards every task, thought and treatment of others. I have found that when I treat myself, my mind and body with more love and understanding that I treat others in this way also. But not always. I have come through the fast track schooling of "My way or the highway" so it has taken some adjustment for me to realise that life's journey is not always on my terms. Sri Anandamayi Ma in her book *Matri Vani* said, "Do you think that God does everything just to please you? He certainly does what is best for you even if it does not seem the case at the time!"

The Great Master often said that heaven and hell are within us and not in some imaginary place in the sky where we go at death. When I am happy with life, I am in heaven. When I am unhappy, I am in hell. If my mind and breath are relaxed then I am normally in heaven. I have no consciousness of an afterlife but I can feel more divinity inside of me which is not connected to my mind or body. This leads me to believe that this invisible divinity or consciousness within me is separate and will continue to exist after my life is over. For those who do not believe in the afterlife, there is no reason to take life so seriously and worry so much!

MEDITATION

What is meditation? To find out the answer one needs to go inside the space between two thoughts. This is the place of meditation. Without ever contemplating or attempting to go into this space, my life would just be peppered with desires and dreams. Those desires that manifest will make me happy temporarily and those that do not will make me unhappy. Surely this cannot be the truth of life. It is my experience that the more my desires and expectations diminish, the more stillness and satisfaction I feel inside. This conflicts with the material world that encourages us to chase our rainbows even if we are not equipped to do so. Once this stillness comes, worries fade and joy arrives. The Great Master told me that the blissful state is beyond happiness and unhappiness. I cannot say that I have experienced this state but when in deep meditation I do not know who I am, where I am and have no awareness of my body. There is no technique to be in this state. My experience is that Kriya Yoga prepares my mind and body to be still so that I can enter into meditation. It does not work each time however, so even advanced meditators as well as beginners need to be prepared for mixed results. As soon as I judge one meditation experience as being better than another, the trouble begins. I just continue regardless of my judgement of the result. But how to get to this still point and what is the point of getting to that point? How did I come across Kriya Yoga and how did I know which meditation path was the best for me?

I should emphasise that my perception of meditation changes according to new experiences. What I thought meditation was one year ago is different to today. It is a process which continually evolves. Experiences change and consciousness subtly reveals itself. Before Kriya Yoga I thought that meditation involved sitting in a circle with like-minded people with meditative music in the background being guided on some kind of imaginary journey. When I went to Dan's guided meditations in this environment I found it incredibly wacky and off the wall. However I could actually feel the energy change when the meditation began. As much as the cynical part of me wanted to, I could not deny the experiences that were coming to me however strange they seemed at the time. Fortunately, after meeting the Great Master, Dan and I soon realised that in comparison to him we knew nothing about spirituality. Luckily we recognised our shortcomings early on and wanted to learn from someone who knew rather than rely on what we thought we had learnt. By the way, I do not for a moment criticise those who meditate in their own way. It is a start to the journey, but like discovering any great teacher or role model, I have found that a true living guru can really assist the spiritual seeker. Experience wins over theory every time. My experiences are not bound by some edict and while hearing about the spiritual journey of others can be interesting, when the inevitable comparisons take place, doubt and confusion can arise. It is comforting to have a teacher when problems come or experiences or feelings change. The Great Master teaches that we should go beyond our imagination and experiences to see what is waiting in the silence.

In my early years on the spiritual path before meeting the Great Master, as well as visiting Egypt and Tibet, I also went to "energy centres" such as Avebury and Stonehenge and holy places and old churches in the UK and Europe. When going to these places I could feel more concentrated energy and it was easier to meditate.

When this new area of life opened up to me I continued my work in finance which became more successful, as I meditated more. As I worked I became more aware of this "hidden" energy even outside of my meditation time. It became more present rather than just being switched on and off when I meditated. Sometimes I would even sit at a computer in my office to do some highly concentrated work and I would see circles of light for thirty minutes before they disappeared. This still happens occasionally.

So at this point, those readers who have never meditated before may well close the book thinking I am making this all up. You will be surprised what might happen to you should you ever start to meditate. If a run of the mill "unspiritual" person like me can be affected, then you can also and for the good. Instead of losing my day-to-day faculties, on the contrary my efficiency and success increased. Meditation brings gain and not loss. When I started Key I always said that I would remain the driver of the train. After I met the Great Master this idea of control changed: I was on a one way bullet train being driven by him! So is meditation just for the sake of spiritual experiences or to help me to be more successful materially? Growth in both areas has developed hand in hand. The continued subtle theme that meditation creates is that there is more to life than my parents or teachers have taught me. My life has a new agenda and it is slowly showing itself to me. It is now my path as a human being to discover my true nature which is hidden beneath the surface and beneath the obvious. Did you ever ask yourself and contemplate what is the real purpose of your life?

HOW TO MEDITATE?

When I worked flat out I nearly always meditated for thirty minutes each morning which gave me spiritual energy for the day. Successful people have the ability to concentrate. Kriya Yoga helps develop more concentration because it brings more oxygen to the brain. I have never missed a day of practice. Even ten minutes per day can be beneficial.

I meditate after a shower when the body is warm and before I eat breakfast. I follow this pattern most of the time. For those unfamiliar with meditation, it is not the same as contemplation or listening to music. I have recently come across the term "active meditation" which means that people relax when jogging or swimming or doing some other physical activity. Whilst these activities are all of great benefit, they are not meditation. However the Great Master advocated often that we should be conscious of every breath in every activity as it is beneficial and promotes more awareness.

A simple technique to practise, when you are not driving or flying an aeroplane, is to find a quiet place and to sit on a chair with your spine straight or cross legged on the floor with your chin slightly down. If you cannot sit then lie down. It is better to sit unless it is at the end of the day and you want to fall asleep. Close your eyes and your mouth and slowly breathe in and out of your nose. Do not hold your breath or breathe with discomfort. Observe the breath without controlling it. You are now going to focus in various *chakras* a couple of inches inside in front of the spine for anywhere between two to five minutes depending on how much time you have. Start with the forehead. Observe inside. Just watch your inhalation and exhalation. Be relaxed. Calmness will come. Focus there. After a few minutes, move your attention down to the throat area again a couple of inches inside, watch again, then follow this process by observing inside the centre of the chest, the belly button area, genital area and at the bottom between the genitals and the anus. Can something so simple really bring benefit? See what happens to your breath. Many people say they are open-minded. Are you? This is a very basic way to begin meditation and can be practised anywhere. If thoughts come, just continue. Find a specific time each day to practise. Should the desire come to go deeper into meditation then find a path or teacher that suits you and your mind. I have close friends who have had no interest at all in meditation, but they have all benefited from practising this simple technique to help relieve stress. It is very easy to tell someone to be more relaxed but how to achieve this is not generally taught by parents or teachers.

CALMNESS IS GODLINESS

The Great Master often repeated that, "Calmness is Godliness." The main benefit of meditation has been the receipt of more inner peace and awareness. I cannot deny that some of my old reactions and agitations may still manifest, but I am more aware of what I want to change in my behaviour and meditation creates the platform for me to do so. I have found that a calm mind possesses the potential to succeed; a restless mind misses the potential.

When I sit down to practise Kriya Yoga, sometimes I go into the state of nothingness known as *parabhasta*. It does not always take place or last a long time but it gives me encouragement to continue. I may have experiences for months on end and then no experiences for months thereafter. Yet the Invisible Hand keeps driving me to persist. What I now notice after many years of practice is that stillness comes very quickly, often within minutes of starting to meditate. Ten years ago, I would never have believed that this would be possible.

It is really difficult to describe the experience of meditation in the same way as it is nearly impossible to accurately describe the taste of food to someone who has never eaten before. You have to taste it to really know. Meditators often talk about detachment and yet I do not think that many are really compassionately detached. Masters talk about detachment with love and this is one quality that I would like to develop more. I am only too aware that wanting to be more loving is one thing yet loving with detachment in practice is quite another. I have subtly experienced detached love in a relationship and it felt quite strange at times because it was new. My best description and experience of loving detachment so far is disassociation with the world around me (and sometimes my mind or body) but not in a cold, rejecting manner. It is a feeling of peace without running away from the world. I am in the world but not of the world. It is neither contentment nor discontentment and more like total neutrality. Experiencing this inner peace is not always easy to communicate in words; nor can words describe that deep inner silence and joy. What is certain is that unless I had experienced meditation I would never have been able to find an antidote to stress that did not involve alcohol or other intoxicants.

CHAPTER 5

KRIYA YOGA: THE ANCIENT PATH OF MEDITATION

The only reason I was attracted to practising Kriya Yoga was because I was impressed by the Great Master and latterly Smiling Swami. I had never been interested in yoga before. The Great Master often said that Kriya Yoga was the safest, surest, quickest technique to gain calmness and godliness. He did not say this in an arrogant way but more as a matter of fact. *Kriya* means the "Soul is doing the work or activity." The common meaning of *yoga* is "to be united" or "union". I am told by Smiling Swami that *yoga* has 32 meanings including friendship, devotion, an opportunity, carrying on a business and even being a thief or a spy! So everyone is an unconscious yogi, it seems. Kriya Yoga encompasses all of the 108 authentic yogas mentioned in the ancient Indian Vedic scriptures and is described in *Autobiography of a Yogi*, one of the best selling spiritual books of all time by the great Kriya Yoga master Paramahamsa Yoganandaji.

If you are like me and cannot touch your toes or sit on the floor cross-legged then that is not a barrier to learn Kriya Yoga. I can still practise the techniques and receive the same benefit as anybody else. In fact my lack of physical suppleness has been an advantage as I spend more time on the breathing techniques which take the student into deeper meditation. The practice of Kriya Yoga gives all round development of mind, body and spirit, but this does not mean that other yogas are not beneficial. Kriya Yoga is non sectarian and is not a religion. Beliefs or religious practices do not need to be given up to practise this technique. Those who love God through their own religion can still also enjoy the benefits of Kriya Yoga.

AS IS THE BREATH SO IS THE MIND

The Great Master said "As is the breath so is the mind; as is the mind so is the man." When he said this he was referring to both genders. The key ingredient to calmness is the breath. If my breath is still, my mind is still. If my breath is restless, then my mind and body will be restless. If the breath is not still and I am not relaxed then I cannot go into deep meditation. In fact in deep meditation my breath almost seems to stop. It becomes feeble, as if there is no inhalation or exhalation taking place.

In spite of my experiences you should not be under the impression that I am advanced in meditation just because I am writing about it. After fourteen years of Kriya Yoga and four years of other meditation I genuinely see myself as a beginner. However I can tell you that I am more peaceful and joyful and this is 100% correlated to the state of my breath. As soon as I become agitated by someone or something, I notice that my breath changes and becomes more uneven and restless. When I am relaxed and feeling detached and loving then I react more positively and calmly as negative situations arise. This is almost the opposite of how I would have reacted when a problem arose in business. If I could not get what I wanted when I knew it was possible, I became restless or agitated and would not rest until a solution came to me. This did not mean that after such a reaction that I ran around like a headless chicken.

After reacting I would search for a practical solution. Yet the more I was agitated the more stress I placed on my body and mind. Kriya Yoga has changed this reaction. If I reflect, it has been deeply transforming and totally life changing.

Meditation is now firmly embedded yet in spite of this I genuinely wonder whether some of my old patterns of behaviour would reappear if I went back into the aggressive work environment. The nature of running a business is aggravation and it is not easy to be non-reactive. However if I had not meditated at all when I was working all hours then my life would have been far more difficult. As I practise more, my aim is to become even calmer regardless of the circumstances. In conclusion, restlessness is often unavoidable but can be "treated" and reduced through meditation.

The solitary path

Both the spiritual seeker and entrepreneur follow a solitary path. They have much in common. They come across difficulties, obstacles and aggression. In business, being the boss can bring the rewards of being more in control and the potential to earn more money. Independent decision-making has always appealed to me. Self-employed people or entrepreneurs should not be so naïve to think that meditation will cure everything. What it did for me was to keep me sane under intense pressure. So why not just listen to music or watch TV to relax? I did and still do. But while the mind is still active during these activities, meditation helps it to switch off and rejuvenate completely. After a good meditation my mind and body are far more relaxed. This means my health is better and I rarely suffer from illness.

Meanwhile the spiritual seeker may find he or she

becomes less interested in external activities which can bring underlying criticism from friends and family even if such criticism is subtle. People do not generally welcome change. Choosing to go on retreats instead of beach holidays can also cause tension with partners. To keep balance between family, work and children, meditation time has to be carefully managed. The gurus I have met re-emphasise the importance of family and responsibilities but also remind us that there are 24 hours in the day and we should not waste time. Making space for meditation is vital but not in a way that is damaging to others.

IS CALMNESS CONTAGIOUS?

When I was stressed at work I sometimes asked Laid Back Cigar Man why he was not taking a crisis seriously because he was so non-reactive. He would reply that there was no point in both of us being stressed. He was right of course. So I should not really be surprised that now I am calmer others around me can become agitated by this. I also learnt that just because people meditate they are not always calm. There are rare people in the world like Laid Back Cigar Man who does not meditate and who are far more relaxed than me. I am working towards being calm in all circumstances and if I do not always succeed I do not beat myself up too much.

THE THREE BODIES:
CAUSAL, ASTRAL AND PHYSICAL

After Kriya Yoga initiation, I experienced seeing light, hearing sound and feeling vibration. The light and sound were infrequent but I felt the divine vibration constantly. I can think of any part of my body and it will vibrate. All of these experiences are aspects of AUM. AUM is actually a sound to hear, feel and see rather than just to chant.

"A" is for Sound and represents the causal body. The causal body is the cause of everything. "U" is for Vibration and represents the astral body. This is the body of mind and thoughts. "M" is for Light and represents the physical body. Some people experience all, some or none of these qualities even when they are not meditating. It must be very troubling for those who are not being guided by a master to have these experiences as most vicars, rabbis or priests are unlikely to have any idea about these occurrences.

There are many philosophies on how many planes of existence and bodies there are. The Great Master teaches as follows:

The causal body is the cause of everything, both good and bad. It is the cause of all thoughts and it provides the environment where the seed or sprout of karma can grow or remain dormant. It creates the veil of ignorance resulting in forgetfulness of our true divine nature. The causal body is experienced in deep sleep in the state of non-awareness of time, thoughts or the physical body.

The astral body consists of our mind which apparently we do not use anywhere near to its full potential. Smiling Swami teaches that if we think of the past then that event is still taking place in the astral body.

The physical body experiences the net result from the astral and causal bodies. The physical body sits inside the astral body. The causal body is invisible, is the size of a small dot and sits between the third eye and the fontanel in the engine room of the bodies, the pituitary gland.

As more consciousness comes, more light can be

experienced. The astral body expands with this light. The physical body feels lighter. I asked Smiling Swami what happens at realisation. He explained that for some there is an explosion of light which is indescribable. At that moment the three bodies are no longer bound by karma.

In the next life and those that follow, the realised person comes back clean and unaffected by future actions but with past memories. In deep meditation there is no awareness of any of the bodies. I have experienced this sometimes but clearly not for long enough!

MEDITATION EXPERIENCES

Initiation into Kriya Yoga and the experience of AUM was like being given a key to the door of life. It is up to the recipient what they do with this key. After years of Kriya practice I still experience vibration, occasional light and occasional sound. As discussed earlier the main change is being aware of a very still breath. When I inhale this "still breath" it is like pure nectar. There is a gentle pulsation inside of the head coupled with extreme peace of mind. When I am in this state of total serenity and it continues throughout the day, little affects me. It seems that the breath is moving inside of my forehead and not through the lungs. A shallow breath without effort or strain would be the best description. As time progresses I have even experienced this for weeks on end. The yogis call this the *udana* breath. When I experience this "special" breath consciously in daily life it is like constant effortless meditation without the eyes being closed. The mind becomes still and is active only when required. When this "special" breath disappears it is a shock as I am pushed back into the world fully again and affected by what is happening around me. If I meditate for a long period of, say, three hours this breath may return but I regard this experience as being out of my control. However, the Great Master talked about another breath when pointing to the top of his head – the short breath. This is the breath which takes the spiritual aspirant to enlightenment.

In Kriya Yoga there are different techniques to learn. I have noticed that when I learn a new technique, the one that I had learnt previously becomes easier to practise. When I first meditated and had spiritual experiences I really felt that I was on a continuous natural high. However I did not give up if the experience diminished or did not repeat itself. I have come across people who run from guru to guru or from spiritual course to spiritual course to chase that high constantly. The Great Master observed that it is very difficult to go down a river with your right foot in one boat and your left foot in another! The boat will eventually arrive at the other side but surely the passenger will drown.

Experience is not what my spiritual journey is about. Experience is not enough. I want to know what is beyond experience.

MIND IS THE RECEIVER, THE PERCEIVER AND THE DECEIVER

When I first started to meditate I noticed that my mind was really busy. Meditation was supposed to still my mind yet it seemed to become really active instead of being calm. My take on the matter was that it was probably no more busy than usual so why worry about it? I had just never stopped to observe the mind without other distractions. Meditation is the real medicine for the mind. Like a well prescribed medicine it still works even if I do not believe that it will. "Is meditation dangerous?" I once asked the Great Master. He replied that finance was dangerous!

MONKEY MIND

Many people who meditate find their restless minds to be a problem. Instead of continuing they stop practising, giving the excuse that they are too restless to meditate. Their minds will still be restless even if they stop meditating so what do they have to lose by continuing? It is natural for the mind to be restless so why give up so easily? Restless people make good meditators because they need it so much that they see the benefits quickly. I decided early on to ignore the mind rather than engage with it as the thoughts ebbed and flowed. Being logical I told myself that if it is the job of my mind to be restless then let it do its job. These thoughts do not need to control me unless I allow them to do so. Why worry about it? My mind imagines most of the time and luckily my thoughts do not always manifest. So the next question is, will meditation work if my mind is busy? Yes absolutely. Will meditation work if I only have limited time each day? Yes absolutely. My experience is that sometimes when I meditate the thoughts are strong and sometimes they are not. This does not prevent me from meditating so why make it a barrier? The main excuse people give for not meditating is, "I do not have the time." However these same people manage to find the time to use mobile phones, Twitter, Facebook and emails when before these technologies existed nobody had the time to meditate either. We find time for what we want to do and are experts at finding activities that keep the mind busy rather than still.

Time analysis

Have you ever thought what you spend the most time doing in your life? Breathing. Up until my 48th birthday I have breathed over 368 million times, assuming an average of fifteen breaths per minute and 21,000 breaths per day. It is the most important thing that I do but before meditation I never paid attention to it.

I have also slept approximately 109,000 hours assuming six and a half hours sleep per night and meditated for approximately 8,000 hours in eighteen years. This excludes contemplation or thinking of the Divine.

Some yogis believe that we are given a certain amount of breaths in our lives and the speed we breathe determines our life span. If we are angry and agitated then we breathe far quicker and without natural rhythm, which can lead to poor health and premature death. If we observe the animal kingdom, giant tortoises are believed to breathe four–five breaths per minute and live between 100–200 years. Meanwhile elephants and whales breathe for a similar length of time and also have long lives compared to other animals such as dogs that breathe 24 breaths per minute and live on average fifteen years.

I was asked to speak about meditation to a group of fifty people who were going through divorce. 95% had never meditated before. I asked them how many minutes were in the day. There were no mathematicians in the room so I told them the answer: 1440 minutes. I asked them:

What percentage of the day did they smile?

What percentage of the day did they say thank you?

What percentage of the day did they say something positive?

What percentage of the day did they spend helping someone?

What percentage of the day were they stressed or angry?

What percentage of the day were they thoughtless or selfish?

What percentage of the day did they worry?

What percentage of the day did they watch TV or use email or mobile phones?

I then enquired how they used each 1% or fourteen minutes of their day carrying out the above activities. The latter three options proved to be the most popular and can be carried out simultaneously!

At the end of my talk I asked everyone to close their eyes and observe their breath. The room was totally silent. I timed this mini meditation to last fourteen minutes and then thanked everyone for giving 1% of their day to meditation.

If everyone on the planet gave just 1% of their day to meditation and kept the remaining 99% for other activities surely the world would be a better place. There is always time.

Silence is golden

When I first went on silent retreats I found it was almost impossible not to speak. On my first retreat in 1999 in a bleak snow-filled Germany, I was sharing a room with Joy. The silent retreat had a programme for each day which included three meditations with classes and lectures in between. This was a full and tiring schedule especially for those of us who were quite new to meditation. Initially Joy and I had to force ourselves to stop speaking about who would shower first.

After a day we got more into the rhythm of silence and it became more natural. We were also told that while on retreat we could read a book but if we could avoid reading we would be following "noble silence". By day three, my mind was screaming. Then slowly the mind began to calm down. I could hear inner silence in the form of the AUM sound. By the end of the retreat I felt totally chilled out. As I watched what was happening internally I became more aware of the part of me which felt like my essence or my soul. Each year I continued to attend these retreats and found real benefit and a welcome escape from the stresses of work.

PRACTICE MAKES PERFECT

When new students learn Kriya Yoga, they promise to practise every day. Most break this promise within one week! Meditation is a necessity rather than a chore. Why would we deny ourselves a practice that increases efficiency and makes us calmer? In order to change existing habits, discipline is needed. It took me at least five years of daily meditation before it became as natural as brushing my teeth each morning. It was helpful to practise at the same time each day. So when is the best time to meditate? The short answer is any time, although some advocate that it is preferential to meditate before sunrise and sunset. It is *never* not a good time to meditate. Once my mind became used to the regime of meditating at the same time of day, it accepted this and became quieter. I knew immediately that meditation was good for my mind, body and emotions. I have never looked back. I could not miss a day of meditation. Not because of the attachment to the experience but because it is as important as breathing.

NEW CAREER

Since leaving finance, my full time job has been inner reflection, change and growth as well as writing this book. This has not been a narcissistic pursuit. Retaining sanity is vital on this path of inner work. Good progress can only be achieved with a balanced approach and my gurus have been essential in this. It is difficult to proceed with anything in life without being able to consult an experienced teacher. I am aware that others who yearn for material or spiritual success are not so fortunate. Not finding a good teacher or role model makes life harder. Meditation is the best remedy I have found but how many take it? It is good for me and contrasts starkly with the long term negative effects of seeking happiness through excessive intoxicants, loveless and addictive sex, compulsive gambling or continuous over-eating. If we follow the latter path are we really so deadened and unconscious to the harm we are causing to ourselves? Why is it that when we should be doing something good for ourselves at times of stress that we end up doing something bad for ourselves? An example is a smoker who lights the first cigarette of the day who coughs continually as he or she fills their lungs with carbon monoxide when we know oxygen is what we need to live. Of course there is nothing wrong in enjoying a few drinks or our favourite food in moderation, but can we stop at a few?

Desires are linked to certain *chakras*. By watching desires closely as they arise I can discriminate which ones I want to manifest. This does not mean that I should follow all of my desires. I watch some diminish of their own accord like a fruit dying on a tree. I am also learning to watch my thoughts more before making a decision. Often I fail dismally and then try again. This is totally the opposite to my attitude in business which was to proactively seek a solution or remedy to a problem quickly. However in business, Laid Back Cigar Man and my father acted as my anchors giving balance to my decision-making process as problems arose.

CLEANING

Once the Great Master and Smiling Swami were in Germany. They walked onto the street in their orange clothes. On the street were cleaners who were also wearing orange. The Great Master commented that they were in the same profession. The street cleaners cleaned the outside and the yogis cleaned the inside!

In the same way that it is necessary to clean the house where we live, the house that we were given at birth, our bodies, also needs cleaning. I am not referring to the obvious outer cleaning but the inner cleaning. Many spend time following diets or keep fit regimes and sleeping yet how many do anything for the mind? Meditation helps the mind to rest. The mind can still be overactive in sleep which does not lead to a satisfying rest. When I watch my breath in the *chakras* within before I sleep, I nearly always have a peaceful rejuvenating rest. Meditation is essential daily maintenance.

CHAKRAS

There are seven main *chakras* ("energy centres") in and around the body. The Great Master referred to the body as a house with seven storeys representing the seven main *chakras*.

These are detailed below:

A *chakra* is an energy centre which is invisible to most of us but visible to a few. Imbalance in any of these *chakras* gives trouble mentally, emotionally and physically. Meditation helps to balance the energy in the *chakras* resulting in a more peaceful life.

A balanced *chakra* can be compared to the pilot light in a gas boiler. The pilot light stays on permanently and burns gently and evenly. When energy is needed, the thermostat clicks and the pilot light fires up the boiler automatically. Once the house or water is warm, the fire subsides back to the original flame. If the fire continues to burn vigorously non-stop when no longer required then eventually this will cause a fault with the boiler. If it burns too much the boiler will break down. Conversely, if it does not burn enough then the boiler will not work efficiently. In each *chakra* a fire or *agni* resides. The energy and "flame" increases in a particular *chakra* when an activity is carried out relating to that specific *chakra*. If the energy in a certain *chakra* is overused or abused through living in excess, then, like a candle running out of wick, in time the fire will not burn evenly, causing an imbalance in emotional, physical or mental health. Meanwhile if the energy in a certain *chakra* is deficient, then a person will have low energy levels or difficulty carrying out daily activities. A constant deficiency in a *chakra* can lead to poor physical, mental and emotional wellbeing and even fear. If the pilot light goes out in any chakra then death occurs!

The guru or spiritual teacher is like the boiler man who knows how to make the repairs and advise on maintenance. The three lower *chakras* are particularly active in our daily lives. They are sometimes referred to as the "animal centres" because these are the centres in which animals live their lives.

Survival and the material world reside in the lower centre which is located between the anus and the sexual organs. It is also known as the *muladhara chakra*. This is where the fire for material desire and wealth is situated. If this fire does not burn evenly then the person will have a hard time surviving in the world and have financial problems. If the fire burns too much then greed and overindulgence will follow while too much aggression can result in stress and heart problems. Too little money gives trouble as does too much money.

Procreation and relationships operate in the second centre where the sexual organs are located. This centre is known as the *svadhisthana chakra*. It is where the fire for family, relationships, sexual energy and procreation emanates. If someone has too little fire in this area then family problems will prevail and the person may have sexual and relationship problems. Too much fire or overindulgence may give rise to unhealthy relationships which can lead to agitation, fear, sexually transmitted disease, unwanted children and broken homes.

The vitality of life and health reside in the third *chakra* which is also the food centre located in the area of the belly button. This centre affects the mind greatly. The third centre is known as the *manipura chakra*. This fire controls the desire for food and digestion. If we eat too much or overindulge in alcohol, or other substances, then the body will be strained and the mind agitated. I have observed that what I eat influences my mind and its state of restlessness or tranquillity. Eating healthy food results in a more balanced mind. If I overdose on desserts or sugar, my mind and body react. In fact if I consume too much sugar in a short period of time even the thought of having something sweet will make me sweat. Often people with low fire in the third centre will have low energy and have a desire for spicy food to give them more fire. Those who already have high energy and eat spicy food will be highly restless and probably suffer from insomnia. Those who overindulge in food and alcohol increase the risk of suffering from diabetes or far worse illnesses. Under-eating or too much fasting can also lead to acute mental imbalance.

A day off from eating now and again may be beneficial for the body and mind. Some spiritual masters fast two or three days per month to rest the internal organs but the lesson of Buddha was that fasting and a total disregard for physical health is not the balanced way. The Great Master ate three small meals a day and he did not advocate fasting as a way to attain balance. Fasting in an extreme way can lead to a person having an erratic mental and emotional state. Such a diet gives imbalance and contradicts the teachings of my masters. In addition focussing on not eating food can make the mind very restless. In conclusion, an imbalanced diet either through eating in excess or in paucity leads to mental unhappiness and possible disease.

The fourth centre is in the centre of the chest. It is known as the heart centre or the *anahata chakra*. This is where the fire of emotion is located. If we lack emotion then this makes us cold and if we have too much emotion then it affects our rationality, judgement and balance. A balanced heart *chakra* will lead to healthy expression of emotion with love and openness.

The fifth centre in the throat area is known as the *vishuddha chakra*. This is where the religious or creative fire is located. It is the place from where communication emanates. If imbalanced we can become over-expressive, radical and extreme in our views or religious opinions. Fanaticism can become dangerous for all of us. Tolerance and kindness in speech can on the other hand help and not hinder.

The sixth centre is in the centre of the forehead. It is commonly known as the third eye, the Soul centre or the *ajna chakra*. This is where the spiritual opening is located and is the place of intuition. Life's energy charged with divinity descends from here. The yogis believe that the pituitary gland behind this area is the powerhouse of the brain, body and entry point to divine consciousness. Through the practice of Kriya Yoga a yellow circle of light can appear when meditating and concentrating in this area. Other colours may also appear. It is not imagination. I have experienced it.

The seventh centre known as the *sahasrara chakra* is located around the fontanel. This is the small soft spot on the top of the head which is more prominent when we are born. By concentrating here, the Great Master taught that the formless stage can be experienced, beyond the five elements in the body (earth, air, fire, water and ether). He often referred to this area as Infinity North. Only with a tranquil mind can the changeless, immortal soul be witnessed. Heavenly bliss is here.

Animals spend their time in the lower three *chakras* to survive, procreate and eat. If we stay active in these centres only, then we are not much different to animals in our behaviour. If we use the positive feelings and emotions of our heart *chakra* and express ourselves in a balanced way from the throat centre, then we are not as bound to the lower three centres. When we focus on the Soul Centre and the fontanel which are activated more through meditation then we become more conscious of our divine instincts and have less animal tendencies. The Great Master taught pointing to the top of his head, "You are to roam in here." He also said that metaphorically if we remain in the top two centres we are in heaven, but if we remain in the five centres below without consciousness we are in hell.

My experience of the change in emphasis and operation of my *chakras* is as follows:

In the first period of my life I had to learn survival and to keep my emotions in check. This was necessary to survive boarding school and the trauma of a difficult home environment. Controlling emotions helped me to develop the drive to achieve. All these basic and essential needs in the world require the use of the bottom three centres. From the ages of 18 to 31 I also stayed in the lower centres more, enjoying food, wine, sex and working very hard. Hopefully I also used some of the positive qualities from my higher centres, otherwise I would have been a ruthless, uncaring person in business and relationships. At 31 my consciousness changed quickly through my spiritual experiences. Overnight I no longer drank alcohol and my food became simpler. I became vegetarian and then mainly vegan.

From my mid thirties I continued to be driven to succeed materially but while the target was the same, the purpose changed with more focus on the higher *chakras*. It was as if the Invisible Hand had sent me in a direction from a young age with ambition to succeed materially whilst all along this was not the real plan. I began to realise that this success was not just for me. I could help others also. At 49 years old I notice that the fires in the centres are burning quite evenly and that my mind is generally still and not overactive, yet old patterns of agitation may still arise occasionally. More and more I am avoiding these situations and feeling less attached. Being removed from the responsibility of work has of course made a huge difference and fortunately I have not had the desire to start creating new businesses and ventures.

I have no doubt that by practising Kriya Yoga, the regulation and balance of my *chakras* have improved. The breath has begun to flow more evenly and gently. My health is good and I keep physically fit. The fires within the *chakras* are more inactive now which is due to my changed lifestyle. It really feels like the energy from the lower five *chakras* has "returned" to the source which is more apparent in the sixth and seventh centres as I need this energy less.

I also aspire to avoid the isms – fanaticism, criticism, extremism – which reside in the throat centre. The spiritual aspirant needs to attain excellence in all of the five lower *chakras* to stay rooted in the sixth and seventh *chakras*. Escapism is not an option.

CHANGES IN DIET

If the lower *chakras* are not looked after, then the foundation for a healthy life will not be strong and cracks will appear later. So how to take care of the seven storeys? Moderation in drinking and eating is a good start. A little exercise which does not just involve going to the fridge when the TV adverts come on is also important!

On my 31st birthday I went out and enjoyed a fillet steak. The next day I announced that I would no longer eat meat. No longer eating fish and chicken soon followed. When my intake of three bowls of chicken soup on a Friday night reduced to zero then I knew that a permanent change had taken place. For someone who loved bacon and sausage sandwiches this was quite a shift. As a child the only vegetable I would eat was peas. However giving up being a carnivore happened very naturally without any effort at all. In a similar way I stopped drinking alcohol shortly afterwards. Same pattern; I woke up one morning and said that I would no longer drink. At first friends, work colleagues and business associates did not believe it. The desire had gone naturally of its own accord. You should not now think that to meditate it is necessary to give anything up. The Great Master observed that if spiritual advancement was only down to diet then all of the cows would be realised as they are vegetarian.

I recently spoke to a psychologist who was very suspicious of me when I said that I did not drink. I could hear her brain ticking over assuming that I had suffered from a drink problem! When the desire for alcohol ended it was without any struggle. My body just did not want it anymore. Sometimes there is no reason at all. In a similar way in my early twenties, I gave up cigarettes and went from a packet a day to zero overnight. Unlike many smokers, when I started to have pains in my chest, common sense prevailed and I gave up smoking immediately in spite of the discomfort of the detox that followed. I believe that it was through grace that I stopped smoking.

If the desire came again to drink, smoke or eat meat, then there is nothing stopping me. I did not have to fight to give them up, so I am not fighting a desire to start again. My body and mind surely appreciate the changes. I certainly do not advocate that others should follow what I have done. But, what is clear is that a huge contributory factor to my health and happiness is my good diet. If I had continued over-eating, drinking or smoking in excess for short term happiness and escapism, poor health would more than likely have manifested sooner or later. Poor health cannot be passed onto someone else. Abuse of the body through excess is not the answer. I now know that what makes me happy can only come from inside. Do you lead a lifestyle that is really good for you?

Regarding eating meat, fish or chicken there are enough scare reports to put me off for life. However I respect those who have a different view as I did before becoming vegetarian. After giving up meat I did then think about how much fear I had been eating. Animals when slaughtered are afraid. Fear of any kind is generally contagious. I never heard of an abattoir where the animals went joyously to their slaughter.

So, I eat what is good for me, cook and eat with love and am grateful for the food on my plate. I am also grateful to the people that planted, grew, picked and transported the food to my table. The love and care required to grow vegetables and fruit is incredible. I also normally remember to say a prayer of gratitude at the start of a meal. It really makes the food taste better.

PURPOSE OF LIFE

Last year an old friend remarried. On the night before his wedding he emailed me at four o'clock in the morning thanking me for my friendship. He told me that for the first time he was contemplating his life and his future. How often does anyone take time to look at themselves and their lives? Do we take the time to even ask what is the purpose of our lives? Why should we? I would never have asked myself why I was here, but the Great Master was very clear to me. He said that the only purpose of life was to attain Self-realisation. He told me that life was not a broken dream. The only purpose of marriage or to succeed or fail was to realise the truth. Self-realisation is to be in conscious union with the Divine or the Invisible Hand at every moment. Buddhists refer to this state as enlightenment. The Great Master's reality check made me pause for thought. Your trigger when it comes to stop and look inside could be quite different. Such a moment might come at any time and act as a mini realisation for changes in your life for the good. I know that these special moments with the Great Master put me on a new course. I asked him often to help give me more sincerity. Although I sacrificed my time and energy in creating my business which paid dividends, I always had a goal in mind rather than constant career progression and the accumulation of more and more wealth. Achieving this material goal was nothing more than an unconscious spiritual practice to achieve other goals in my life. It is practice for the next task. Like most readers, when I was working flat out even when visiting the Great Master, I found it really difficult to make time to reflect and meditate sincerely as there always seemed to be an urgent activity to do. Now I have all the time in the world which is a potential recipe for even more restlessness. In my case my mind was ready to rest so I experienced less restlessness. Most of the time the mind needs a purpose.

WHAT CAN I DO?

Sometimes I ask Smiling Swami if there is anything that I should do. He has told me to be the most relaxed man in the world! It is not as easy as you may think. Restlessness and agitation still arise especially as my mind is less active than when I worked. So what is my life purpose? Whilst my natural inclination is to think that it is indeed my life, is this really the case or is it a gift from the Universe? After all I cannot control how long I am here and when I will leave. Yet if it is not *my* life how can *I* attain this state of consciousness if so many events around me are out of my control? I am strangely comforted to follow the spiritual philosophy that I am not the doer but not to escape from life or responsibility. Some spiritual people I meet claim they are not the doer yet when something negative happens to them they conveniently blame it on a past life, someone else or God. Conversely, when events are going well it is easy to be happy and take the credit! However like all theories and philosophies, talking about them is very different to experiencing them. My experience is clear. I no longer accept that my mind needs to be unhappy and restless. However as I continue to watch TV or read the newspapers I find that my mind is still influenced and even polluted.

For the first thirty years of my life my purpose was to learn, play and achieve materially. I thought that this would create the happiness which I sought, wanted and needed. When spiritual experiences happened of their own accord consciousness gave me new purpose. Yet strangely I did not apply the same focus as I did with business success. I wanted to advance spiritually but without achieving spiritually as I sensed that any achievement was not in my hands. So there was a clear difference in my approach to material and spiritual aspirations. I let the spiritual journey unfold gradually without making it my ambition to progress spiritually. I recognised from the beginning that it was not of my doing. In terms of ambition, with regard to material success, I had been striving towards a goal of being materially successful because I believed that wealth in its basic form would give me freedom. Yet halfway through this journey of striving for wealth, when spirituality arrived I saw that the goal for wealth was not going to be enough. I still wanted material success but with a spiritual purpose to life. Every achievement is vital for spiritual growth and learning.

The Great Master describes the real state of love and detachment through his experience of deep meditation where "the seer, the sight and the seen are one". This is a comforting description of where I hope that I am heading. I am more open-minded and watchful about my different states of emotion and how I express love. If I am in a bad mood when I wake up, I observe this state especially if it appears for no apparent reason. Watching the reactions inside of me good or bad is a way to develop detachment rather than escape or denial. I have to believe that when I am unhappy it must be through grace, and, that same grace also applies when I am happy. Perhaps unhappiness makes me appreciate happiness more. So unhappiness has its purpose. It is easy to forget that everything has a purpose.

CHAPTER 6

FAITH, BELIEF & ABILITY

When I worked I never stopped to think why success had come to me. I later realised that the main ingredients to any success in my life have been faith, belief and ability. A little impatience helped also! The Great Master said that we need "faith, good company and practice which will lead to perfection".

What do I mean by success? Firstly I should clarify my success. Although I retired at 42, I have no desire or wish to make out that I know something that others do not or can give you any secret formula. Perhaps my mix of business and spiritual experience and knowledge is unusual. Although I achieved financial success, I was helped by many people. With regard to my negatives and positives, I followed the policy of smothering my negative tendencies with my positives. I did not spend time focussing on what I could not do but rather on what I could do. This did not mean that I did not want to improve myself or learn new things and I most certainly have not overcome all of my negatives.

Enthusiasm counts for a lot in life. I love learning from people who have rare knowledge or think in a different way to me. Luckily Laid Back Cigar Man always knew something I did not and I hope vice versa. Now that I have retired I have more time to think deeply about issues that arise or to ignore them completely. Taking time for self-analysis is vital for anybody who wants to advance whatever their profession or hobby. Those who do not contemplate their lives are living in poverty and could become beggars in the world searching for happiness. Those who theorise, imagine, talk or dream about success, will not change their circumstances one iota. Imagination may make me aware of the dream that I want to achieve but will not produce results. It is like looking at the menu of a restaurant for hours on end; it shows me what is available but will not satisfy my hunger.

I am intrigued rather than put off by other people's negatives and "cannot do" attitude. Enthusiasm is a must and helps make the hardest tasks easier. If I am not enthusiastic, the journey to achievement will be devoid of joy. It is up to me to change my attitude if my appetite wanes. I have found that with a little lateral thinking and faith most things are possible. Every problem can be solved. When the imaginary brick wall appears, how do I overcome it? Change direction, walk through it or climb over it? Obstacles overcome are no longer obstacles. Turning back has never been my way when a challenge arises. The same attitude is needed when a meditator has problems concentrating or even making time to practise meditation. What is to be gained by giving up?

A positive outlook helps to find a solution. For example, if you see a glass half full of water, will you perceive the glass as being half-full or half-empty? The positive person will see the glass as half-full and the negative person will see the glass as half-empty. The Zen master will enquire which glass? Meanwhile the yogi will see the glass as full. Half-full with water and half-full with air.

BECOME GOOD AT SOMETHING

Successful people are good at being successful. They focus on what they know and not on what they do not know. If they do not know they find out. They make fewer mistakes or they could not succeed. Everyone is good at something.

Doubtful people spend too much time on what they lack which is unproductive. Even lazy people are good at being lazy! Laziness can be transformed into relaxation by slowly introducing positive habits. Angry and stressed out people are good at being angry and stressed out. Meditation can help rebalance these negative qualities so that they can in the words of the Great Master become "Calmly active and actively calm".

In case you think that I was totally organised or calm in everything that I did, this was not so. I was not always the tidiest worker but I knew where everything was except for my car keys which I lost periodically. As a solution, I bought a bleeper system that found the keys. This solved the problem until I could not find the bleeper! Another bad habit was creating lots of different computer passwords to keep myself sharp. This caused me no end of trouble and cursing when I tried to reopen an old document and had forgotten the password.

Many have far more money and many are far more spiritually advanced than me. My real success (which I now question is even mine) is that I have found and experienced peace and happiness inside even though it does not always last. I can sit down and enjoy my own company without any external factors influencing this happiness. This was not the case when I worked so I know the difference between happiness and unhappiness.

FAITH AND BELIEFS

Holding onto rigid beliefs can become an unhelpful smokescreen and burden in life. If my belief system is based solely on someone else's belief or what they have heard or read, then how much practical value does this belief really have?

I view my beliefs as being impermanent. I leave space for new beliefs to come in and for old ones to go. Just believing blindly in God would not be enough for me. After spiritual experiences came to me spontaneously of their own accord, I no longer needed to hope or feel that some mystical presence was behind me every step of the way. I now knew. Perhaps my confidence in life is based on this intuition that the Invisible Hand has always been with me even if I never really knew it or thought about it before. I feel so fortunate to have found some peace, as a life with constant doubt and fear must be miserable. Many "successful" people in business or even spirituality can be pretty downright miserable. The more confidence I have in God, the more confidence and faith I have in myself. This brings more joy but does not mean that my beliefs change substantially or that I jump from ship to ship. Beliefs based on ancient alleged facts can lead to fanaticism. Such beliefs can be misguided at best and dangerous at worst. I am happy with my beliefs. Are you happy with yours? The more impermanent my beliefs the more open I am to tear them up.

Beliefs have some importance but are surely not as relevant as experience. Good experience leads to good knowledge and can bring wisdom beyond knowledge. Wisdom leads to stillness. My jewel in the crown is to have belief, faith and trust in myself. When I am strong with faith in myself everything works out. I now realise that faith has been given to me. It only seems like "my faith" but I am sure that it is generated from a hidden invisible force which exists internally and externally. The Invisible Hand is silently operating through me. When my faith in myself weakens, this is caused by restlessness in the mind. Doubts come when restlessness is present. Doubts cause no end of trouble. Kriya Yoga is the only antidote that I have found to dissipate restlessness, fears and doubts. It works like magic. When calmness, strength, intuition and belief are present, doubts disappear, which is comforting. Even when I do not believe that a result may turn out to be positive, "feeling the faith" cultivates positivity. Pessimism then quickly turns into optimism. Often I have an inner expectation of the result which then manifests but it does not always go to plan. I see the picture of the result that I want and it normally turns out that way or even better. This expectation is totally natural to me. Yet it is not that I feel that I deserve anything. I believe in myself more than I believe in others. This means that if I believe something is possible and others do not, I trust my own judgement rather than the belief of others. My inner belief has been reinforced more after meeting the Great Master and Smiling Swami. What they teach and practise fits generally with my rhythm and mindset even though they tell me things that have never even been contemplated by me. For example, I never thought about life after death or even considered that I might be here on this planet for any other reason than having fun and making money. Perhaps these thoughts come as a result of age and experience but I know several people in their seventies who never think like this and who are afraid of death. I do not fear death at all but would prefer to go quietly without suffering.

TRUST NOT TRICKS

In my second job in the finance industry the company motto was "trust not tricks". Trusting myself is more important than trusting the tricks of my mind or others. Although I trust myself more than others that does not mean that I do not value the advice and support of people around me without whom success would not have been possible. There is a saying that it is good to be friendly with many but to choose our friends carefully. My faith in myself is not arrogance but those with little faith may read it that way. When someone else has more ability than me, I admire their qualities and enjoy learning from them. Although I put a large amount of faith in myself this does not mean that I do not know my limitations. On reflection, over the years, many people have put faith in me and I hope for the most part that they have not been disappointed. Sometimes people divulge their secrets to me, knowing that I have no interest in telling others. In finance it is normal, or was the case, to keep information confidential so perhaps people sense something in me when they share their secrets.

It is probable that those with little faith or confidence do not trust others at all or are poor at choosing who to trust as every decision is tainted with doubt. This can lead to mixed results. People who are lazy and do not have faith in themselves or who do not care, experience the results accordingly. This lack of care or faith may also translate into poor judgement in choosing a mentor or adviser. I cannot see how someone can be successful without faith in themselves or the Invisible Hand or a mixture of both.

SO WHAT ABOUT MY FAITH IN GOD?

I did win the divinity prize at nine years old and spent half an hour as a choirboy before I ran out of the door. Some might argue that it was downhill from that moment! I really did not think about God so much. I went to church every day at boarding school for nine years and through parental pressure I went reluctantly to synagogue once or twice each year. It did not help that I was unimpressed with the rabbi who seemed rather condescending when he delivered his sermon. Another factor that put me off the Jewish religion was my father's expectation that I should marry someone who was Jewish, even though he was liberal and would pick and choose which aspects of the faith he wished to observe. I understand the reasoning behind his belief that I should marry someone from a similar cultural background, but the rate of divorce is just the same across the spectrum of same faith marriages or mixed faith marriages. Unsurprisingly I married a non-Jewish woman but to be fair to my father he did finally support me and my decision. It is a good example which shows that when parents impose their views rigorously the opposite of the desired result manifests.

It is obvious to me that the reason I and many others do not follow religion is due to the zealous way religion is sometimes presented. Luckily God understands me even if I do not follow religious worship or practices, but I respect others that do. We all have to find the rituals that suit us. If I want to pray to great prophets or masters like Buddha, Jesus, Mohammad, Moses or Krishna and feel their presence I can do so without having to follow any religious practice. Their love is for all of us. To be a scholar of scriptures is quite different to experiencing the presence of God. I once heard of a rabbi who lost his faith in God and had to be persuaded by some of his community that God did really exist! Doubt is of course natural and surely as more God consciousness comes to us then this dynamic consciousness overtakes blind faith. Those who teach with God-consciousness or humility are inspiring compared to others who preach religious dogma. I accept that tests of faith come to us, but the story was troubling to me as the rabbi must have been teaching theoretically rather than from his own inner truth. Another time, I went to see a famous rabbi speak about kabbalah, the mystical side of Judaism. The rabbi opened his talk by translating a verse from a scripture. He said that the meaning of the verse was that we should be "afraid of God"! After this comment I switched off. My God is about love and not fear. I was accompanied by a friend who is a scholar in Aramaic and Hebrew and practising Kabbalah. He told me that the rabbi had translated the verse incorrectly. The correct translation was to be "in awe of God". That made more sense to me.

Meditation has certainly increased my faith in God. With this faith my journey is to discover what is behind my experiences and the knowledge in the world. What is the truth of life?

FAITH IN THE GREAT MASTER

I have a close friend called Katie. She is in her sixties. Although she is older than me I feel and care for her as if she was my younger sister. About eight years ago, her body suddenly lost all energy and she could not move. An incredibly busy person's life changed literally overnight. She was diagnosed with Chronic Fatigue Syndrome. Her situation became precarious very quickly as her husband's health was poor and money became very tight. Neither could work any more. However, she had enormous faith in the Great Master who was no longer alive. Firstly she managed to obtain early retirement from her job which was not easy to achieve and received her pension lump sum which was not usual. Slowly her health improved but whenever she had more energy she overdid things and went back to square one. Then unexpectedly their landlord told them that he would be doubling the rent at the end of the lease which expired two months later. They were in real trouble. Nobody in the family had money or space to accommodate them. She prayed to the Great Master. In the following week a strange thing happened. She received a letter from a private housing trust whose list she had joined many years ago but had forgotten about. A house had become available and they wanted her to attend an interview to assess her financial circumstances. In short they were selected and ended up paying a small percentage of the rent that they had been paying, with secure tenancy for life.

Katie believed in the Great Master throughout her difficulties. Miracles do happen. I admire her faith and gratitude even though her life is still very tough.

SINCERE FAITH AND PRAYER

So do we all need a guru or to believe in God for a prayer to come true?

I am sure that sincere faith and prayer helps with or without a guru. However, it is not so easy to have faith in an intangible, invisible God. The guru acts as the divine representative who is conscious of God. The guru shows me how to go inside to become aware of that invisible force operating within and around me. Even if a prayer does not seem to be answered, it gives the person who is praying mental support, which is invaluable. Perhaps we all have a guru or an angel watching over and helping us even without our awareness. The tricky question to answer is why some of our prayers manifest and others do not. I cannot answer this question through my own real knowledge and experience, but believe that only good comes from sincere prayer and meditation. Some people link the results of prayer to karma and destiny which I will expand upon in the next chapter.

WHY DO DIFFICULTIES COME?

I do not claim to have the answer categorically from true personal knowledge, but I know that I have to live with circumstances that I cannot control even if I find them to be unfair or troubling. What I can do is help myself to overcome them using the faculties I have been given. I can control my fitness, what I eat and drink and whether I use intoxicants. I can decide whether I spend my time in good company and whether I behave honestly or dishonestly. If I abuse my body or live stressfully, I do not need a doctor to tell me that such a lifestyle will bring me trouble and illness. Amazingly we are warned how important it is to see a doctor before going on a diet but not advised to do so before overeating, smoking or abusing our bodies through alcohol! Instead of complaining about what we cannot control, perhaps we should be asking how much difficulty is brought about by our own negligence? 80% of us know about the 80% that we can and need to change about ourselves for our own benefit yet I doubt that more than 10% do something about it. Others in the world have little choice through poor education or terrible living conditions so those of us who are more fortunate have no excuse. We have to play the cards we have been dealt and make the best of each situation. It helps to have the comfort, support and guidance of the Invisible Hand.

Krakow: survival and faith in adversity

In 1997, the thought came to me to visit Auschwitz. I had never felt the urge to go there even though I had lost relatives in Poland in the Second World War. I made a call to a contact in London who gave me the name of Moniak, a holocaust survivor in Warsaw. When I told Moniak that I was vegetarian and did not speak Polish, he told me that I would have difficulties. Unperturbed and totally out of character, as usually I like to be prepared for holidays, I located some possible places to stay but did not book anything. I decided that as the idea had come from nowhere I would trust in the Invisible Hand and be guided accordingly.

I booked my flight and off I went. I sat on the plane and meditated. After some time the food was served and the lady sitting next to me started talking to me. Her first question was how long had I been meditating. We instantly had something in common. We chatted and when the plane landed we said goodbye. She was from Australia and was just starting her spiritual journey. I hailed a cab at the airport to take me to a Christian Centre close to Auschwitz that I had located in my guidebook. It was a cold December day and there was snow on the ground. Auschwitz is situated in a remote part of the world. One car was parked outside the centre and only one light was on in the building. I knocked on the door. Eventually someone answered. The young man who greeted me spoke good English. He told me they were just closing for Christmas. However he invited me in for some tea and cake and offered to take me to another hostel close by to see if there was a vacancy. Fortunately a room was available. I was being looked after.

The next day I went to Auschwitz concentration camp. I

walked around and imagined what terrors had taken place there. In the museum there are piles and piles of spectacles and mounds of human hair. I could touch the wooden slatted triple-layered "bunk beds" where the prisoners used to sleep. When I met Moniak later in Warsaw, he told me that disease was so rife that the strongest would climb to the top bunk. Those sleeping below them would rarely survive because they would suffer the ignominy of human faeces and urine coming through the slats whilst they slept, leading to more disease. I stood inside one of the gas chambers. It was natural for me to say prayers for those who had died there and I could sense that many others had prayed here before me.

As I was walking around Auschwitz I stumbled across the Australian lady from the aeroplane. She was on a guided tour. I was already planning on leaving the next day so after some discussion, the tour leader allowed me to join them for a lift into Krakow. I found a room in the same hotel as her. She came to my room and I offered to give her a healing session. In hindsight I thought it was very trusting for a woman to come to a stranger's room. We then had dinner and said goodbye. Occasionally thereafter we exchanged letters and she told me how her spiritual path was unfolding.

In addition, by chance in Krakow, I was walking around a park area and saw a restaurant. It was vegetarian. I went inside and the food was great. A concert pianist practised there every night which was wonderful. In Krakow itself I felt at home.

In spite of the warnings from my father's friend about the difficulties I would have about language and food, the Invisible Hand was looking after me and even putting me together with likeminded people. My faith was being rewarded on a basic level.

The black madonna

While in Krakow, I heard that the Black Madonna, one of the most religious sites for Catholics in Europe, was in Czestocowa. I had never heard of the Black Madonna and had no idea if it was a statue or something else. When I discovered that it was four hours away by bus I decided to go the next day. I sat next to a nun on the way who did not speak a word of English. When the bus reached its final stop, I followed the signs to the cathedral and started to walk around for an hour not really sure what I was looking for at all. Finally I found myself downstairs in a small chapel and walked towards the altar. On the wall was a painting of Mother Mary with Jesus. I read on the wall that this was the Black Madonna. Apparently it had oozed blood centuries ago when the painting was damaged when stolen. There were twenty seats in the small area in front of the picture so I sat down and started to meditate. After some time, I became aware that people were now sitting around me and many more were standing behind me. A service had just begun. I later discovered that the small chapel where I was sitting with the Black Madonna was rarely open outside of religious festivals, so I had been "lucky". I felt blessed for the experience.

In this environment I could feel the presence of the Invisible Hand and my body was vibrating from head to toe. My unplanned journey in Poland was unfolding of its own accord.

The last leg of my journey was to Warsaw. Warsaw was totally erased as a city in the Second World War and was then rebuilt. My contact Moniak, a survivor from

Auschwitz had helped me book the hotel. It was a dreary looking building that reminded me of a London office block from the 1960s. The next day I met him. I went to his office which was situated in an old concrete block. He was a successful publisher. He had agreed to spend the day with me and take me around Warsaw and the old Ghetto by foot. He told me that he was in his teens when the Occupation began and how as teenagers they used to throw home-made Molotov cocktails at the Nazis at night. The Nazis were afraid to go out at night. He showed me where one of his friends had been killed and where the resistance met. Then he took me to Treblinka, a concentration camp in the countryside one and a half hours from Warsaw. I had never heard of Treblinka.

On the way we passed over old railway tracks which the Germans later tried to hide in an attempt to cover up their evil activities. Then we arrived. A beautiful forest welcomed us. Lurking behind the forest was the site where the atrocities had taken place. Apparently the birds had not come to this area for fifty years after the Second World War. They must have known somehow what had taken place here. The Nazis, as cover for their atrocities, put a zoo there. One million people were exterminated here, mainly Jews. As I type these words it is almost unimaginable that I stood where such horrors had taken place in such a small, beautiful area. The picturesque surroundings made it seem even more chilling to me than Auschwitz as this spot was one of beauty rather than dereliction. There are 17,000 stones placed in remembrance of each village where a victim had come from.

FAITH AND SURVIVAL

As we were driving back to Warsaw, Moniak encouraged me to ask him questions about his concentration camp experiences. He proudly told me that when he had been found by the British at Buchenwald, having survived the death march from Auschwitz, he weighed five and a half stone (35kg) and had many diseases. He had even become a case study reported in a scientific journal as it was considered a miracle that he had survived.

I was interested to know whether the people who survived the concentration camps had faith in God. He told me that many survivors had been interviewed. One third believed they survived because of their faith in God. One third did not believe that God existed or the atrocity would not have happened and therefore relied solely on faith in themselves. One third, (the category in which he put himself) believed they had survived because they had faith in their friends or family in the camp. The common theme is that many survivors had strong faith even though what they had faith in varied. These answers demonstrate that any form of sincere faith is a positive attribute and can have an equal effect. Moniak told me that when he arrived at Auschwitz he was fifteen. He wore glasses. On his first day they broke. If the Nazis would have found out that he needed glasses to work and that he did not have any, they would have killed him instantly. His friends went without food for nearly a week to buy him glasses on the black market so that he could survive. It dawned on me how amazing human nature can be when put in extreme circumstances. This was an act of true friendship and true spirituality. To keep busy, Moniak read newspapers smuggled into the camp to inform others what was happening in the world. Later he realised that this was a fruitless exercise, but at the time he felt he was doing something worthwhile which gave him a sense of purpose keeping him active and useful. If Moniak could find purpose in such awful circumstances why do some of us find it difficult to stay focussed and upbeat in our lives? His job in the camp was to cart dead bodies to the cremation area.

Towards the end of the war, they were sent on a death march from Auschwitz. He remembered finding and eating a raw potato to survive. I began to think and feel ashamed of the food I have bought and wasted. He was very ill but unlike others who were dying around him, he and some of his closest friends survived. They lived life in an environment of humiliation, pain and suffering, yet if Moniak was anything to go by, the survivors came out with incredible humility and dignity making something of their lives. Just as we were speaking and driving back on a dual carriageway a man ran out in front of the car. We just missed him. Moniak was a little shaken. Immediately I thought of God and then I asked him if he thought that it was a miracle that we had not hit him. He stumbled to answer. I had no doubt that a grave incident had been averted as the speed we were going would surely have killed the man on impact.

When I met Moniak he must have been in his seventies. It was a great blessing to hear directly about his experience and how he had survived such a terrible ordeal. Unlike many survivors he decided not to record his experiences on film so I felt honoured and humbled by our meeting. After the concentration camps many survivors became very successful in the world.

Faith appears in many guises even in the most trying circumstances.

TO BELIEVE OR NOT TO BELIEVE, THAT IS THE QUESTION

So regardless of belief in God or otherwise, believers and non-believers survived. Religious people might argue that you need strong faith in God to survive such a trauma yet the statistics given to me by Moniak show that in fact two thirds survived with no faith in God. Perhaps we can demonstrate even unconsciously our faith in the Divine by putting faith in ourselves and other people.

So does the businessman have more faith in his or her business ability than the spiritual seeker has in God? Faith in myself is nothing more than faith in the Invisible Hand whether I am conscious of that or not. Many spiritual seekers could learn a lot from the busy successful entrepreneur about faith in adversity. Yet where does this faith come from? Can it be explained by us humans who are only using a fraction of our potential? Can we put faith in scientists who also have limited understanding? Do we judge a scientist because of something he or she has previously discovered? A stockbroker may have been good in his previous stock recommendations but he is only as good as his next tip and the scientist only as good as his next discovery. Should we wholeheartedly put our faith in religious leaders who claim to have faith in God? Clearly many of us are unconvinced or religion would be more popular.

OTHER STORIES OF FAITH:

SHATTERED ILLUSIONS

Near to my office there was a small health shop run by a kind and helpful Indian lady and her husband. On Christmas Eve 2004, a huge tsunami hit Thailand. Many people died. The owners of the shop were on holiday in Thailand with their children. Her son who was 23 did not share his parents' belief in Hinduism. When the mass of water hit the hotel he found himself trapped alone in the bathroom which was filling quickly with water with no route of escape. In his moment of fear and panic he instinctively called to Krishna, the family deity, to help him. At that moment the window broke with the force of the water and he escaped through the window. His mother told me that after that experience, he now had a different attitude to religion and God. This "impact" moment changed his life.

FLASHING LIGHTS

I met a teacher of Kriya Yoga on my travels in India. He was a longstanding disciple of the Great Master. He was a serious and well educated man. He told me about his friend who was a professor of science and did not believe in God. This friend went to a lecture where the Great Master was speaking. The friend listened but did not really believe anything that the Great Master was saying. At the end of the lecture to his surprise the Great Master summoned him and said, "You come with me." The Great Master told him to follow him to his room and to shut the door. The Great Master removed his shirt and the professor was dazzled by blue lights around the Great Master's *chakras*. The professor was humbled and realised that his knowledge was really quite limited and he asked to be initiated by the Great Master.

RING RING

I heard another story of a physician who visited the Great Master for initiation into Kriya Yoga. The Great Master told the people attending that they would hear sound, see light and feel vibration. The doctor was cynical. He had become well known and he knew about science and how the body functioned. He took initiation and heard the AUM sound. Scientifically he could not believe it and thought it was his imagination. He asked the Great Master what he had done to him. The Great Master, sensing the arrogance in the doctor, replied that as he was the doctor who knew all about the body, surely he did not need to ask a simple monk such a question! Days later the doctor returned and begged the Great Master to help him. The sound was becoming so loud that he could not hear the heart beat of the patient when he used his stethoscope. The Great Master advised him to pray to God and before using his stethoscope to speak about day-to-day matters with his patient. The sound reduced thereafter when he was carrying out his work.

FAITH IN THE GURU

After Kriya Yoga initiation, the initiate is given a flower. This flower is infused with the purity of the ceremony. I remember going to a programme in Paris and hearing a woman recount a story of how her whole house burnt down. She said everything was burnt to a cinder except for two things; the picture of the Great Master and the box containing her flower.

On another occasion, a friend of mine was standing in a queue waiting to see Hugging Mother. When Hugging Mother arrived to go into the building, she stopped in front of my friend and told her she knew that she had epilepsy. Hugging Mother touched her head and told her she would never get it again. To my knowledge she was cured.

These stories are from real people. It is encouraging for me to know that even in adversity everything is possible.

FAITH IN THE POWER OF THE DIVINE NAME

On arriving back from my Egypt trip to the Great Pyramid my cases did not turn up. I spoke with the airline Egypt Air in London who told me they would need to telex the airport and wait for a reply. As days passed by and nothing happened, I took matters into my own hands. I telephoned the Egypt Air handler at the airport. He told me that he could not locate the cases. I inquired where all of the lost cases were stored. He described a huge mountain of unclaimed luggage. I asked him to look for me. He said it was not really possible as there were hundreds of cases. I changed my approach and said to him, "I am praying that you look for me." These words had an impact on him. He was obviously a religious man. "All right," he said, "I'll do it." To make matters worse I did not have a name tag on the cases so I had to describe what they looked like. We spoke an hour later. He was very excited. He had found the cases. The word "pray" had struck a chord with him. It had come to me intuitively.

FAITH IN MY ABILITY TO SUCCEED

Putting faith into action needs confidence, determination, drive and inspiration. Even if "failure" sometimes comes, I see it as part of the process of success. When I started to write this book, Sarah, a very successful entrepreneur asked me why anybody would want to read my story. I told her that I felt that few people had first-hand experience of success in business while simultaneously pursuing the spiritual path. In addition, I felt that there are many consultants advising people what to do with little actual hands-on experience themselves. My real experience of building a business was based on fact and not theory. Regarding spirituality, a guru from India can advise us to be calm in the office environment but few gurus would be able to quote from their own real life business experience. Also a book written by a new age or religious person compared to someone with my background would be less likely to be read by an agnostic who might dismiss spirituality and *chakras* as airy fairy. Sarah then responded that I needed to accept that there may be failure. I was surprised to hear this from a successful person. The thought of failure never crossed my mind. It was obvious the book may succeed or fail but I have never started anything with the thought of failure. If I think that something will fail then why waste my time doing it? If problems arrive, they are just bumps on the road to success. It does not mean that the destination will not be reached. I may anticipate and prepare myself for problems ahead but I will not be paralysed by the fear of failure.

REAL SUCCESS IS NOT TO BE AFRAID

No doubt success can also be achieved through fear, but what type of reward is miserable success? Apparently even realisation can be experienced by miserable people but it is far more enjoyable to be joyful in everything. A fearful "successful" person will soon find something else to be afraid of such as losing everything that they have gained. Cultivating consciousness of the Invisible Hand increases confidence and reduces fear. I accept that surprises will come no matter if I think I am the doer or not so there is little point in being afraid of the unknown. On a deeper level as I cannot comprehend why events happen or do not happen, can I really claim the credit? I was always and am still fiercely independent by nature but I realise more that I am at the same time dependent on the Invisible Hand. If this is true then when I think that I am making a decision is this really the case?

To conclude, to be successful in life we need to believe in something, whether it be ourselves, God or others. Faith is vital to success. I never met anybody who achieved anything without faith. Faith overcomes temporary doubts and perhaps what we achieve can be measured in terms of faith.

Simple events help me to see the Divine and to have faith that everything is possible.

CHAPTER 7

KARMA & DESTINY

"There is nothing accidental in this world, it is all incidental.
There exists no such thing as chance in the universe."

– THE GREAT MASTER

DESTINY CANNOT BE AVOIDED

My meeting with the Great Master changed my life. It was my destiny to meet him even though I had no desire to find a guru. The run-up to my meeting him was far less dramatic than the story of some others I know.

I heard a beautiful story of an Indian professor who met his guru in 1982. He was a well-known scholar who came from a large well educated family. He had no belief in God and any worship that he had been taught by his family was forced and mechanical. One day at the age of 42, he experienced a feeling of being in a dark crater. He heard strange sounds and his body started to shake. This happened for 24 hours and it left him perplexed and worried. He became afraid of the dark and was unable to sleep. Seeking solace he went to visit his uncle who could see immediately that something was wrong. His uncle told him to eat and relax and then sent him to say a prayer at the famous Jagannath temple in Puri. Although he felt a little calmer he knew that this would not be enough. He went back to his uncle. He was advised to go to an ashram some distance away to see a guru who could help him.

In those days transport was sparse in rural areas so he had to walk a long way in the scorching sun to get there with only a handkerchief to cover his head. He felt hot and uncomfortable by the time he reached the ashram. He received a curt welcome by an ashram resident who told him that the guru was out and would not be back for four hours. The professor asked whether he could go to the meditation room to bow before the picture of the guru as is customary in India before leaving. The picture or image of a guru is seen as the living guru and not just a representation. The unhelpful resident shrugged his shoulders. Although he had requested the whereabouts of the meditation room, he had no idea what he should do when he went inside. A young man dressed in white saw him in the room and asked him why he was not smiling and why he was full of melancholy. He explained his situation and the young man said that the guru would be back soon. The young man in white encouraged him to sit down next to him. He closed his eyes. The professor started to speak to him but he did not reply. He had gone into deep meditation. The professor was surprised he could not hear him and so touched his arm. The professor felt a strange tingling energy in his body. He then decided to close his eyes also.

After a while there was movement around the ashram. They both got up and went outside the room. The guru had arrived. He sped past them with large strides growling like a lion. The young man in white and the professor followed the guru, almost running to keep up. When they arrived in the room where the guru had gone, it was full of people. The professor panicked and wanted to leave. The young man in white prodded him forward. The professor bowed in front of the guru. The guru touched his head with his hand. He felt a cool energy enter into his body. The guru said, "Calmness, calmness, calmness," and smiled at him. The professor started to leave and the young man in white followed and asked why he was going. He was encouraged to stay and they ate lunch, facing the guru. The professor's gaze was transfixed so much on the guru that when he ate he occasionally missed his mouth altogether. After lunch he left the ashram feeling better. His fear had gone.

Fourteen years later after continuing his life as a professor and coincidentally, just before the Great Master was leaving to live in the West, he decided to go back to the ashram again. He had kept in touch with the young man in white who welcomed him when he arrived for the celebration of foundation day of the ashram. The young man in white encouraged the professor to ask for initiation and told him what to do. On the morning of his departure the Great Master strode forward purposefully towards the meditation hall. The professor stood up barely able to speak. The Great Master asked him what he wanted. He asked for initiation. The Great Master told him to come with him. They walked through the crowd in the room and the professor was aware of people asking and whispering who he was. He was given initiation.

The Great Master never returned to India alive. The professor never saw him again. After his initiation, the Great Master pointed at the monk who had been the young man in white and told the professor that he would look after him. Now many years later the professor is a humble monk living in India following the direction of Smiling Swami, the young man in white.

ANOTHER MEETING WITH THE MASTER

In 2002 a young woman called Srutima went to a lecture on Kriya Yoga in Cuttack, India. Her grandfather had been initiated many years before. After the lecture she went home and carried on with her life. One year later, accompanied by her mother, she was going to a meeting in the car. There was a road block ahead and the police told her driver that they had to take a detour. After a few miles, there was a banner on the side of the road advertising a Kriya Yoga programme. She told the driver to stop. There were many people there and she enquired if she could see the head monk. She did not know his name but was told that he was far too busy to see her so her mother suggested they leave. Srutima told her mother, "Let's wait a few minutes, you never know." She had barely finished the sentence when the same monk who had given the lecture a year before was standing in front of her with a big smile. After watching him for a moment, she spontaneously requested if he would initiate her. He agreed and asked her to come back tomorrow. The next day came and she was initiated. Afterwards Srutima saw how everyone paid their respects by bowing at the monk's feet as is the custom in India. She wanted to do the same but having had a serious car accident fifteen years earlier this was impossible as she was wheelchair-bound. She wondered how she could touch his feet. The monk then approached her without warning. He smiled and lifted his foot onto her head and said, "So?"

Some weeks later Srutima's health took a turn for the worse. She was experiencing internal bleeding and clotting. The doctors at the hospital said they could not stop the blood flow and there was nothing more they could do. Srutima went home. Her mother and younger sister were distraught. Srutima could no longer speak and was drifting in and out of consciousness into a semi-comatose state. Her mother was up all night crying and then thought of the monk who had initiated Srutima. She prayed to his picture and thought, *as you have initiated her, she is like a daughter to you so how can you let her die?* It was 1am. A few minutes later the telephone rang. The voice down the phone said "What is the matter?" The mother cried even more and did not know who it was. He told her, "It is me, Srutima's guruji." Her mother was astonished. She told him, "She's dying, she's dying and the doctors cannot do anything about it." He told her mother to give the phone to Srutima but she told him she was unconscious. He instructed her to do it anyway and put the phone near her ear. Her mother said to Srutima, "Hey, hey. Your Guruji is talking to you." Her mother took back the phone. Srutima was still unconscious. A few minutes later the bleeding stopped totally. She was amazed.

The next day Srutima woke up as if it was a normal day, feeling no after effect and no weakness in her body. She asked her mother what had happened. Her mother told her the story and added, "I didn't do anything. I just prayed."

Srutima then asked, "How did he get our phone number?" Her mother replied, "I don't know. I just know he gave your life back to you." Srutima's guruji is Smiling Swami.

These stories demonstrate the power of fate and faith, of karma and destiny. The professor found solace out of deep fear, while the faith of Srutima's mother made the impossible possible.

WHO IS DOING AND WHO IS NOT DOING?

Who decides what or who I am attracted to? Who decides my tastes? Is it true that every good action has a good result and every bad action has a bad result? A series of events occurs for some and not for others such as meeting a partner, having children or suffering illness. What determines whether the mosquito that bites me has malaria or whether I am born healthy or unhealthy? These events seem to take place quite randomly, but is it really the case?

Have you ever stopped to think why if the sun shines equally over a field that some plants grow better than others? Perhaps grace is given in the same way, but through genes and conditioning some of us develop more than others or are more successful than others. Genes and conditioning are inextricably linked to karma and destiny.

The Great Master taught that human life has three important elements which influence our outcome and destiny. They are Heredity, Environment and Culture.

Heredity accounts for 20%. By this he meant that we come into the world with our soul and our karma from previous lives.

Environment accounts for 30%. This relates to our parents, our teachers and the environment in which we are brought up as well as the people with whom we interact.

Culture accounts for 50%. By Culture he referred to our own effort. But where does the effort come from? Effort does not always come easily. The more flickers of consciousness that come to me, the more I see that effort is given through grace.

Apparently all of us arrive in this world with karma and destiny. Karma, contrary to popular belief, is actually a neutral quality and is essentially neither good nor bad.

It means "present" action and the present is a consequence of the past. From past karma a small fraction becomes destiny and some of that destiny impacts on the present life.

In deep meditation where there is no thought or action and total stillness of breath, karma halts. Conversely, in daily life it is human nature to decide whether our actions or the actions of others have a positive or negative effect on us. An advanced yogi will accept an experience instead of judging it. On a human level the effect of karma and destiny can be described simply. If a person has good karma and good destiny then these two elements work in harmony together. If a person has good karma and bad destiny then the two will lock horns and work against one another. Good destiny and bad karma have a similar discordant effect. Finally someone may be born with bad karma and bad destiny. Their life will be difficult. So what is good destiny? Good destiny might be expressed by being born into a loving, caring or spiritual family, receiving a good education and being brought up with moral and ethical values. Success in a career, a healthy mind and body, also reflect good destiny.

SO WHAT IS KARMA?

My knowledge of karma comes from what the Great Master and Smiling Swami have taught me. Karma describes action or activity and the results that follow. Karma represents action and even inaction. Karma is associated with the concept of doership or ego. Events or clashes happen because of a battle of egos. When we see the divinity in each other a good relationship exists. Karma reduces by mentally reinforcing the thought that "I am not the doer" or this evolution happens naturally especially for those who meditate.

Smiling Swami says that when we have bad dreams we generally release bad karma. It is important not to attach too much relevance to dreams. I am not worried about my karma but want to be calmer! The more I perceive or think that I am not the doer the less I associate with personal ownership of karma knowing that the Invisible Hand is taking care of everything.

He also points out that karma from previous lives has a cumulative impact on our present life but the karma from our last life has even more influence. For most of us spiritual growth from life to life is negligible. With karma, we reap what we sow although the harvest does not always arrive instantly because the fruits of good or bad actions may take time to manifest. If we eat badly for all of our lives then surely at some stage there will be a negative effect on our health. If our diet becomes more healthy, the years of bodily abuse will not disappear so easily and illness may still manifest later.

Where karma is inactive, this is good news as it means that not all karma needs to manifest. My observations are that the seeds of karma often take time to grow as can be the case in business. At times one must be patient and stick to the path in order to achieve a good crop. Good always comes in the end. Several masters like Sri Anandamayi Ma and Ramakrishna Paramahamsa have said that one act of good karma wipes away 100 acts of bad karma. So there is hope yet!

Bad karma can mean that we are continually attracted to those fruits in life which are not good for our evolution. One day this may change by an impact moment or through effort or natural evolution. This is where destiny comes in. If one's destiny is good then in time even that small desire to do things that are not good for us will manifest less.

Thoughts also create karma. If I think negatively of another person or do something in a negative way towards another, I receive negative karma. The receiver of my thoughts or actions will simultaneously receive some of these negatives. The opposite applies also. If I think or act positively towards another person, both of us will benefit. Smiling Swami often warns us to be careful of what we think. I am certainly far from being the finished article in this department!

Apparently a true spiritual master is unaffected by karma because he or she has surpassed its influence. Yet, karma has to go somewhere. I therefore asked Smiling Swami what happens to the karma created by the master in his or her life or created by the people interacting with the master. The answers were as follows: the positive actions of the master go to those who speak and think positively of the master. As the master is beyond karma, no actions by the master are negative. If the master tries to correct someone and a person thinks negatively of the actions or speech of the master, then that person receives the negative karma. However, if we think negatively of the master of our own volition, we receive a double helping of negative karma! One amount of karma from our own thought and the same amount again because our negative thoughts reflect back to us from the master. So the true master is beyond karma and the effects of positive and negative.

When we carry out an action in God consciousness the karmic effect is good. If we intervene for instance with a bully and use force to stop a fight then this is good karma. However, if we intervene with vengeance and hate for the bully then the karma created for us is negative. Good karma is even demonstrated simply by earning money from work and then receiving more money from others. It accumulates more and more.

So a good attitude in all that we do is essential to proceed in life, spiritually or otherwise. Every thought and action has an effect.

THE POWER OF GRACE

Regarding the grace of the master or the guru, this arrives regardless of karma or destiny although I wonder whether it is destiny that brings the guru. A guru can neutralise karma through his prayer. I have observed how Smiling Swami often tells people with problems that he will pray for them. Once I asked him if he just prayed generally for people as he must have made this promise to thousands. He told me that when we are asleep he is praying for each person individually! This is his daily ritual in the very early hours of the morning. Grace of God and gurus is inseparable as a true guru is in total union with the will of the Divine. More meditation helps me to appreciate that the main driving force in my life is grace.

Some gurus teach that we should go beyond our desires and control them. Yet this conflicts with the principle that the Invisible Hand is doing everything and giving every thought. Logically my desires come from the same source, so why should I be concerned? The more I remain in tune with the Invisible Hand then the more the desire is seen by me as one desire and not "my" desire. This allows me to be more detached from the result of that desire and to realise that it does not matter. The problem is that the more a pattern becomes engrained mentally and physically in the body, the more I become attached to the thought or the experience. Having given up alcohol and cigarettes and meat easily and naturally, I have not suffered any battles with addiction which many people do. Was this my willpower, my destiny or my good karma at work? It is not possible to separate these areas as all are prevalent like a good dish enhanced by many different ingredients. What I can say is that little effort was required to give up alcohol and cigarettes which in the long term could have been detrimental to my health. Good karma and good destiny were certainly present.

ARE WE BORN GOOD OR BAD?

The Great Master taught that on the left hand side of the brain reside love, joy, humility, kindness, purity, perfection and happiness. On the right hand side of the brain reside anger, pride, cruelty, insincerity, hypocrisy, resentment and unhappiness. Because of this every human being has the potential to be good and successful or to be bad and unsuccessful. Negative and "evil" people are living in ignorance. They misuse the freedom that everyone has been given to be happy and loving human beings. If that freedom is misused then these actions accrue from life to life and return in different guises as negative karma. For those with difficult lives, it is harder to find the proverbial light switch so they continue to live in darkness. However, just as a person who shines a torch into a hidden cave which has been in darkness for thousands of years can introduce light for the first time, the same immediate transformation can apply spiritually to a person in ignorance. Our inherent nature and habits dictate which qualities manifest more. If I am given a knife I can do harm to myself or another or I can use it positively to cut vegetables and make a beautiful meal. So a lethal weapon can be used for good in the same way as choosing what we say. A good person will not think about using a knife to harm someone else.

THE BLAME GAME

Anyone can blame their genes, parents, lack of education or others for their faults. If I have faults then it is up to me to do something about them irrespective of their origin. I have never followed the "poor me" approach to life. On a human level my success in the world is down to my efforts and attitude, regardless of my conditioning, but being in the right place at the right time is unexplainable. I have always maximised my personal attributes rather than thinking about the ones that I do not have. Surely it is better to focus and put to good use what we know rather than waste time thinking about what we do not know. In business to succeed it is vital to make the most of the resources and opportunities available. In spirituality the same applies.

Successful people get on with life, have as many difficulties as anyone else but seem to get much more done than others who complain about their lot. I like the mantras: "If you want something done give it to a busy person" and "There is no rest for the blessed" and "Do your best and God will do the rest." Give a job to a person who is lazy and inactive and they will take longer to do it, if they do it at all.

Both "wannabe" entrepreneurs and "wannabe" gurus who fall short in their aspirations do so because they fail to take the opportunity to tap into the talents that they have been given. When the spiritual aspirant has a problem in the world I often hear them say, "I will meditate on it."

The divine complaints department must be really busy! I often say a prayer of thanks when things are going well as surely the Invisible Hand deserves to hear some good news now and again.

Wannabe entrepreneurs who have trouble succeeding rarely look inside at what they need to change about themselves in order to advance. Those who finally recognise that their lack of success is to do with them and not outside circumstances will then have a chance to proceed more favourably.

Changing myself is always harder than telling others what they should change about themselves. It is never too late to make changes to my life.

DESTINY CATALYSES A MOMENT OF CHANGE

When I learned Maths at a young age my father made us learn our tables by rote but I struggled with the theory. When I related numbers to money, it all made sense! When I was twelve years old I could not swim. The teacher told my father that I never would. From that moment on I began to swim. What is the hidden ingredient that triggers sudden change and success when "failure" looks certain?

IT'S ALL IN THE PALM OF MY HAND

My elder sister had her palm read when she was sixteen. The psychic asked her if she had a brother who was an Aquarian. She told her that I would be successful. This information was enough for me so I never investigated having my fortune read and I was afraid to hear something about my future that was unpalatable. Yet one day in 1995, soon after my first spiritual experience, as I was walking along the pier in Brighton, Joy encouraged me to go inside a gypsy's caravan to see what she had to say. I was reluctant but decided to go with the flow. The gypsy dealt some tarot cards which I had never seen before. There were five cards. She turned them over one at a time. I had no idea what any of them meant. She told me that the cards showed a time of great change. They signified that my life had entered a new era for spiritual growth. I was then informed that I would become involved with a spiritual organisation in the USA and would travel back and forth many times. This was three years before I became involved with Kriya Yoga and met the Great Master in the USA. She also told me that I would write a book and be published when I had never contemplated writing a book! None of these events were on my radar and yet they have taken place.

WHY AM I MORE FORTUNATE THAN OTHERS?

It is very hard to witness atrocities or difficulties especially when they happen to those I know and love. Creation is full of innate beauty and natural disasters. Sometimes these affect us directly and other times not. When others are afflicted I have the opportunity to give them more love and pray for them or help them practically. Those who explain away negative events glibly in terms of bad karma or bad destiny, might imply that the receiver deserved their fate. However, when I have heard my gurus speak about karma it is never done on this basis. Planes fall out of the sky; trains crash; earthquakes happen; people become unwell. It is life. Instead my gurus are full of compassion and spend their lives helping others who are less fortunate than them.

If I have been given good karma and good destiny then I should help others who are less fortunate than me.

The Great Master said many times that through sincere prayer and meditation we can change our destiny. What do we have to lose by practising meditation as an antidote to our difficulties?

STORIES OF GOOD AND BAD DESTINY:

BULLET-PROOF MONK

Once I saw a TV programme where a scientist put a Buddhist monk in a laboratory and carried out various tests on him. Without warning, as he meditated, a bullet was fired next to him. The monk did not move. I was impressed.

When I relayed this story to Smiling Swami he asked me what would have happened if the bullet went off and the monk was not meditating? What would his reaction have been then? This made me reflect that while I can prepare to the best of my ability for all eventualities, the true test comes when I am totally unprepared and an unforeseen circumstance happens.

AVOIDING DANGER

When I look back on my life I could have been in trouble several times yet somehow I was protected. When I was sixteen I went away to Alicante in Spain with an old school friend called Rusty. One night we went out to a nightclub and Rusty became very drunk to the extent that the barman had to help me kick down the toilet door to get him out as he was lying on the floor nearly unconscious. When we went outside to go home with my girlfriend, all three of us were suddenly surrounded by fifteen young Spanish men who started to harass us. My friend was almost comatose and we were propping him up. The Spanish men wanted my girlfriend to go with them. Suddenly a few of them produced batons from a car and stood right in front of us. We were in trouble. Without any thought or fear my adrenaline took over. I grabbed the arm of my girlfriend and Rusty and we walked straight past them into a taxi and sped off.

At that crucial moment I thought, acted and proceeded without showing fear. Somehow through the grace of the Invisible Hand courage was given to me and we were saved from what could have become a nasty situation.

A few years ago I was in a bank waiting in a queue and the security guard standing three feet from me was robbed by a youth brandishing a knife. Luckily minutes before I had just handed over £5,000 to the cashier from a charity weekend I had arranged. The handful of us in the queue were unharmed as was the security guard who handed over the money.

A week before my honeymoon the news showed people being shot in the lobby of our hotel. I had to cancel our arrangements. More recently, I missed the awful terrorist attack in the Taj in Mumbai where I normally stay, by only three days. Through God's grace, destiny and probably good karma, as the above stories illustrate, I have been very lucky and feel protected by The Invisible Hand. I do not take this good fortune for granted. Others are not so lucky. For example, I knew a fitness coach who I played squash with when I was younger in Portugal. He was in his late twenties with a young family. One year he went to the Caribbean on holiday and he was shot dead for the money in his wallet. In an instant his life was taken yet on that same day even minutes before or after other people would have walked down that same beach unharmed. Why him?

DESTINY IN BUSINESS: SHTUM IS THE WORD

Whenever I returned back from holiday, within the piles of letters awaiting me in the office, a different, normally unpleasant surprise would appear. "What do you mean we have to move out in a month's time?" I cursed loudly as I read the letter which had been cleverly hidden halfway down the pile by Fiona, my admin manager. The new landlords had looked at the technicalities of our lease and had refused to allow us and another tenant to let out the floor jointly which had been partitioned, even though this arrangement had stood for many years. Of course for a huge fee they were prepared to "listen to our offers". We had been at the offices for six years and thought that renewing was a formality. Now we were in trouble. There were very few appropriate offices in the area.

As I left the building that night, "by chance" I met the secretary of the other tenant who had received the same letter as us. She told me that they had found an office close by and described where the building was located. I had seen the property a year before and knew the agent very well. I picked up the phone to him and was viewing the property ten minutes later!

If both of us had not left the offices to go home at the same time then I would never have known about it. I put in an offer on the new office space which was accepted the next day.

GOOD KARMA AND GOOD DESTINY

In 1999 I was thinking about changing my seven-year-old car. I was pondering whether it was spiritual to buy anything more than a standard A to B car. After a group meditation, I overheard a woman speaking to her friend about the very same topic. She said she could not understand why people bought expensive cars. She said if she had £30,000, she would give the money to charity. This struck a chord. Was this a message from the Invisible Hand? Should I upgrade or downgrade? After much research I found a trader who offered to import the car straight from the factory in Germany for a 35% discount. I knew this would help me obtain a good resale value. Luckily my judgement was good as I obtained 33% of the original value back seven years later. However, to keep my conscience clear I also paid an equivalent amount to charity!

When the car finally arrived, everything seemed rosy until twelve months later I was driving down a busy road and the car lost power totally. The accelerator pedal did not respond and the car came to a halt fifteen seconds later. Fortuitously it stopped directly outside my favourite Chinese restaurant! The car would not restart. Had I been on a motorway, I would surely have been chop suey! Luckily for me, the problem was resolved after the company sent an engineer from Germany with a new computer chip.

I also had another car incident when I discovered a nail in one of my tyres. I went straight down to the tyre repair centre. What looked like an inconvenience soon became a blessing. The manager at the tyre centre noticed that there were some large cracks on the surface of the tyre. He then proceeded to check the other tyres. I was shocked to hear that every one had the same cracking problem which he told me was dangerous. Had I been driving at high speed I would have been in trouble. The manufacturer eventually replaced all four tyres.

Blessings often come in disguise.

Chapter 8

TRUST, HELP AND LOYALTY

Whose success is it anyway?

What really made me successful in my career? Surely my ability and effort contributed to this success, but can I honestly claim that I "own" this skill and take credit for the efforts? I cannot walk around proudly as if I have achieved something. I say this not out of humility but because I believe it to be the truth. I realise that without my clients and the people I employed, nothing would have happened regardless of any supposed abilities. Timing and opportunity cannot just be created by me alone. I may have been the physical doer but when I was in tune with the universe I was aware that success was determined by my karma and destiny which were bestowed on me. Otherwise everyone would be successful at what they choose to do. If I had no spiritual awareness I would tell people that the success I enjoyed was down to me. Destiny or not, success has made me more humble hopefully and more grateful.

When I am conscious that the Invisible Hand is behind everything, my life is richer. My early upbringing instilled self-belief and I was confident in my abilities. Eighteen years of effort at Key and my earlier work experience paid off as did my stubbornness to stick to the path ahead. An accumulation of effort certainly leads to effortlessness. Effort if directed properly leads to effectiveness. In spirituality, the effort required to change is where the real work begins. Although I have worked hard, when I look back at any achievements, the amount of work required seems to have just taken a minute and appears effortless. Faded memory clearly helps as the effort and sacrifice were huge.

STICKING TO THE PATH WITH THE GURU'S HELP

When I have a clear vision I am not put off by others who say it is not possible. If I believe something is possible then it probably is so I go for it. Normally the way is shown to me either conventionally or unconventionally, for instance when I had only a month to find a new office as described in the last chapter. I think of the Divine when things are going well as well as when things are going badly. When I reflect deeper I know intuitively that the same source that brings success also brings failure. What is the determining factor? It must be fate and I have the advantage of knowing that I am being helped by my masters which is also fate. It seems to be one of the "jobs" of the guru, whether in the form of teacher, parent or spiritual guide to help me to exhaust or fulfil my desires and to give a helping hand. As my worldly desires are fulfilled perhaps I can be of more service to others. Smiling Swami tells me that even in dreams desires can be fulfilled which means that they do not need to manifest in the physical body and the material world. Teachers come in a positive and negative form. However I have noticed that those who live in theory often advise others about what they should practice yet those who live in theory rarely practise!

STANDING UP FOR WHAT I BELIEVE: WHY SUFFER IN SILENCE?

I have no problem in standing up for what I believe to be right and just. If I did not then my life would be far more difficult, inhibited and tedious. When difficulties come I believe that God will give me the skill to deal with them or send someone to help me. In my personal life, instead of following my old pattern of burying and masking the emotional suffering inside, I am now more open with those around me and this helps greatly. To continue a repetitive habit which is not good for me is not the way I want to lead my life any more. There is a theory in psychology by Dr Ernst Weber from the nineteenth century called Weber's theory. He observed that after carrying an emotional burden for so long we begin to think it is normal and forget about the damage it will do in the long term. This sounds all too familiar.

I respect those who fight to establish themselves and overcome issues that in the beginning are really uncomfortable and unnatural to them. I shall give examples later of friends who have overcome their difficulties or weaknesses. It takes real courage to make a stand, but once it becomes a habit there is no need to look back. For example many people stay in their job when they are unhappy. Confident people change their job quickly if they are unhappy with their career advancement, their salary or are badly treated. Others suffer in silence or complain behind the scenes. Which type of person are you?

Fear to express oneself cannot be healthy. Confidence is the opponent of fear and with increased confidence, fear erodes. Half-hearted, timid complaining leads to poor communication and results in misunderstanding and no change.

Be fearless and tearless; be cheerful and not fearful.

MOANER LISAS

Why do certain people moan a lot and then manage to find others who are in the same boat as them and assume everyone in the world has the same problems? What defines us is how we solve our difficulties. Successful people do not moan about life generally. Contentment normally manifests when a person is content with what has manifested. If I ever moaned, this would become the catalyst to achieve something or to change. If we are unhappy with our lives then we should stop moaning and do something about it. Long-term moaners can only be miserable. Discontentment manifests when a person is discontent with what has manifested.

There is a story of a master in India who was punched to the ground. When he was discovered and being helped up the person asked, "Master, who did this to you?" He replied, "The same guiding force that knocked me down is now lifting me up. Everything is God." The master had no complaint about what had just happened! The true yogi will accept "good" and "bad" in equal measure as just part of life. By now you will realise that I am far away from this ambivalent attitude! To accept life as it comes is a utopia which cannot be forced. What I can do however is watch when I am happy or unhappy and look at the cause and my reaction. What is unhappiness really? Normally it is either my mind or my body that are unhappy. If I allow events and others to make my mind unhappy then that is something I can help control by watching my breath. This leads to the mind being more relaxed and less agitated although the latter still takes place sometimes.

THE BULLIES AND THE VICTIMS

Fortunately I did not meet too many bullies in business. Perhaps this was because they intuitively sensed that I would not put up with that type of behaviour. The weaker and less confident someone is, the more likely they will be bullied. Take Gina, a nursery nurse. Blonde, blue-eyed, attractive, very kind, gentle and softly spoken. No matter how many times she moved job and no matter how many people she worked with, she was singled out and bullied. She was bullied even if she worked with only two or three other people. No doubt her looks and demeanour sparked jealousy. There was always one person amongst them (normally a woman) who would give her a hard time.

My friend, Helen, had a similar problem at the opticians where she worked. She is a very kind and caring person yet people take advantage of her. Slowly she became stronger and started to confront the bullies in her work place. She had thought her new approach was working and was gaining confidence and respect from others. However after receiving a bonus from her boss, who assured her she was being rewarded better than the others, she found out that she received the lowest bonus in the shop. She had even thanked her boss for the bonus. Her self-confidence was really knocked again. Amazingly, she is still smiling and beginning to meditate. She has now realised that she needs to change herself to attract different types of people as the same pattern keeps emerging. The good news is that she has finally quit her job and is much happier elsewhere.

Another friend Annabelle was beaten by her father from two years old. He bullied her into her teens. She was in and out of hospital with injuries from a young age. Her mother and sisters did nothing. Even today they seem to imply that it must have been something to do with her. Incredibly she has forgiven her father and spends time with him. I am not sure I could forgive so easily. She has really forgiven and forgotten. I am humbled by her attitude towards her family.

One bully I came across myself, was my ex-landlord from whom I rented a house for a few years. He reminded me very often that he was worth £60 million. I assume that he thought I would be impressed and that it would make him think that he had the upper hand over me. He believed that I had no right to stand up to him when he was being unreasonable. He was certainly a bully and one of the most unpleasant men I have ever come across. I stood up to him especially when work was required on the house. He disliked this immensely.

I recount these stories to encourage us all to be bold and courageous in difficult circumstances. To remain loving and forgiving in adversity is certainly a challenge and the friends mentioned all keep going with a smile on their faces.

Hate the sin and not the sinner

Smiling Swami teaches us to hate the sin and not the sinner. This is a teaching which I find hard to incorporate in my life and still have a long way to go. So, as hard as it is sometimes, courage is required in difficult circumstances. A bully hates to be stood up to and normally will back down quickly as it is only a defence for his or her own lack of confidence.

The deservers

The deservers believe that they should be more successful than others around them. They often say "should" and "would" with a plethora of excuses as to why they are not in a better position in their lives compared to others. They commonly suffer from the deadly disease called envy. This disease is fortunately not contagious to all, but is like a slow poison working from the inside out. Fortunately, I rarely come across these people or not knowingly anyway. They are present in both the spiritual and material world. The Great Master repeated many times that we should, "Keep good company." In this context he was referring to the people we spend time with as well as our minds. Keeping the company of a balanced mind is better than keeping the company of a distressed mind. For someone who is honest enough to acknowledge that they are a "deserver" and who wants to change these traits, there is a yogic technique employed where you roll up your tongue inside your mouth. It is impossible to speak with the tongue locked in this position. The Great Master said that the tongue is the most dangerous weapon that man possesses. It can be sharper than a sword and deadlier than a revolver and can fire repeatedly without reloading.

SO WHO CAN I REALLY TRUST?

When I worked in the merchant bank I witnessed internal fraud for the first time. The only manager in the bank under 45 was a real high-flyer called Bob. Everyone trusted and liked him. He was very clever and became a troubleshooter for the bank. One day a crisis in the Far East office arose. Bob was called away to see how the problem could be resolved. In his absence a loan came up for renewal for one of his clients. In the office we searched high and low for the client's file, but it could not be found. As the search continued, it soon became obvious that the client did not exist. Destiny had called him away unexpectedly. He had been carrying out the fraud for years. He went to jail and a potentially great career was ended. All of us who worked in the same department were shocked. It left an indelible imprint in my mind not to be taken in too much by people who appear to be really impressive and clever. In addition it demonstrated that a smart perpetrator can be very creative and resourceful. What a shame that someone so gifted did not use his skills to create something honestly. The short cut and dishonest way will always be found out in the end.

At Key over the years we witnessed some fraudulent dealings and stories of clients' money going missing. No matter how clever I thought I was, or how robust our controls, one always slipped through the net.

After three years of trading we were saddled with our largest bad debt of £94,000 which wiped out the year's profits. We lent the money to a medium size legal practice. It was for an office refurbishment. The practice was profitable and we advanced the monies. Laid Back Cigar Man visited Nick, the Senior Partner to sign up the necessary paperwork and he even saw the plans. We required two signatures, so Nick told Laid Back Cigar Man to wait in his office and he disappeared to obtain another signature. As a matter of security we also sent a copy of the loan agreement to each of the other partners.

All went well for three months until they stopped paying. We later discovered that Nick had defrauded us and many others. One bank was "taken" for over £2 million. It transpired that in our case, Nick had forged another partner's signature when he left Laid Back Cigar Man waiting in his office. Had Laid Back Cigar Man been really canny, he would have asked to witness the other partner signing. It later transpired that the company accounts on which we had based our decision to lend the money were also fraudulent. We had no recourse to the auditors, because partnerships do not need to have an audit. Even more amazingly, when the partner whose signature had been forged by Nick received a copy of our loan agreement, instead of calling us he raised the matter with Nick who promised to send the money back to us! Nick went to prison.

So diligence and care may not always be enough and I have to accept that I am not always right in my judgement.

Loyalty and betrayal

One of the saddest stories of loyalty which turned into betrayal and stupidity concerned an ex-employee of my father's called Roger. He had worked for my father for over thirty years running his small printing business and became a close friend. The business just ticked over and my father did not make any money from it. It was a marginal decision whether to keep it going but he did so to give Roger the chance to top up his pension and earn a living until retirement. My father even decided to employ a sales manager to help Roger to build the business. Steve, the new sales manager seemed very good at first and brought in some new clients. A year later, my father suggested to Roger that he and Steve take over the business and pay him for the machinery and other assets. He heard nothing further from them and the business continued as usual. One day he came in to the office. There was no sound from the printing factory. Roger and Steve had gone without leaving as much as a letter or a message. They had decided to set up on their own using another printer rather than pay for the assets. The printing business had been abandoned overnight and they also stole the clients. Suffice it to say the business never survived. My father was devastated and felt so betrayed. He never spoke to Roger again.

Roger and Steve lasted six months together before their new venture failed. Roger had trusted someone who he had known for one year instead of my father who he had known for thirty years. I had grown up spending time with Roger who was very good to me. I was shocked to hear what had happened.

One moment of madness can destroy everything in life. Lahiri Mahasaya, a great Kriya Yoga master, summed this up by saying that, "Man is unreliable until he is realised."

MONEY AND FRIENDS

A story about trust and money comes to mind. Mixing money with friends and family is not a recommended path. The Great Master commented that friendship is damaged when we ask for something. He illustrated this with a simple tale.

I had a friend. The friend asked me for money. I gave the money to my friend. My friend promised to repay me. I asked my friend to return my money. The friend never repaid me. I lost my money and my friend.

THE BANK'S TOP CLIENT!

Once I was invited to a dinner at a country club to celebrate the promotion of one of the bank's directors. Eight major clients were there including me. It was a fine affair held in a private room. One of the clients, Phil was a successful high-flying chairman of a top 500 public company. He was extremely well spoken and later I discovered he was championed by senior politicians. The government promoted him as a role model, in particular to young black people. I remember observing how impeccably he was dressed in a handmade suit with a crisp white shirt and tie. One year later, I read in the newspapers that the bank had been defrauded to the tune of a rumoured £100 million by his company. The stock of the aforementioned public company became worthless overnight. Phil had created a company that built turnover and profits on fictitious sales.

When I spoke to Harry who had previously been the manager at that branch, he told me that he had often been approached by this company for funding but that he could never understand what the business did. He therefore used the tried and tested motto: "If in doubt leave it out." It acts as further confirmation of my policy not to invest in anything which I do not understand. If more businesses and banks followed this dictum, I suspect the world might be more boring but ultimately more solvent!

INTERVIEW TECHNIQUES: SECRETARIES

When we started Key and some would even argue towards the end, our interview techniques were primitive and we were rather naïve. It took us a few years of employing secretaries who could not type in spite of their claims of competence to test their typing skills at the interview stage. It was also revealing to see how many people turned up late for their interview. Not a good start. Unless there was a valid excuse we rarely employed them. I was always impressed if a candidate brought their exam certificates along with them or even reference letters. This demonstrated their initiative and organisational skills. Meanwhile Laid Back Cigar Man prided himself in asking the odd trick question. In the interview of one of our earlier secretaries, he enquired whether in an emergency situation she would work an extra thirty minutes even on her anniversary. She answered automatically that "her bloody husband always kept her waiting so if it happened, then he could wait for a change!" Two years later the moment of truth came. We had a crisis and needed her to work late on her anniversary. She had forgotten what she told us at the interview and was really unhappy.

Our next secretary could hardly type but made excellent tea which she loved doing. She made tea nearly every hour to avoid working which was too much even for Laid Back Cigar Man. She also had the habit of banging on her keyboard and tutting when she would make mistakes or when her computer froze. She was the only employee I ever fired on the telephone. I had called the office late one afternoon after a meeting. To my surprise Laid Back Cigar Man answered the phone. "Where is Natalie?" I asked. "She has gone early to have her hair and facial," he replied "What do you mean?" I asked. He thought that she had asked my permission which she had not. Her career with us was over!

ADMINISTRATORS

When employing administrators, I assumed, rather foolishly in hindsight, that if someone had worked for a bank or a finance house they would be a prime candidate for us to employ. One afternoon I was very hopeful. The prospective candidate worked in finance. She was nervous yet she understood our business. Then the written test came which had five simple arithmetic questions with addition, subtraction, long division, and multiplication. She answered all of the questions incorrectly! I was shocked. How could she possibly be working in the pay-out department of a busy finance company without basic maths skills? We even knew her employer. I wondered how many mistakes were hiding in their files. I gave her the benefit of the doubt and gently asked her to try again without us being in the room. She still answered them all wrong! We did not employ her.

The lesson I learnt was never to overlook the result of a test in an interview no matter how pleasant the candidate or impressive their background.

Following my instinct

When we hired new employees, we asked them to complete an application form in their own handwriting. It helped to see if they could write and spell. The results were mixed. We always took written references from ex-employers sometimes going back more than five years even if they were not offered as referees by the applicant. In fact if an applicant did not put the most recent employers as a referee, I became suspicious. For us, in particular, searching for the right accountant was as hard as finding the Holy Grail. I have not met many business owners that actually understand how to operate accounting software or know what a trial balance is. Laid Back Cigar Man and I took years to understand how the trial balance could balance but still be wrong! With this lack of understanding, any accountant from the street could create havoc. To protect ourselves we employed an external firm of accountants to monitor on a monthly basis what the internal accountant produced and to check that they used best practice.

My policy of "prevention is always better than cure" paid off when we were about to employ an internal accountant. When our internal accountant was leaving after six years with us, in my absence Laid Back Cigar Man and Fiona interviewed her replacement. They offered him the job subject to references. Three of the four references came in, even going back ten years. They were all good references. When I returned back to the office I was told the news.

He was due to start the following week. Laid Back Cigar Man told me that he was a bit of an "anorak" but seemed to know his stuff. I reviewed his papers. Did we really need the fourth reference? I decided to telephone the employer that had not supplied the reference as it seemed strange to me that two weeks had passed without a reply. Most people would not have bothered. I just had a feeling that now was not the time to forget my attention to detail. The Invisible Hand was guiding me. The HR director at the previous employer I called was reluctant to supply a reference. I pressed her and told her that she could talk to me "without prejudice". She was still hesitant but agreed to tell me what was already in the public domain. My ears pricked up. He had gone to prison after being convicted of sexually abusing children. We checked this out independently through a contact and it was confirmed. He had also changed his name several times.

So now we had a moral dilemma. Was it right to punish someone who had served their sentence and paid their dues to society as prescribed by law even though the crime was so abhorrent to us? We employed many women in the office who had children. How would they feel if they found out? We had agreed in writing to employ him but had made the offer "subject to references". I looked at his CV again. During the period in which he had been in prison he had written that he had been on "study leave". We were not obliged to employ a liar and the offer was withdrawn.

Thereafter on the application form we directly asked if a person had ever had a criminal record. A candidate could still lie but we added it anyway. We always took out a credit reference (with the candidate's permission of course) on each potential employee. This was especially important in finance, as those that were in a dire financial situation or had a history of bad debts would be more likely to steal from us.

We also asked candidates to supply their exam certificates or proof of qualifications. Once we offered a job to a nineteen-year-old who became angry when we asked for copy certificates on the grounds that nobody had asked her before. She also claimed to have lost them. "No problem," I told her. As she had only left college a few years ago I suggested she obtain copies from the college. I never heard from her again. How sad that someone so bright and young had to start her career by lying. From an employer's point of view it is better to find out earlier rather than later.

I firmly believe that if someone lies on their CV, they will surely lie when they work for you. In spite of the protective systems that we put in place, it was still possible to end up with someone who passed through the interviews with flying colours who ultimately did not make the grade. However, by asking these questions we surely eliminated potential problems. At least when we found good staff, they generally stayed and some came back after going elsewhere or having children.

HONESTY

No matter how tight the controls, entrepreneurs who run cash businesses such as a pub or a restaurant, will find that some of their money will go missing. The temptation is too great for some staff. I know a restaurant where the owners test new staff by leaving some money outside of the till on purpose. The honest employee will bring it to their attention and give it to them. 50% of staff fail the test. I would not be the right person to run a 'cash' business. I would have sleepless nights. Proprietors of "cash" businesses need to know their industry backwards to know how much the business should be producing. If it is below the necessary return and all other areas are in line such as overheads and clientele, then they will have to tighten the controls or find out who is stealing the money. Any unusual behaviour by staff such as never wanting to take a holiday should be noted. One bank I knew had been defrauded by a staff member who had never taken two weeks holiday in more than twenty years. Dishonesty can extend beyond money. If staff are dishonest about what they are doing or have lied to a client then this can cause difficulties. We sometimes received CVs from prospective employees in company envelopes with the prepaid postage mark of the employer they were hoping to leave! Not a good start on the honesty front.

Once we had a tax inspection. The tax inspector was amazed to see cash receipts where I repaid the company for personal mobile calls and stamps for my own use. Even though it was my business, I kept personal expenses separate from business expenses because it was the right thing to do. As the leader it was my responsibility to lead by example for my staff to follow even on such minor issues. If I cheated the company then how could I expect them to do differently? As a leader of a small business I certainly made many mistakes but I can say I really did my best.

Ramping up the expenses

On the question of staff honesty, I was picked up by a taxi at Heathrow airport to travel to Central London. When I paid the driver, he asked if I wanted a receipt and whether I wanted him to leave it blank. I enquired how many people asked for it to be left blank. He said 90%. He then volunteered that he was usually asked for two blank receipts! It is a sad indictment that many feel they have to rip off their employer. If the employer treats them badly and this is their revenge then it becomes a spiral of negativity. If 90% of employees do this I wonder what else they take from their employer.

The moral of these stories shows how difficult it is for an employer to know who to trust even before they have set foot in the door. To progress in business and spirituality some trust is needed as it is impossible to succeed on our own. In business it is evidently vital to have good staff. Good leaders know how to help and support their staff when things go wrong and give them the training they need to become more efficient in their work. The recruitment stage is so important and all businesses need to become experts in finding good candidates and avoiding the bad ones. In spirituality, I am the student and not the leader which is a role reversal, although I did arrange the programmes for the organisation for many years in London. The Great Master and Smiling Swami teach by their own example. Like all leaders they give out instructions which are not always followed, and they demonstrate infinite patience and tolerance.

CHEATS NEVER PROSPER

So why do people feel that they have to lie or cheat to proceed in the world? Is it in their genes or due to the environment in which they have been brought up? If a restaurant forgets to charge you for a dish will you tell them or not? If a shop gives you back too much change will you give the money back or not? Some cheats clearly think that they deserve to be in a better position than they are and through laziness they motivate themselves to take a short cut. Others cannot resist the temptation to steal, often to fuel an addiction. The last category turn to crime through desperation having dug themselves into a financial hole. Surely 99% of people are hardworking and honest yet 1% can cause a lot of trouble for society. What should society do?

The guru is watching

An ashram story comes to mind which illustrates how the Great Master taught about honesty. When Dan was living at the ashram, he went shopping for food. It was a sweltering hot day so he bought himself a small ice cream from the change and ate it on the way back. When he returned the Great Master summoned him to his room. He told Dan never to take anything that was not his without asking. How did the Great Master know? Dan was alone and nobody knew he had taken the money for an ice cream. The Great Master showed that he did not need to be in someone's physical presence to know what they were doing. Dan received as did I from hearing the story a profound teaching in a clear, non-judgmental way.

How a guru deals with a thief

There is a true story about two Indian businessmen who were publishers. Both were realised masters. One day, one of them was walking along the street. He felt a hand in his pocket and knew it was the hand of a thief. He put his hand tightly over the hand of the thief so he could not escape.

He pulled him to the side and asked him why he needed to steal. After hearing about the difficult life of the thief, the master offered him a job to give the thief a chance to reform. One day in the factory some money went missing. The manager summoned everybody to empty their pockets in front of him. The owners knew that the thief had taken the money. It was his conditioning. So just before the time everybody had to report for the search, the owners sent him on an errand. The thief knew that they had saved him. He felt guilty and returned the money to the owners in an envelope. The thief was transformed from that moment and followed a life of honesty thereafter. This is a great teaching for me in how to deal with a problem with love. What a way to help transform someone who has lost their way.

Another incident closer to home took place when I was assisting at a Kriya Yoga programme in Europe. I had already been the Centre Leader of programmes in London for some time. At the opening seminar 100 people attended. The entrance fee was €5 per person. Excluding unemployed people there should have been €500. I counted the number of people from the back of the hall and checked the money box out of habit and not because I was suspicious. There was just €350 in the box. Two volunteers were on the door taking the money. Smiling Swami was giving the lecture. I was certain which person had taken the money and he confirmed I was right. Smiling Swami told me that the perpetrator would deny it but it would be a good lesson for the organiser to speak to them to explain the problem. As predicted both denied all knowledge and the matter was left. It is not advisable to steal money especially from a charity when a realised master is present! I would not have put the perpetrator near money because I knew he had financial difficulties. The organiser thought everyone was trustworthy because people were offering their time for the charity out of the goodness of their heart. He never thought to look at the qualities of each volunteer and give them an appropriate task. Smiling Swami told the organiser that it was "our fault and our mistake" for putting him close to money to give him the temptation to steal. This acted as a reminder that organisers and leaders have responsibility for others who are working for them even in such a situation. It is a good lesson that a leader should give the right job to the right person.

TRUST MYSELF

I have normally trusted my judgement and instinct. I cannot see how success can come if I do not trust myself. I was a sole signatory on cheques for tens of millions of pounds. I was never going to defraud myself, my company or our lenders. It is not in my conditioning. I hope that I am never put in a desperate situation where I would behave differently. Through hard work, I trusted that the business would always give a better service than our competitors. I never wanted our quality of service to be compromised even if we had to work all hours to achieve this standard. It should not be difficult to deliver what is promised. People generally break promises when they do not think through what they have promised. For me, making a promise is a commitment that I want to fulfil. Businesses that give a poor service or do not carry out their promises are taking clients' money in a dishonest way. Apparently even companies have karma!

WHO CARES?

Nowadays it is rare for companies to give confirmation in writing or by email. Some do not even allow staff to do so or phone a client back. Such companies clearly do not trust their staff and prefer their clients to call expensive numbers which earn them money. Such arrogance or poor training leaves a gap for entrepreneurs to set up in competition. I find that when something is not confirmed in writing it normally goes wrong. When clients give repeat business year in year out, instead of imbuing a sense of gratitude which is reflected in a better service, large companies often do the opposite. It seems to be more a case of familiarity breeds contempt rather than contentment. A foundation of great customer care breeds healthy growth. Healthy growth breeds success. This is my experience. No clients results in no business. Unhappy clients are the start of a downward spiral.

Luckily there are people in business who are moral and ethical, and actually care. So are meditators more or less honest? I would hope that more honesty comes as consciousness increases through meditation.

CHANGE OURSELVES

This leads me on to the mantra "Change yourself" which is commonly heard in spiritual retreats or self-help courses. When I was a child I accepted who I was and never thought anything was wrong with me. This has carried through into my adult life. I never thought I had to change anything unless my parents or teacher told me. Thoughts and fears came and went.

Smiling Swami once asked in a lecture, "Who told us that our minds are restless?"

The mind just existed when I was young. Many courses focus on the mind. I decided to follow the advice of the Great Master who told me to focus on the breath. When the breath is slow the mind is slow. The mind is then peaceful.

How to be great

Great people do more than the minimum. They do the maximum. People who moan about their lot, do the minimum and complain to the maximum. What gives great people the drive to get where they want to go? It can be helpful to have an aim, a target or a goal. The few great people that I have met are humble, do very little for themselves and everything for others. In addition they have a huge capacity to work and incredible concentration and do not measure their results or expect or want credit. Even with such humility they are still criticised. So if people want to be extraordinary rather than ordinary, they need 90% attention and 10% "healthy" tension. They will then have a good chance to fulfil their dreams. If they have 90% tension and 10% attention then you know what will happen!

Speculate to accumulate

In the early 1990s everyone began to buy shares. Penny shares were a favourite and somehow whatever I bought, everyone else had bought also. Even while standing in the queue in the bank, I would hear people discussing their share portfolios. When I was studying for my exams for the New York Stock Exchange, I learnt about a theory called the

Short Interest Theory. Basically the theory states that when the public starts to buy, the professionals are already selling. It was so true. After many years of dabbling in and out of shares I saw that year on year I rarely made any money, so I stopped and decided to invest in my own ability instead.

I have so many discussions with friends who know nothing about finance or shares. Even though they are intelligent they are taken in by the glamour and the press and then gamble their hard-earned money in stocks and shares. Past performance or graphs never ever indicate what will happen tomorrow. This was proved time and time again when I worked in the markets in spite of what our economist would tell us "should happen". I always ask myself how much my life would change if an investment went up 20% and how it would be affected if it went down by 20%. I know if it went down I would be really unhappy. So I do not take the risk for the upside. For those thinking of investing their hard-earned cash it might help them to calculate how many hours they need to work after paying tax to recoup any losses. Very few enjoy looking at this option. Meanwhile those who retire without enough money and decide to risk what they have on a last roll of the dice, should instead contemplate why they do not have enough money. It will normally be because they chose to work less hard than others or have overspent and not saved enough. This is a simple example of karma in action. Our actions from the past affect our present and future. I recently met an old client of mine who at the age of 58 has consistently earned over £1 million per annum in the last fifteen years. I was shocked to hear he could not afford to retire. I asked him why. He hung his head slightly in shame and said he had been profligate. The Invisible Hand helps us but we have to help ourselves!

Professional advice

It has always helped me to find someone impartial whom I can trust to bounce my ideas off. I am not necessarily talking about consultants, accountants or lawyers who advise on technical matters. They would not be my first port of call on a practical business issue. The greatest advisers are those who follow their own advice. It also helps to speak to someone who has already "made it". It is no doubt difficult to find a good adviser. I observe the questions advisers ask as much as the answers they give. Take Stanley, a 65-year-old stressed-out, conservative, man, who four years ago was advised to put his pension pot into a fund that had at least twenty different investments including shares, commodities and overseas funds. He was advised that the fund was low risk and that he would not lose any money. He quite reasonably trusted the adviser who he had known for over 25 years. He asked me to take a look after the investment had been made. I immediately questioned the advice. I suggested to Stanley that beyond the age of sixty, it was ludicrous to invest in anything other than cash or guaranteed fixed income. To risk all his hard-earned pension so close to retirement when the stock market could crash at any moment, was not sensible. Fortunately he listened and badgered his advisers who eventually agreed to return the money. Luckily he received his capital back just before the credit crisis came and the "safe" fund where his advisers had put his money reduced by 30% overnight. So my simple strategy is never to risk pension money close to retirement. In fact I do not risk it even now. I worked too hard. If people need to make a fund grow because they have not saved enough then it is still not sensible to risk what one has however small. If people want to gamble they should pop down to the casino.

SERVICE WITH A SMILE

I remember one year signing two deals close to Christmas. One was for a client in the Midlands where there was heavy snow. It was normally a two-hour journey but it took me four hours. I arrived at the offices of the firm. I was told that the senior partner, Lance was out having lunch with his wife. He was expecting me. Could I go to the restaurant to find him? A strange request. Apparently, he had not seen his wife for weeks because of work and it was a "peace" meal before Christmas. I was slightly embarrassed to interrupt. In fact he and his wife were really impressed that I had fought through the snow to see him. We kept that client for many years. Clients never forgot when we put ourselves out for them.

We had another client called Keith, who was an overweight, aggressive but humorous individual. On the afternoon before Christmas Eve, Laid Back Cigar Man received a call from one of Keith's sons as he was making his way home. The family wanted to surprise Keith and buy him a new Bentley that he had seen. Could we finance it? Laid Back Cigar Man called me from his car. Would I go in the snow and sign the deal up the next day? No problem. I sped into action. We later discovered that they had asked another finance house (where we knew the manager) who had said it was impossible to do the deal at such short notice. This made the deal even more satisfying. Off I went to their posh residence. I went in to sign the paperwork. His sons were there and we shared a glass of champagne. The car was arriving that afternoon. Keith said to his sons, "You see, boys. That's what you call service".

The art of self-destruction

We had another relationship with a loyal client. After we had agreed to fund a substantial deal which did not go to plan, we fell out with Henry, the Senior Partner, who became racist towards me, a first and only experience in business. It took time to unwind the situation and recover our money. Henry ended up backing a "duff" firm which we were not prepared to support as it was making heavy losses instead of the promised profits. He then licked his wounds and carried on with the successful main business. Several years later we heard that he had sold the business. Unfortunately for him, old habits die hard. Henry was negotiating the sale with the Finance Director (FD) of a huge international practice. The price had been agreed. However apparently during a crucial meeting Henry lost his temper and insulted the FD who was of Indian descent. Cool as a cucumber the FD left the meeting. He telephoned Henry the next day and informed him that the price they were willing to pay had just halved! Because of financial pressures Henry had no choice but to accept the offer.

Anger is an expensive liability. Uncontrollable anger can destroy everything including health and financial wealth.

All of the above stories demonstrate the need for caution and diligence which reminds me of a saying by Smiling Swami: "Be careful in a careful way."

CHAPTER 9

SOMETHING IS KILLING THE ROSES

The purpose of this chapter is to observe how business owners, managers and others treat their clients. I recall some of my experiences of good and bad service in business and seeing how people overcome their difficulties. Some stories relate to my own company. Each story has a straight-forward message. Many would not look out of place in a Monty Python sketch.

I admire companies that really care about their clients. On other occasions I have come across businesses who expect me and other clients to accept bad service delivered with a bad attitude. From a spiritual viewpoint they are in ignorance whether they do it on purpose or not. Can we be blamed for what we do not know? Absolutely not. If we are in ignorance it is not a mistake. However ignorance has a cost especially when we have been taught what to do and trained properly. If we change our behaviour then the same mistakes may happen but they will diminish. Nevertheless, if we keep making the same mistake again and again through lack of care or thought then we cannot expect success or goodwill from others.

However, on some occasions helping others is of no help at all. When the Great Master was much younger, he was walking along the street with his master, Shriyukteshwarji. The Great Master saw a man pulling a cart with fruit and vegetables and one bag fell off. He instantly chased after the man to tell him. Shriyukteshwarji scolded the Great Master asking him why he had interfered. The Great Master was surprised as he thought he should help everyone wherever possible. His master explained that the man never took proper care of himself or his possessions and needed to learn an expensive mistake so that he might be less careless next time!

As someone who always likes to help people when I can this is a great lesson when not to interfere. I have also found that some of the best lessons I have learnt from others, are how *not* to do things.

The actions of people, employers and employees alike, contribute to the success or failure of a business or even a spiritual organisation. Failure may not happen overnight but if an employer does not know what is lurking in the undergrowth of the business, then the consequences will surely be costly or even terminal. An entrepreneur who thinks that all is well if five new clients use his services but five others leave at the same time is naïve to the nth degree. The canny business person will know otherwise. Good service is important in both business and spirituality. A business cannot survive for long without always improving its service and caring about its clients. An ashram will not prosper unless people serve selflessly and a badly run charity which does not use the hard-earned cash of its donors properly will eventually be found out.

FEAR OF COMPLAINING

If I order a drink in a bar I quite reasonably expect to receive it, yet on two different occasions I have been with friends who ordered tea and received coffee instead.

On both occasions my friends accepted the coffee without saying anything to the waiter. They told me they did not want to make a fuss. Such an attitude may well be admirable in a social environment, but surely when a person is paying for a drink they are entitled to drink what they ordered. Otherwise what is the point of ordering? They may as well have asked the waiter to bring any drink!

Both of these friends were struggling to earn money and these incidents showed me the reason. You may think that I am being over-analytical, but how can we expect to achieve anything if we do not have the courage or confidence to ask for what we want by sending back a drink when paying for the privilege? Fear of confrontation cannot be helpful for anybody's growth. For those with less confidence, starting with small steps is the way to gain confidence on the bigger issues. This is also true for the entrepreneur. If a person cannot get what they want in a coffee shop, then what hope do they have when it comes to winning a contract or negotiating terms on something far more important or substantial?

Regarding spirituality, I have also met many people who are afraid to ask the guru a question. If I have a question to ask, I ask it. I certainly will not receive a response if I follow the motto "Don't ask, don't get."

HARD WORK BUT NO CONFIDENCE

Neil is a brilliant craftsman. He is kind, generous, caring and a hardworking man who many people would love to employ. His former boss owed him money and everyone else was paid except for him. Neil is afraid of confrontation in spite of being physically strong and tall. I encouraged him again and again to claim what was rightfully his, as I hate injustice. Eventually he did approach the wife of his boss. She promised that her husband would pay him but he never did. On a spiritual level this would be a marvellous lesson provided the person who is taken advantage of is non-reactive and unbothered by the result. Turning the other cheek is quite different to silent suffering and there is a huge difference between humility and stupidity.

SERVICE DEPENDS ON WHERE YOU ARE SITTING!

Once I visited a hotel in Israel with Dan. We went into the empty lounge for a drink. After ten minutes we finally managed to attract the attention of the disinterested waitress. She said she could not serve us. We asked why. She replied rather aggressively, "You are not in my row!" We asked which was her row. She pointed to the armchairs and tables to our left. We stood up and went to where she had pointed so that she had to serve us. She was not amused!

PSYCHIC WAITER

I was having lunch in France, overlooking Lake Geneva. I signalled with my hand for the waiter to come to the table. He rushed past me without even a glance and told me that he would bring the bread. Unfortunately he was not a psychic waiter. We already had bread. We wanted water. I then stopped to think and reflected how easy it is for me to think I know what someone wants without asking them and I do this many times. Lessons can be learnt everywhere so I should thank the waiter for bringing this to my attention.

SOUFFLÉ WITH A STING

At a close friend's fiftieth birthday celebration, as a surprise, I arranged for a special chocolate soufflé dessert in a very expensive restaurant. There were eight of us and when the bill arrived, the restaurant tried to take advantage of the occasion by adding a 50% service charge for the desserts. The soufflé was magnificent but why should I pay 50% more? I refused to pay the extra charge. They clearly misread the invisible sign on my forehead that said "hug me" and not "mug me"!

The only way for us to stop companies abusing their clients or giving poor service is to complain and not be bullied, otherwise they will just carry on regardless.

HARDLY BREAKFAST AT TIFFANY'S

One of my more memorable breakfasts was in Canada in a highly rated hotel. Breakfast time came. It was 9.00am. I went downstairs with my partner. There was a queue of at least thirty people. No problem, we thought. In order to find a solution we asked whether we could have breakfast in the empty lounge upstairs but were told this was not possible. Being relaxed, we decided to go back to the restaurant half an hour later. When we returned there was still a long queue so we decided to wait. Having stood in the queue for a further twenty minutes it was now 10am. I insisted on seeing the manager who took fifteen minutes to arrive. He could see that I was unhappy and gestured for me to speak with him away from the people in the queue. I declined and told him we could speak in front of everyone. I told him the problem and asked him what he intended to do about it. The people in the queue were nodding their approval. He told me that he knew about the problem as this happened often and that he was going to make changes on the following Monday. As it was Friday and we were leaving on Sunday I asked him what use that was to me! Now I was annoyed. I asked for his card. He had lots of letters after his name and a master's degree in business. I should have known better. No offence to those postgraduates with common sense and practical skills. Eventually we had breakfast and when the bill arrived I told them to give it to the manager.

There are two reasons for telling this story. The first is that the people in the queue accepted their fate unhappily but were unwilling to confront the situation. When I complained they were glad that someone else was complaining. Secondly, however many letters managers or directors have after their name, common sense is the key to good leadership and managers need to be trained how to deal with real people face to face.

GOING DOWN THE TUBES: HOW NOT TO BE AN ENTREPRENEUR!

WHEN THE CHIPS ARE DOWN

I love to visit new restaurants. I find myself automatically working out their likely success or failure. A few years ago, a restaurant opened close to where I live. The décor was simple but well done. I decided to have lunch there. I went inside and was "welcomed" by a miserable waitress. I ordered an egg mayo sandwich with home-made chips. I was told that I could not have chips because I needed to have the fish to have the chips. I told her I was vegetarian. She told me then in that case I could not have them. I had to have the fish. I asked for the manager. He told me the same. I could not have them. He said that they only cut enough chips for the main course of the day. I was astounded. I thought they must be joking. I was hardly asking for Italian food in a Chinese restaurant. If the diner has a pleasurable experience, he or she will return and tell their friends. Equally if the experience is poor, the diner will not return and tell their friends not to either. Surely I am stating the obvious. Unsurprisingly, I did not return again and within a year that restaurant had gone bust.

Last year another new restaurant opened in a prime location in town. It had taken over the premises of another restaurant that had previously failed. There is a possible stigma attached in these circumstances where the new restaurant needs to distinguish itself pretty quickly to show that it is not a remake of the old failed business. I went inside for a drink and chatted with the new owner who was very pleasant. The menu was bistro-like and the restaurant had the advantage of having outdoor seating. The new owner who had no restaurant experience told me she wanted to offer something different and only serve food that she liked. A recipe for disaster, I thought to myself. She told me proudly that clients had already asked for sandwiches and chips but she had declined as it was not that type of place. I was amused that at one end of town was a restaurant offering chips only with fish while at the other end was a restaurant refusing to serve chips at all! Call me old fashioned but surely ignoring client feedback is the kiss of death. The new owner also informed me that she did not want to be too busy at the beginning and wanted to attract a certain clientele but she had decided against advertising or even putting a menu in the window. I was amazed. I am glad that I was not an investor in the restaurant which must have lost money from day one. This business also met its fate.

One more restaurant story! Some years ago, Dan, and his girlfriend, Joy and I were in Florence for New Year's Eve. We stayed at a hotel which surprisingly is still in business today. It was absolutely freezing. The hotel seemed quite pleasant but was obviously empty. We ordered tea and snacks. Joy requested a cheese sandwich. She had the image of a delightful ciabatta and some fresh cheese. The waiter arrived with two rather stale pieces of bread with a slice of processed cheese in the middle. I sent it back. Ten minutes later the same sandwich arrived back with a small British flag on a cocktail stick in the middle of it!

I know nothing about running a restaurant but surely the above examples illustrate certain failure. It is hard enough to make money in the first year of operation for any business but why make it a certainty by not advertising or marketing? All losses have to be recouped later. Effort and enthusiasm are needed from day one. The moral of the story irrespective of the type of business is to give the clients what they want and serve them in a helpful and friendly way.

BAD HAIR DAY

Suzanne has been going to the same hairdresser for years. She was not content with her hairdresser but continued to go out of habit as did her mother. I asked what invisible power the hairdresser had over her. I could not understand why someone would pay for a widely available service continually without being happy. Finally with my encouragement she plucked up the courage to change hairdresser.

However, old habits die hard. She chose a hairdresser who had previously cut her hair badly many years ago. When she returned home she noticed that the colour of her hair had changed dramatically and she was close to tears. She was unhappy again. I asked her why she had gone to a place where she had received a bad experience before. Third time lucky – she has now found a much better hairdresser. This is not quite the end of the story. When we went to her parents for tea, the subject of hairdressing came up. Her mother told us that she had been unhappy with the hairdresser for years. She has also now changed hairdresser. Family karma in action!

Sticking to what we know is really good only as long as we are happy with the result.

A LESSON IN BUREAUCRACY

The following story is an example of not giving up, trusting yourself and not always listening to others.

Buying a car can sometimes be a painful experience but have you ever tried buying a car in Switzerland?

I had the unenviable experience of helping a Swiss friend buy a car. She lives in a suburb of Geneva. We started looking for a car after some preliminary research within an hour of her home. She said she would not go further afield as it was better to buy the car close to home. I found this attitude very strange and limiting especially as after researching car prices, they were significantly higher in Geneva than anywhere else in Switzerland. The Geneva car dealers must have been well aware of the innate mentality of the laid back wealthy people in the city. I hasten to add that my friend is not financially well off at all, so every penny counts for her. However the day proved successful as we identified the exact car that she wanted. She suggested we buy the first one that we saw, but I persuaded her that the price was too high and it was not in very good condition. She needed a car urgently as hers had been written off.

After searching for another week, the stress of looking became too much so she wanted to wait until the New Year even if going without a car was inconvenient for her. There was no logic to this at all as she was proposing to do what was bad for her and not what was good for her. My attitude was that as we had started the exercise we should finish it. I offered to help her to find the car. She reluctantly agreed as I had now returned home. I located a car in Zurich. I do not know much about Switzerland but I can tell you that Zurich and Geneva may as well be in different countries. In Zurich they speak German and in Geneva they speak French. The problem was that the dealer only spoke German. No English and no French. My friend did not speak German, so I summoned the help of a German friend in Portugal to ask all the questions and to negotiate on our behalf. The deal was finally done and I offered to pick the car up from Zurich and drive it to Geneva.

I assumed that, like in the UK, when you buy a car, the insurer would send a provisional insurance cover note to the dealer. The dealer then supplies the car with a new number plate after payment. In Switzerland, things are not that simple. Firstly Swiss drivers are obliged to keep the same registration number and number plate for life unless they change canton (region). This resulted in the ridiculous scenario of us having to physically post the number plate to the dealer! There were only two days to go before I was due to arrive in Zurich. I called a courier company and arranged everything. When my friend went to the courier's office at the railway station it was closed at a time when she had been told it would be open. As a result she had the added inconvenience of going to the post office on her way to work and her stress levels were rocketing.

She then called her insurance broker. He said that we needed to take the registration plate and details of the car to the Bureau des Autos, a local government department to register the car. Until they approved the transaction she could not have her new car and he could not issue the insurance. We explained to the broker that as the dealer needed the number plate we had sent it off. The insurance broker refused to budge from his normal procedure. There must be another way, I thought. To make it worse the Bureau des Autos was closing for two days that week unexpectedly. This would mean that the procedure would not be done in time for my flight which had already been booked. But now my friend was becoming really stressed. Luckily the dealer was far more advanced than the insurance broker and had already carried out the procedure online with the Bureau des Autos. The broker employed by a multi-billion dollar insurance company expressed surprise that this could be done online. He had caused his client unnecessary stress by not knowing his job.

So finally I arrived on a gloomy day in Zurich. Now the risk was that we had paid the dealer up front without inspecting the used car we were buying. This is strictly against my principles when buying anything. I took a train to a station twenty minutes from the airport and was met there by the dealer who was highly amused at the way the transaction had been negotiated. He gave me a bunch of flowers for my friend and then unveiled the car which was hiding under a silk cover tied with a ribbon as if it was a brand new car. The car had only 3500 kms on the clock and although three years old, it looked brand new inside and out. The effort to overcome the obstacles had paid off.

So my Swiss friend learned that everything is possible regardless of what other people tell you and that perseverance pays off in spite of the obstacles. How I deal with small problems in life helps me to deal with the bigger ones. A positive, enthusiastic, unyielding attitude is often necessary. When I know that something can be done I do not give up easily. Do you?

Here is the last story from Switzerland. In the block of apartments where my friend lives, workmen were carrying out urgent repairs to the water system. On the Friday that I arrived, we went out and on returning in the early evening we discovered that the water was off. However the water was working in all the other apartments. So we had to get the buckets out and fill them up from her neighbour. Our original plan to stay in the apartment was not going to be so comfortable. She tried to get in touch with the repair contractor but to no avail. It was a Friday night. Her attitude was that we should put up with the inconvenience. However I had other ideas. I asked her why we should be put out. I was only visiting for a few days and the contractor did not work on the weekend so I went online and started to call the local hotels. I told my friend that she would be reimbursed by the contractor but she was worried that they would not repay us. I had no doubt but she did not believe me.

I called various hotels trying to find a last minute deal. It was 9pm. I managed to find a hotel and we had an enjoyable evening followed by a full day in Central Geneva. The director of the contracting company finally called back, apologised and reimbursed the money without any objection and put the water on the next day.

My Swiss friend was amazed. Her family conditioning was to accept everything even when inconvenienced by the inefficiency of others. The "stiff upper lip" or "put up with it" attitude seems therefore not to be an exclusively British characteristic.

The lessons from these events show that two different approaches give two quite different results. Both stories contain lessons for me in both business and spirituality.

ÜBER-GERMAN EFFICIENCY

I recently bought two wonderful devices that allow me to connect to the internet by using a plug that goes into a normal electric socket rather than using Wifi. I choose to believe the reports that Wifi is not a healthy option to use. Installation was supposed to be a simple procedure, but the plugs would not work. So I called the helpline. I waited five minutes and after pressing various automated options, a human finally came to the phone. The helpline was in Germany. The customer relations representative asked me what the problem was. I told him and politely asked if he would run through the process with me. He curtly replied, "As long as it does not take too long." I was a little taken aback by his response and politely pointed out that I had spent five minutes waiting on the phone so he could at least have the courtesy to help me patiently. So we waited for my computer to boot up as I engaged him in pleasantries. He asked me to confirm that I was using the same electric supply and was not trying to put my plug into the neighbour's electric socket. No I assured him, I had not gone into my neighbour's house! Then in the middle of the conversation the line went dead. Either he had died of boredom or had just gone to the next call. Am I the only person in the world that these things happen to? I really hope not. Before he disappeared unceremoniously, he told me to check each plug individually which I did. One plug did not work. I called again and after the obligatory five minute wait, spoke to another curt German customer service representative. I was immediately told that I should have realised that one of their brand new plugs was probably broken. Now apparently I am the expert. No apology. "Go back to the supplier," he told me. So I went back to the supplier in the UK. I spoke to Sam, who was helpful. He asked me to double check again to test it did not work and to call him back. When I returned the call Sam was on the other line and I made the mistake of speaking to someone else. Sam had made getting my replacement plugs sound so simple. Young Anthony had other ideas. When I asked him to send me two new plugs, he replied that he needed the two plugs back in his possession before he could send replacements. I told him that I was concerned I might receive another faulty plug so wanted to hang on to them so that I could use the one that worked and mix the set if needed. Why should I be inconvenienced any more? If they wanted the plugs they could deliver new ones and pick up the old ones at the same time. I was told they could not do that. If I wanted new plugs I would have to pay again and when I returned the old ones they would reimburse me. I was not prepared to do that. I asked for a director to call me. They were all in a meeting but he told me he would leave a message. A director never called, so the next day I spoke to Sam again who agreed to send me the new plugs and arranged for the old ones to be picked up. Nobody ever came to collect the old plugs.

Both Anthony and the two Germans worked in customer support. I did not feel supported. They made me feel like it was my fault that the plugs did not work. In business, knowing how to handle a query or a problem is as important as knowing how to handle a sale. Where are the directors who are running these companies? Good leadership comes from the top, not the bottom.

Mea culpa: leading from the front

As much as I dislike poor customer service, I also enjoy great customer service and love remembering the good experiences. I am equally happy to applaud good service as I am to berate poor service.

Take the example of the ex-Chief Executive of Barclays Bank plc, Martin Taylor who clearly led the business from the front. This event took place over twenty years ago. As someone who spent his life in finance, my good credit rating was sacrosanct. When my bank was sorting out a new joint account for myself and Joy, I used my cheque book as usual. I paid my local deli man £12 for my ritual Saturday smoked salmon, bagels and chopped liver. A few days later, I was horrified to receive a letter informing me that the cheque had bounced due to insufficient funds. So I drafted a pretty blunt letter to Mr Taylor, requesting that his bank courier the cash over to the deli. I also expected compensation due to the insult and possible loss of my reputation. I could not have the deli thinking that my cheques were no good in the future because I had a dodgy credit rating! The same day Mr Taylor did what I asked. I also received a letter back from him apologising for the problem. The deli did not even know that the cheque had been rejected when the courier arrived with the money.

Now I was interested to see what level of compensation they were prepared to give me. I took advice from an ex-bank manager who told me that the smaller the amount on the bounced cheque the bigger the insult. Banks love to charge us for our errors or going overdrawn but hate to be charged for their own errors. Negotiations with the regional office were taking too long so I wrote again to Mr Taylor. It may be hard to send an instruction up the line but I have found that any instruction from the top moves downwards at lightning speed. The regional director was instructed to credit me with £1,000.

When the Chief Executive of an organisation leads from the front and pays attention to detail, irrespective of the size of the organisation, this is really impressive. I doubt that many CEOs have ever faced a small client or even really genuinely care about what is happening on the ground. It is a great shame that so few CEOs would do the same and actually say sorry.

Another great example of leading from the front comes from the CEO of a top, family-owned hotel in London. The staff are very helpful and friendly, and I always enjoy staying there. However, in the early days I had a few negative experiences and this is the amusing but constructive letter I received from the owner which really showed how much he cared about his business and his clients.

"Dear Mr Green,

In reference to your recent problems, I would like to repeat my apologies about some of the lapses in service. I have been looking into the detail.

The orange juice is squeezed here every morning at 5am, and disposed of by evening. Occasionally, during a change of season (funnily enough we are coming into a change right now), the oranges are extremely bitter no matter where we buy them, so we cut the mix with mandarins to sweeten it. I think we may have either missed a bad batch (despite the fact that the night chef tastes it!!), or, even worse, failed to rotate the containers from the previous day – a cardinal sin!

Our lounge team have, by their own admission, been under par due to a combination of circumstances that I should not bore you with. I am satisfied that the three factors have been dealt with and that you will see markedly better service when you are next here. There are still some issues but I am confident that we are resolving them.

As for any member of staff saying no to any request, I am massively embarrassed and have personally spoken to the perpetrators. We don't have many rules here, but the number one rule is that the answer is always yes!!!! I am Horrified. You can have vegetables, or afternoon tea WHEREVER, WHENEVER you like when you stay with us. If it's 3am, there may be a slight delay though!

I have instructed my staff to offer you a substantially discounted rate for your next visit, as well as a very handsome upgrade. This represents a very large saving and I hope that this is suitable.

I also wanted to ask you if you would like to have dinner in our Dining Room with a guest, as my guest. It would be a small gesture of apology but one which I very much hope you will take up.

I do look forward to meeting you hopefully in a few weeks time.

Yours,

Jeremy Goring"

The above examples show two rare incidents where CEOs lead from the front and actually care about the quality of service being offered. If it is possible for some CEOs to lead from the front why do so few do it? If I had the power I would enshrine in law that the CEO or Chairmen were legally obliged to deal with complaints or at least sign off on monthly reports. They would soon start changing their company's working practices as they would soon become bored of dealing with so many complaints.

SAY IT WITH A SMILE

Everybody wants to feel wanted and loved even in business. There is an old proverb that says, "A smile is worth a thousand words and a tear can hide a thousand sorrows."

It took us weeks to train new staff to speak with a smile on the phone. Our meticulous training really worked as we received many positive comments when we met clients. Smiling is a free gift. I fail to see how a business can give a good impression if employees are miserable when they speak to clients. In addition a lazy or unhappy attitude can spill over when staff reply to emails. Owners will find it hard to create a business with ethos or value going forward if their employees have a poor attitude towards customers. Training and leadership from the top are vital.

CHAPTER 10

ASKING FOR WHAT I WANT

Knowing what I want and asking for it in business especially has been essential. Asking is an asset that has helped me to be successful. As discussed earlier, knowing *how* to ask is the real skill. I am rarely shy to ask a question or feel the need to apologise for asking. Why ask someone if they mind if I ask them a question? Why waste a question? Just ask it. It is not impolite to ask a question. If I ask a stupid question then I may get a stupid answer. Perhaps some believe that if they ask for what they want they will not get it due to their own lack of self confidence. Alternatively, they may not wish to put others out or they lack self worth.

In both business and spirituality asking is wholly justified. Sri Anandamayi Ma comments in her book, *Matri Vani*, that the child asks the mother for everything, yet the adult easily forgets or through pride or arrogance is unwilling to ask for help. I have noticed how meditators when having problems with their practice prefer to ask a fellow student who is less likely to know the answer than the teacher. The Great Master referred to pride as a negative quality. In these circumstances pride restricts growth and makes the spiritual aspirant's path more difficult than it needs to be. The same applies to business – being ashamed to show a lack of knowledge or understanding can only limit growth. I take a logical approach. If I know I know. If I do not know and want to know then I find out by asking someone who does.

Can't pay or won't pay

When I was a finance representative in my second job, occasionally we had to help collect money from non-payers or to decide who needed to be sued in court. There was an "arrears" customer who avoided all calls from me. I could not get through to him. What was worse was that he knew my father. I was not deterred so I asked one of our sweet secretaries, Jane, to put on her sexiest voice and ask for the person by his first name. When the receptionist enquired what the call was about, she said it was personal. After she was put through to the client she passed me the telephone. Now you may say that he would hang up at this stage but this rarely happened as he was caught off guard. My bolder colleagues would be put through by advising the receptionist that they were calling from the STI clinic! Creative thought is required when dealing with devious people.

Asking more than once

A few years ago, I rented a car in Amsterdam to drive down to Eindhoven. I had requested a small automatic Mercedes. When I checked in at reception I was offered two different automatics and was told by the receptionist that they did not have the car I requested. I opted for another one and made my way to the pickup area. When I was at the pick-up area I asked the person there if I could change the car. I told him that I had originally wanted the compact Mercedes. "No problem," he said. "I have one here." I was happy but amazed.

Another time I was with a shy friend who was shopping for some trousers in a small boutique. She found a pair that she liked but her size was not on display so she asked the assistant if they had her size. She was told that they did not. I approached the assistant, smiled and asked if she could look in the store room to double-check. The assistant came back shortly afterwards with the trousers in my friend's size who subsequently bought them. My friend was surprised and wanted to know why my approach resulted in success and her approach failure.

These two short stories illustrate the need to persevere and not to take no for an answer. Being proactive and asking twice never hurts and often yields the desired result. Perhaps when we pray we also have to ask more than once. Surely if everything exists then everything is possible.

ASKING FOR MONEY

Take Laura, a painter friend of mine. She is fun and exuberant but struggles for money month after month, often because she under-charges for her work. She dislikes asking for money and dislikes being without it! Something has to change or the same suffering will continue. Not long ago, she told me how much time she was spending on a painting for a client and that she was going to charge him £200 but was concerned it was too much. On analysing her hourly rate and materials I suggested to her that her price was far too low. I recommended she charged £325 and give £25 towards my charity walk if he agreed to the price. I gave her guidance on how to put the price to the client, simply without too much explanation or over justification and without apology. She reluctantly agreed to follow what I suggested. This was uncomfortable for her. When she presented the picture and the price to the client he did not blink. He thanked her and paid her what she asked. She learnt a lesson of value here.

Another friend, Gabby, is an excellent lawyer. Having run her department for years without the title, her firm decided to recruit a partner from outside and made him her boss. This new partner was given twice her salary and produced just 10% of the fee income that she generated. He also asked her advice on what to do on his cases and the staff continued to report to her and not him. Gabby hates confrontation but I encouraged her to pluck up the courage to approach her Senior Partner with her fees and salary statistics for the past three years. She told him that the balance of reward had swung more in favour of them than her. He was speechless. They automatically increased her salary and gave her a pension. It took her at least a year to find the courage to confront her bosses and it paid off because she could justify it. She finally grew in confidence and realised that she was too good for them to lose. Three years later the partner above her was fired. She is now plucking up the courage to ask for the salary of the failed partner! Sometimes we all need encouragement from another person to get what we deserve especially if we are really good at what we do.

A good boss will always want to reward employees well, even if occasionally the boss may need a nudge. If the boss does not recognise the results or value of good employees financially or otherwise then they will leave and his or her business will suffer. On the other hand, the employee may not be as good as they think they are! An honest and reflective approach helps to justify more money and should be backed up with factual achievements and information.

Helping your boss build your case and make a positive decision is a smart way to achieve what you want. Once again it
is following the simple philosophy of asking but being able
to justify the request making it difficult to be turned away.
However if the ground underneath is insecure because
the employer is unhappy with an aspect of the employee's
performance then it is sensible to repair these areas before
requesting a pay rise.

Spiritual reward

As the above examples demonstrate sometimes our work
in the world goes unnoticed and unrewarded. A really
advanced meditator will be unperturbed by the result of his
or her work and concerned only with their consciousness
and spiritual attitude during the task that was carried out.
The Great Master emphasised that every meditation and
every thought towards the Divine is credited to our spiritual
advancement. Unlike money or dignity, it cannot be taken
away. Our spiritual practice is always rewarded even if we
or others may judge it to be below par. Goodwill towards
others is also banked. Spiritual wealth is the real treasure.
Every small action for good is noticed and has value.

One day God sent an angel down to earth to witness a
farmer in a field. God told the angel that the farmer was
one of his most devoted subjects. The angel observed the
farmer. The farmer did not sit down to meditate or pray.
Instead he went about his work on the farm looking after
the fields and the animals from early in the morning to late
at night. The angel was unimpressed and returned to God
questioning whether God had made a mistake. The angel
told God that the man never prayed or meditated. He just

worked. God scolded the angel. He replied that at every moment the farmer was seeing the Divine everywhere in his work. The farmer saw God in the animals and in the fields. He did not look for results in his work. Whatever the fields produced he gave thanks to God rather than being ungrateful for what had not been produced. His attitude was that God would take care of everything and if things did not go to plan then God obviously had a better plan. The farmer had surrendered his work and himself to God completely. He was united with the Divine.

SPIRITUAL PHILOSOPHIES ON ASKING

As a spiritual aspirant, should I be humble and accept what I am given and ask for nothing or ask for everything? The first philosophy is simple. If God knows everything then why is there any need to ask? Surely I will be given everything I need. The second philosophy is to be like a child who asks the mother for everything. This is a loving and not a begging way to communicate internally with the Divine and raises divine consciousness by constantly thinking of God. As time goes on I believe that if I want something materially or spiritually then it will manifest if it is supposed to, with or without my effort. However, I was given intelligence and a voice for a reason. As I feel the presence of God more, my effort and his effort seem more like one effort and the two philosophies become unimportant. I am still carrying out actions and thoughts but no longer think that I am the "real" doer although I forget often. Neither path is "wrong" and it is surely beneficial to choose a philosophy which is conducive to one's own mind but to remain flexible in our beliefs.

Success in spirituality can lead to success in the world and success in the world can lead to success in spirituality. The more love I manifest the more fear is dissolved. Successful people have less fear.

FIGHTING WITH THE BULLY

As a child I witnessed my father's forthright approach to life. He knew what he wanted and was extremely ambitious to achieve materially for himself and his family. If someone was stopping his progress, he would first negotiate with reason, but if this did not work he was never afraid to confront obstacles in his way without fear.

My father's business gradually became more successful after years of hard work despite bank managers threatening to withdraw finance during several economic recessions. The directors of the venue where he held his exhibitions were not oblivious to the growth of his company so they decided to profit even more from his success. They increased the rent substantially, knowing that as the largest venue in London, my father had nowhere else to go. At the time the exhibition hall was owned by a huge shipping company. My father was furious with their blatant profiteering. Early one morning, unannounced, he turned up at the Head Office of the shipping company. In those days security must have been non-existent as he took the lift to the director's floor and walked straight into the Chairman's office. My father announced himself and told the Chairman what he thought of the bully boy tactics and con-artists that were running their flagship venue. The Chairman was stunned into silence. He had no idea what my father was talking about but was very uncomfortable.

My father's direct approach had the desired effect. A few days later the directors of the venue came back grovelling to him and apologised. The Chairman was an ethical man who clearly was unhappy to hear that a company in the group was acting dishonourably. My father was never mistreated again. He succeeded in beating the bully because he was not afraid of confrontation. His gregarious personality was his main asset yet he had other weapons in the arsenal if needed.

BE AN EXPERT WARRIOR
AND NOT AN EXPERT WORRIER

These stories explain something about my conditioning. I am a more cautious and calculating character than my father and am not at all physically intimidating. Luckily I inherited some of his fearlessness and boldness. Having inner confidence and a can-do attitude seems to transmit invisibly and visibly to others especially when we want something done. The opposite applies also. Worry, fear and negativity also transmit in the same way leading to more obstacles on the path. Luckily not all of our worries and fears are manifested. When I used to worry at work I took it as a signal that I needed to find a solution. Now I have more time, when I worry I am more relaxed and more prone to let events unfold rather than immediately rushing to find an answer. However freezing with anxiety and doing nothing is unhelpful at best and destructive at worst. Love also has a positive effect to counter worry. The masters I have met have an incredibly strong loving presence and transmit confidence without fear. Receiving unconditional love was so refreshing and new to me. The love I received and gave to others was normally conditional even if it was not my conscious intention. Love overcomes everything. Being able to express love must be better than being afraid to love or loving to be afraid. Our voice counts. Humility is one thing. Fear to express is quite another. Humility and fear to express oneself can easily be confused.

Discipline

Without discipline, nothing can be achieved in daily life. My boarding school education made discipline become more natural. Time management was strict. Breakfast was at 7.45am, not 7.46am. I do not regard discipline as an enemy but a friend. On every spiritual retreat I attend there is always a question about how to increase discipline and how to overcome the mind. For those who wish to encourage themselves to have more discipline, whether it be to give up smoking or another bad habit, introducing a controlled approach slowly can be more effective than radical measures. Even with the best intention the seeds of change need to be ready to germinate. A person who wants to stop smoking could decrease the number of cigarettes smoked by reducing their intake by one cigarette per day each week. A packet per day smoker in week one could smoke nineteen cigarettes per day; week two eighteen cigarettes per day and so on. Gradual change is easier to manage mentally as the sense of loss is not as apparent. Radical change is much harder for most people and real mental strength is required to give up a habit quickly.

When starting a good habit like meditation, a similar but incremental philosophy to giving up cigarettes applies.

I suggest people start with just fifteen minutes per day building it gradually week by week. It is easy to practise before breakfast or on the commute to and from work. Setting aside a routine to meditate at the same time each day helps the habit form.

MIND CONTROL

In order to discipline the mind, Smiling Swami says we need to discipline our senses. What we see with our eyes goes into our memory affecting our thoughts. Can watching horror movies be good for the mind? Can reading about death, fraud and scandal every day be good for the mind? I do not say that we should avoid what is happening around us, but do we ever analyse what is good food for the eyes, the stomach and the ears? This "food of the senses" governs the state of mind. It then becomes "food for thought" and a constituent of the mind. How can we discipline the senses? Take eating. The tongue is used to certain tastes and can hold the stomach to ransom. If food is over-salted or over-spicy then in the long term health can only deteriorate. Reducing salt, sugar and spices may be difficult initially, but better health will surely be the reward with less risk of diabetes. Food affects our mental health as well as our physical wellbeing. People who reduce smoking or alcohol will also benefit by having more money to put aside for healthier pursuits. These habits may be difficult to break as thoughts of smoking or drinking may return. However, with determination everything is possible. By moderating the food of the senses I have found the mind is calmer.

STICKING TO THE TASK

Apart from nearly giving up my career in finance in 1998 to become a healer, I did not have "butterfly" tendencies to flit from pillar to post. Discipline was essential in order to develop the qualities of sticking to the task. At the end of my first visit with the Great Master, he told me to stay with my work explaining that I needed money for my liberation. I had no real idea what he meant at the time but now that I have retired I can see the freedom I have been given to meditate without many worldly distractions or responsibilities. This proved to be the best advice that I ever received from a person I had only just met. However it was tough going, working for years on end knowing that the journey would not be enough to satisfy me. Although I enjoyed my work, after having spiritual experiences it was hard to operate in a business world often filled with false smiles and half-truths. When people in business ask how they can help me, how many really mean it?

MAKING THE SAME MISTAKE TWICE

Laura had been trying to sell her apartment for seven years. It was an attractive building in a popular location but she had two main problems. Firstly, the upstairs flat had been unoccupied for years which put off buyers and secondly, the building had subsidence problems which took ages to resolve. After pulling her hair out for so long, she finally sold it in 2008. Relieved, she decided to go travelling for a year and asked my advice on what to do with the money. I suggested that as the property market was at a high she should bank her equity money from the house sale, earn a little interest and decide where she wanted to live in the long term when she returned. Why jump from the frying pan into the fire? Unfortunately Laura panicked. Stress makes people panic but so apparently does a lack of stress. Feeling insecure without a house, she plunged into the market again quickly arranging an "interest only" mortgage. Within the next two years she lost £30,000 of her equity and is stuck with an "interest only" mortgage at 56 years old without any hope of ever repaying the capital back. After seven years of anxiety she had been finally freed but her fear drove her back to another difficult scenario. On the positive side she had to live somewhere so there has been some benefit.

Regrettably many like Laura have long-term mortgages on an interest only basis. The time bomb is ticking for those in this situation especially when interest rates rise. Time will tell. Planning ahead may be boring for those who are restless but an absence of planning to avoid the truth cannot be the way to proceed. Facing one's options, which do not include winning the lottery, can be a brutal wakeup call but is the only way. Taking advice from others can help but only if the adviser knows what they are talking about. If our debts are too high, then the number of choices is limited. We can either get a better paid job, an additional job or see a debt counsellor. I rarely meet anyone who cannot improve their situation if they review their spending habits or earning potential realistically. It can be hard to face the past when the present catches up because the realisation brings up the truth which has been buried for so long. Often a person will have to come to terms with the harsh reality that they have spent too much or not worked or saved enough. Honesty needs to over-ride the plethora of excuses which may arise and then at that moment change can really begin. Enjoying a life of excess often fuelled by over-borrowing crashes to a halt when the music stops. Everyone wants an easy life but do we make our lives easy? If the mind is untrained it will take time to discipline it again. It will not happen overnight.

WHICH TRUTH TO FOLLOW?

It is always good to be hopeful, but reality dawns eventually, whether we are ready or not. Avoiding realistic analysis and rational action of our true position may defer pain and suffering but it is not a solution.

When a problem arises, once I am clear of the options which I analyse carefully I make a decision without fear and with confidence. Fear is often related to potential loss. I am not afraid of making a mistake. If I make a mistake, then I should heed the words of the Great Master who said "Mistakes are made for correction." Smiling Swami adds that we should not "make the same mistake twice". My take is that it is far cheaper and smarter to learn from other people's mistakes!

JUST DO IT: BATTLE OF THE MIND

When I had my speedy Toyota Celica turbo in my early twenties, I had my "Just do it" Nike sticker in the back window. Having this attitude has helped me in my life but not in a cavalier sense. It is helpful to remember this motto when I want to do something especially when my mind and body are rebelling against each other. "Never say never" is another saying which I have come to accept. As much as I can plan or prepare for what is ahead, the unknown has proved to be far more powerful than me. The key factor is how I deal with the unknown and unforeseen when it arrives.

In spiritual life, many advocate that the main battle is with the mind. I do not agree with this approach at all. If I adopt the attitude that my mind is the enemy then a battle will commence. I am happy with my mind and what it gives me. I let the mind do its job. If my mind does not listen to me then why should I listen to it? The mind is the main source of unhappiness when worries come. When it is calm, I feel content and happy. The Great Master told me to observe my breath not my mind. The breath when slow and rhythmic takes care of the mind. A calm mind possesses the potential to succeed and a restless mind misses the potential. I had never ever stopped to think how important my breath was to my mind and activities before meeting him. When Smiling Swami first came to the West he observed that most people had trouble with their minds here compared to India where more people had trouble physically due to undernourishment and poor hygiene. An uncontrolled mind leads to thinking negatively, speaking negatively and feeling negative. A disciplined mind can be achieved even through changes in diet which I will expand upon later in the book. I enjoy observing how people's minds operate. For example, asking with a negative comes from negative thought and normally leads to a negative response. The question, "I don't suppose I could jump the queue because I am in a hurry", will no doubt bring the negative response "no you cannot!" However smiling and explaining your problem and asking positively for someone to help you will significantly change the odds for a more helpful response.

In business, apologising for a price when quoting or telling a client that there are other companies better than you is unhelpful but it happens often. Quoting with confidence is necessary in business even if rejection follows. Focus and awareness on how I am listening, speaking or asking is very important if I want a positive reaction. Why do receptionists seek permission to ask who is calling instead of just asking who is calling? The above examples are not supposed to be facetious but the smallest details in behaviour on small issues determine how life pans out when bigger issues are at stake. Bad habits grow. To inspire ourselves mentally to be positive even when we feel negative breeds confidence. Life is less bumpy now that meditation has become part of me. Everyone prefers to deal with confident and happy people rather than negative and miserable people in business and in life in general.

SPEAKING YOUR MIND

In sales there is an expression which applies, "If you can't convince them confuse them!" When I reflect on my thoughts I do not see too much value in rhetoric or navel-gazing. If I want to change something about myself, then 50% of the solution is recognising what needs to be changed even if I continue the behaviour. As long as I face up to my negative traits then I am on the way to achieving the change I want. I used to be highly reactive particularly to criticism especially if it was misguided or uninformed. There is a fine divide between telling someone the truth and criticising them. I am more relaxed now if others agree, disagree or misunderstand me. Being relaxed is becoming a good habit. If I still react I realise soon afterwards that

I should not be reacting. Smiling Swami is teaching me through his example. He never reacts regardless of what people say about him. It is tough to master the control of my reactions and the results are mixed. As George Burns once said "Everybody is entitled to my opinion." I used to agree wholeheartedly, but now I am realising this is not always fruitful. Ultimately time will be the judge of my actions.

MISERY

It is really difficult for miserable people to be enthusiastic and successful compared to happy people. Those with a tendency to be negative should seek the company of positive and upbeat people. Playing the "poor me" card alienates others and increases mental suffering. Those who moan that nobody has work or money can never be good role models. It seems surprisingly hard for people to break away from a crowd even if that influence is mainly negative. I never felt the need to be part of a crowd. My independent nature and Get It Done attitude is not dragged down by the negativity of others. I remove myself quickly from negative people and if it derives from family members I keep more distance. When I want to do something, I do not waste energy in discussing it too much with others who are negative. I follow my inner guru. For those who complain perhaps they should stop to contemplate more deeply. Is life really unfair to us or are we unfair to ourselves by not changing our attitude, habits and behaviour?

CHAPTER 11

THE ROAD TO BUSINESS SUCCESS: SALE OF KEY

HOW TO ACHIEVE FINANCIAL AND SPIRITUAL SUCCESS?

I have endeavoured in this book not to speak generally or on behalf of the royal "we". Making the assumption that I know what others are thinking or feeling will rarely be right no matter how intuitive I think I am. However, rightly or wrongly, I believe that most spiritual seekers think that business or materialism is not spiritual and most business people think that there is no room in business for spirituality. I disagree.

True perfection in yoga is the attainment of mastery over the sense organs and balance in the relevant *chakras*. Such mastery is necessary to really grow spiritually. A spiritual aspirant who lacks the energy in the lower three *chakras* to carry out daily tasks, will not proceed well on the spiritual path. Lack of money, poor diet or bad relations with others will result in a restless mind making deep meditation impossible. We are born in the world to experience spirituality in the physical form and in the material world. Any material success or good fortune I have had is due to grace. If I can keep this attitude of gratefulness then I will be happy. My continued reference to grace may surprise you, but this realisation is helping me to manifest and realise the divinity and joy in my life. In business, no matter how successful a person becomes, if that person is dishonest and treats others badly, then problems will follow. Making money is a spiritual activity if it is done with the right attitude of appreciation and joy. Money can also help others as well as ourselves.

When I consider the qualities required to be successful on either path, the skills and abilities are identical: Enthusiasm; Determination; Listening skills; Love; Desire; Resilience; Ability; Energy; Common Sense; Integrity; Discipline; Insistency, Consistency and Persistency!

ENTHUSIASM for life rubs off on other people and creates a stream of positive energy. Waking up with joy to work or meditate will surely bring better results.

DETERMINATION to continue meditation or work when the going gets tough is crucial. The marathon runner does not give up even when he or she is underperforming. It may not always change the destiny of the race, but the next day the true winner will come out fighting to improve again. Perseverance is key to success.

LISTENING SKILLS: The Invisible Hand gave us two ears and one mouth yet I am often guilty of speaking at least twice as much as I listen. In business, every client wants to be listened to and understood. Listening carefully to the needs of a client and then asking the right questions brings success and opportunity for both parties. Listening attentively to a spiritual master can change a bad habit or attitude in a moment or correct a meditation technique.

LOVE makes me do things even better. If I love my work I will be more productive. If I love my *sadhana*, which in Sanskrit means spiritual practice, the more I will practise and love others more.

DESIRE: Healthy desire in business is difficult to master as too much desire can lead to greed and ungratefulness and ultimately bad decision-making. In spirituality, the guru helps the devotee to manifest the desires that need to be experienced and to alleviate the pain and suffering along the way. Yet if the devotee does not take heed of the warnings of the guru to change, then more suffering may follow like taking the risk of going through a red light when we know we should stop. Like a doctor, the guru gives guidance for the wellbeing of the person in his or her care. If the person does not listen to the advice and clings on to bad habits, then their long-term health will be affected.

RESILIENCE: A resilient attitude is needed on both paths particularly when others are negative towards us or do not believe in us. I am respectful of what others say if I perceive their advice to be helpful, but ignore the opinions which are not. Resilience is also needed to combat the negatives of the mind.

ABILITY is given to all of us. In spirituality every person has the same potential to see light, hear the AUM sound and feel the vibration. It is not an exclusive club. In work everyone has abilities to help them succeed.

ENERGY: At work, happiness, enthusiasm and good health help fuel the energy to do our jobs well. Through daily meditation one receives more energy and focus to carry out work with even greater efficiency. I was quite efficient already but became even more focussed by practising Kriya Yoga for just thirty minutes every morning. This is because the techniques oxygenate the brain and body which promotes more energy.

COMMON SENSE is needed to arrange my life, carry out a task and how to think. For example, each week I would quickly calculate the turnover and profitability of the business on the back of an envelope, by extrapolating the figures from different systems. Waiting for an accountant to provide the information six weeks later made no sense to me. The entrepreneur should know the numbers better than the accountant and have a "feel" for the business in case the accountant makes a mistake. Common sense is integral to any success I have achieved. Applying common sense to using my skills well and choosing the company I keep is also vital to spiritual progress.

INTEGRITY: As some of the stories show in this book, I have met people in business who appear to have integrity but later their actions prove otherwise. I have also met spiritual teachers who present themselves piously in public but behind closed doors do not behave that way. I do not mention the above as criticism but one does not need to be a teacher to have integrity and one who is a teacher may not have any integrity at all.

DISCIPLINE: Keeping both eyes on the goal in business and spirituality helps incentivise me to continue when the going gets tough.

INSISTENCY, CONSISTENCY and PERSISTENCY: If I know what I want and know it is possible I ask for it and do not accept no for an answer. This I have followed consistently and persistently!

In summary, it is impossible to argue that the material and spiritual worlds are separate from each other. They are inextricably linked.

HOW TO PROCEED?

Sometimes we just have to proceed! Learning through trial and error works best when corrections are made through unrepeated mistakes. Reading self-help books or attending courses may bring many positives, but there is no substitute for dipping our toes in the water and letting go to gain our own experience rather than rely on the polished truth of others. If we can make time to read or think then we have time to meditate or bring other positive changes to our lives through action. Inspiration leads to perspiration or it just remains another thought. Just as past success does not guarantee future success, past failures and doubts do not guarantee future failure. Initial failure is only deferred success so what is there to lose? Being inspired brings confidence in ourselves and to others.

To be successful in spirituality and business, absolute strength in one's convictions is required. When I was unsure about something, I sought a second opinion. When I was sure, I proceeded with conviction and without doubt. The *Bhagavad-Gita* says, "A doubting person is always in trouble." Smiling Swami advises us to look four steps ahead and then to proceed slowly one step at a time.

SPIRITUALITY IN BUSINESS

A friend who is a psychologist told me recently that the new fad for large conglomerates is to bring spirituality into business. This is marvellous provided the directors are sincere in its implementation. Does this mean that employers, instead of giving smoking breaks to staff which will ultimately kill them, will introduce meditation breaks which will make them healthier inside and outside of the work place? Many consultants and intellectuals are about to be paid vast sums of money to research how spirituality can be merged into the business world. Do we really need consultants to teach us how to be ethical when we know the answer ourselves? Which consultants will be qualified enough to teach us how to be spiritual? Being spiritual is about going back to basics. Smiling and caring from our hearts and being sincere in our actions and motives is a good way to begin. Wanting to help clients or colleagues without an ulterior motive is spiritual. Not claiming false lunch or travel expenses is spiritual! Once the basics have been mastered I doubt that many consultants will be needed.

Spirituality is not only about praying or sitting down and meditating. We all have the potential inside of us to behave like decent human beings otherwise the criminal would never change his or her ways, yet many do. Business is no different. Real change needs to come from the leaders and directors of businesses. Their ethics and integrity set the example for others. A great leader will look at his or her own faults and be accountable and honourable in their actions.

WHY DO BUSINESSES SUCCEED?

Successful businesses offer a service or product which they market and sell. Their vision meets the desire of others. They offer a good reliable service. They get paid for their work. They make a profit after paying their staff. They reinvest and manage their cash flow. They do not rest on their laurels. Success is not guaranteed in the future so drive and determination from the owners and directors is crucial. They build the business on solid foundations ensuring that every part of the process from answering the phone to administration, sales and support works like clockwork. If a problem arises, good managers and directors know about it and then fix it before it is too late.

WHAT IS SPIRITUAL SUCCESS?

Many will argue that ultimately there is no such thing as spiritual success. Some strive for enlightenment or realisation. Others believe that the universe is uniform and organised down to the last detail and we are just playing our part perfectly so spiritual achievement is nothing more than evolution. Natural evolution to enlightenment apparently takes each of us one million years! The good news is that full consciousness will arrive eventually for all of us. As consciousness awakens and ignorance fades, perhaps, for some, restlessness and discontentment arrive to show that pleasure in the world does not last and that they have to seek solace inside. In order to succeed spiritually, the discipline of meditating each day has been essential. Spending so much time with the guru has helped me overcome any doubts as they have arisen. Once, when I was busy working all hours, I asked Smiling Swami about my spiritual progress. He told me that while I was practising diligently I had many leaks like a bucket with holes in it. I knew I needed to shore up the holes by bringing more of the practice into my daily life. For me this meant becoming more patient and loving and becoming less agitated and less reactionary. Smiling Swami has a saying: "Selfishness gets and forgets; love gives and forgives." I observe closely if my behaviour is loving or selfish. Preparation and alertness are essential in business and spirituality. Practising being a good person in all aspects of life is central to progress in the world and spiritually. Regularity of practice leads to sound habits, concentration and purpose, bringing real growth.

Why do businesses fail?

In a nutshell businesses fail for the following reasons: They do not get paid or charge enough for their services; they may have a product which they believe is great but potential clients do not; they give a poor service, are badly managed and have demotivated staff; they do not market or sell their offering effectively; they become complacent and rely on one or two major clients which is unhealthy if the clients go elsewhere; they do not create enough turnover to cover the overheads; they lack the foresight to anticipate potential weaknesses or problems in the business or ignore outside factors which influence their livelihood; they may grow the turnover too quickly and overtrade, meaning the company cannot handle the volume.

In business like in sport, one great performance is satisfying but loses value quickly unless it is followed by success after success. Of course there are other extraordinary events out of the control of a business which can make it fail but the above examples cover the main reasons. A driven entrepreneur will constantly find areas and ways to improve the business especially when problems arise. How we handle problems in business defines the few that will succeed. A budding entrepreneur does not seek solace or excuses; only solutions.

Why do spiritual seekers fail?

As discussed earlier it is debatable whether a spiritual seeker can succeed, so I use the word failure here on the basis that the seeker can always meditate to change him or herself more. Temporary failure is merely an indicator to continue and try harder if necessary. Those who claim to meditate and are constantly restless should find it hard to honestly say they are spiritually advanced. Lack of practice is the common theme that stops aspiring meditators or anyone else for that matter achieving what they want. For some reason those who put in the least effort expect the biggest results. It is more worthwhile to put in the maximum effort *doing* rather than imagining! In spirituality when progress is slow it is worth seeking the advice of a guru who has already been to the top of the mountain and back and who knows how to overcome the obstacles. I have witnessed many who do not practise the Kriya Yoga techniques correctly or who change the techniques or even mix the techniques of one yoga with another yoga. This is purely down to the intervention and boredom of the mind and will give mixed results. In spite of being offered follow-up retreats and classes many do not come again. Kriya Yoga is a key to the spiritual door. Once the door is open it is up to us how far we proceed.

DECISION-MAKING

When I ran Key I was the final decision-maker. One of the reasons that I started a company was because I could not tolerate the poor decision-making and dithering in large organisations. If I have to make a decision I immerse myself totally. Careful and speedy thinking does not result in an inefficient decision-making process. On the contrary I often make very quick decisions. Speed of analysis is an asset. However I do not take decisions that make me feel uncomfortable or unsure. When I have a big decision to make and I lack clarity, I take my time even if this means days and see if I get the same answer each day. Somehow the answer comes eventually and I know what to do. Through good fortune I have normally found a way to proceed. However when a crisis occurred in business I would also become stressed and anxious depending on the size of the problem. The more stupid or illogical the problem the more agitated I became!

Decision-making was second nature to me. Somehow I knew what to do most of the time. It also seems when making decisions it is being done by the Invisible Hand but I have the illusion that I am making the decision even though part of me knows that I am not. This inner sense of good judgement was like a gift which helped me to know and ask for what I wanted in negotiations. Lots of people have this ability so I am in no way different to many others. This did not mean that I was always cool as a cucumber. I certainly was unhappy when a crisis came but I turned that energy of agitation into being more productive and proactive. I never made decisions like a gambler but I tried to envisage the impact of each decision. Pot luck is not involved in good decision-making. This intuitive knowledge is subtly different to knowledge gained through books or training. The Great Master would often refer to the medical student who had studied surgery intensively. He acknowledged how important studying was but commented that nobody would allow a surgeon who had only read many books to operate on them! Technical knowledge is vital but is useless without practical experience on how to apply it.

Decision-makers stand or fall by their decisions. Businesses fail if the decision-maker is no good or nobody is able or willing to make a decision. Leaving a state of flux can be worse than making the wrong decision. Regarding the delegation of decision-making I was very hands-on.

When giving my managers responsibility, I needed to ensure that they were in tune with my own decision-making process. Practically this meant explaining why I made the decisions that I did. If my decision-making had been poor, then the business would have failed and we all would have been out of a job. I was also only too happy if someone had a better idea than me. Anyone attempting to run a business by committee or consensus will soon run into problems. Safety in numbers is sometimes sought by those who are afraid of responsibility. Real decision-makers and "doers" who know what they are doing will not stick around on a committee that makes half-baked decisions. One person's ideas at a table may be sensible and correct but if the others present will not listen, such wisdom is wasted. Consensus decision-making can produce a botched result by trying to take too many views into account. This is probably why governments are so unsuccessful.

Entrepreneurs or ambitious people who like their own way and more importantly trust in their judgement do not need the comfort of a consensus. They would also tire quickly if every committee meeting deferred decisions unnecessarily to the next committee meeting. Also to witness a "poor" decision without being able to change the outcome would be difficult. I accept that I do not always have the best answer, but poor decisions are not difficult to spot. So how do good decision-makers seem to know what the right decision is to make? Are they naturally spiritual and intuitive or do they have the knowledge and experience to make a balanced decision? I suspect it is a mixture of all these factors. Intuition and good judgement are vital on both the spiritual and material paths. Knowing which spiritual practice or guru to follow is helpful even if this changes later. Discrimination to identify the "knowers" from the "talkers" in business and spirituality is essential. I prefer to trust my own judgement even though sometimes the result may not be as I hoped.

ATTITUDE

Einstein said, "It is better to believe than disbelieve; in doing so you bring everything to the realms of possibility."

A good mental attitude may not help the outcome but it helps keep more balance and happiness. If I have the attitude that I am going to succeed, firstly I will believe it more and secondly it will put me in the right frame of mind to accomplish the task. If I do the best I can without worrying too much about what others are doing then I will be satisfied that I could do no more regardless of a result. If by having a poor attitude, I dislike what I am doing, my effort, performance and ultimately the result will more than likely be negative.

When I carry out any task I do not think that failure will come. This is not arrogance but I just do not see the point of approaching tasks thinking in this way. I have always found what I was good at and then tried to excel by playing to my strengths. That is all. I focus on what I am good at and not what I am bad at. It is like being a good weather forecaster who is right more times than he is wrong with his forecasts. A good forecaster will have a feel for the job as well as ability. The greater one's ability and experience, then the less the doubt. I was not the brightest in the bunch by any stretch of imagination. I was never exceptional at anything but a good all-rounder with bundles of perseverance.

Of course it helps if I like what I am doing. No matter how perfect my job was, I had to accept that there were aspects which were mundane and boring. With a better attitude and not too much thought, the job gets done quicker. The art is to have a good mental attitude to the jobs or tasks that I dislike. I often procrastinate over cleaning the house. When I finally do it I wonder what all of the fuss was about. So thinking about a chore can take up more energy and time than doing the job. Delaying what needs to be done over and over becomes a bad habit which repeats and is a waste of time and energy. Such bad habits can only hinder success in spirituality and life in general. Some have the illusion that there is a perfect job which they will enjoy 100% of the time. It is better to realise that this is not the case earlier rather than later on in one's working life. Luckily on the whole I enjoyed most aspects of my career.

Where There Is Love There Is No Effort

Hugging Mother says, "Where there is love there is no effort." Every job in society has equal value and importance – how we do that job – with care or without care – with love or without love is what really matters. The problem comes when the love fades and the work does not match expectations. Gurus teach us to detach from likes and dislikes and to have a neutral attitude. This way of life can be applied to business and spiritual life.

Some people work on the basis that they will spend forty hours per week at their job, get paid and then go home without worrying about work. Their reward is spending what they have earned and not to have too much pressure at work. They are happy with that. As the boss I needed to accept that most people fall into this category. At first I found this very hard as I took it for granted that like me everyone else had the same inbuilt motivation to do things better, learn more and grow. I found it frustrating when the attitude of some staff was not up to scratch. I was frequently amazed when a new secretary came in for her first day's work. At our first meeting to discuss their duties and responsibilities many did not bring a pen and paper to take notes. If I suggested that it would be helpful to do this some replied that it was not necessary because they would remember. By the eighth point I knew that those without a pen were in trouble. If their pride was strong they would remain seated and pretend that they were absorbing everything being discussed. The best ones would hold up their hands, get a pen and paper and would never forget that lesson. The others would not last. I accept that people have different aspirations and ambitions, but to have a positive attitude especially on the first day is a minimum requirement!

The clever entrepreneur realises that the leopard never changes its spots. My father told me this early on but I did not believe him. Experience has shown me that he was correct. We therefore had to discover by trial and error how to get the best out of each member of staff by giving them more of the work they were able to do. Hiring and firing is part of the job lot for a boss but it is a great waste of time interviewing people when their actual skills do not match their CV.

Why did people use our services?

On my last day at Key I gave a farewell speech. I thanked all of my staff but I also expressed gratitude to the thousands of people who were not present without whom there would have been no success. I was referring to all the clients and our suppliers. Without them none of us would have made a living. Those who think that they can be successful in business on their own should go and set up shop in the wilderness and see how successful they are.

Francis Bacon once said "Scientia potentia est" – "Knowledge is in itself power."

For me knowledge is not theoretical business or spiritual knowledge and true knowledge is what I learn from my daily life.

Firms used us because they trusted us and we delivered what we promised. Credibility came once clients had good experiences and they would then recommend us to others. One of the few complaints I ever received was from a client who saw another client with one of our conference folders which he had not been given.

When I left Key, we had a client list of 1,300 legal practices including over 25% of the top 500 in the country. Many of those had been with us for more than fifteen years.

Any entrepreneurs who think they deserve to be successful when their business does not deliver what they promise should contemplate more. During my time in business, the percentage of suppliers that did not deliver what they promised was over 50%. In the case of bankers, 99%! It was a basic rule and blindingly obvious to me that if we told a client we would send out paperwork that night then we did it without fail. The same applied to returning calls promptly. Logic dictates that when a client calls they want to speak to you now and not two days later. Occasionally we told clients that a decision would take three days but got back to them the following day. Under-promising and over-delivering helped Key to succeed. On the rare occasion we could not deliver what we promised we contacted them immediately. Hiding behind a wall of silence just will not do in business yet it is commonplace. We promised what we delivered and delivered what we promised.

Chopstick banking

Once we met an English banker who worked for a Japanese bank to arrange a line of credit. After the meeting, his parting words were, "I'll be back to you in 48 hours." Laid Back Cigar Man had the measure of him and said he would eat his hat if he came back within a week. Six months later, in spite of me chasing him up several times, we finally spoke. He had been too busy! "By coincidence" the case was picked up by his colleague who had just joined who I knew from my first job so there was obviously good reason for the delay! It seems that the Invisible Hand knows best. We did do business with them eventually but they unfortunately closed down a few years later when their Japanese parent got into trouble. When the bank was being wound down, I did manage to negotiate a fee in our favour so that they could be released from their facility. It really makes a welcome change to charge a bank a fee instead of the other way around!

Honest and dishonest bankers in business

The raw material of Key was money so renewing our bank facilities was vital for our survival. If we could not borrow money we could not trade and would be out of business. On one occasion there was a dispute as to whether a previously

239

structured arrangement was supposed to continue for another twelve months or not. I knew I was right as I could remember the original negotiation. I asked my secretary to get the file. I showed them my copy of the letter on which I had put a date of a further telephone conversation clarifying the meaning of the letter. The bank manager read what I had originally written and said that because they trusted me they would still offer the same terms.

However, a few years later the rules of engagement with our clearing bankers changed. They had been taken over by more aggressive Scottish owners. In spite of us having arranged a three-year deal this was effectively torn up by them at the end of year one. The City motto "My word is my bond" had clearly been deleted from the unspoken ethical code of how banking operates. This is a clear example of a non-spiritual approach to business. Changing our main bank after we had invested so much time and energy to educate our bankers in our business made it difficult. In spite of the embarrassment of the local director, we had little choice but to accept the new terms which were more expensive. It was a warning for me to become less reliant on this bank and increase our facilities elsewhere which I did. At the end of year two, the same bank tried once again to get one over us by changing the agreed terms. I had been advised by the assistant director that our £25 million credit facility had been agreed by their board of directors credit committee for another twelve months as before. He told me that the facility letter would be sent to me on the following day. We were both happy to have another renewal out of the way.

The next morning I received a call to tell me that one of the other directors had decided overnight that our fee was not enough and wanted to double it. There comes a point when enough is enough. They thought that they could rail-road me into submission, but when a director gives an oral agreement and changes it the following day it is just not acceptable. I was livid. I demanded to speak to our senior director and the assistant director on the phone. I asked them whether I was dealing with a top international bank or a two-bit bank from the Wild West. I told them that it was unacceptable to treat us as loyal customers like this and insisted they stick to their original fee. A stunned silence then followed. They were shocked that their integrity was being challenged because both of them were honest men who were being asked to be dishonest by one of their peers. The senior director told me he would get back to me. They eventually agreed to stick to the original deal regardless of what the other director wanted. There is a way to do business and treat loyal customers.

BANKS ARE NOT ALL BAD!

As the business grew, we needed more bank facilities. We started to deal with a Dutch bank that loved our business through an old contact who had joined them. Within two years they were matching the facilities of our original bank at £25 million. Andy, the director from the Dutch bank who I had known for fifteen years, had arranged a lunch for me to meet the CEO whom I had met briefly once before. At the meeting before lunch, they told me how happy they were with our business and wanted to double our facility to £50 million. I stayed cool as I smiled inside. This was the first time a bank had really thrown money at us. It was also a spiritual lesson that sometimes we do not need to ask for anything as what we need comes when it is ready. They also advised me that they would reduce the rate of interest that they charged us, but wanted to discuss the exclusivity clause that I had insisted on within our agreement with them. In simple terms this clause stated that they could never deal directly or indirectly with our clients without our involvement. The *quid pro quo* was that we gave them a substantial proportion of our business although this was on an oral rather than written basis. I had insisted on this clause as new competition was entering our market that was also accessing the Dutch bank's funds. It was quite rightly their prerogative to deal with whoever they liked but they had to decide who was their preferred client; the competition or us. I was confident that it was us. Their new unsolicited offer put me in a tricky situation. They understandably wanted something in return for the goodies on the table. I held my ground and reminded them of our long track record and trading experience. This gave them an automatic advantage because they were less likely to have a bad payer through us compared to another introducer. It never hurts to repeat the existing benefits of a business relationship. Nevertheless as we walked to lunch I began to think of some way to give them something back.

Over lunch we discussed pleasantries and before dessert the CEO left the table to make a call. Andy spoke to me. He said, "David, we love your business and are not going to upset you. If you want to keep the exclusivity clause we'll keep it in the documentation." When the CEO returned and raised the point again I knew how to reply – diplomatically of course! The Invisible Hand became the Visible Hand through Andy. A few weeks later, before the documentation arrived I suggested, rather tongue in cheek, that we extend the deal to three years and make it £75 million instead of the £50 million. I suggested to Andy that we may as well plan ahead and to my surprise he agreed!

The moral of these stories is that there are times when I was prepared to stick to what I believed in no matter what the consequences. Also I was not afraid to negotiate the best deal I could get. Being bullied in a business or any other relationship is not worth it. I did not think at the time that I was taking a risk by standing strong but I am not the type of person who picks a battle on every issue. Confronting problems or issues is part of life; the $64,000 question is how to win the battle. Quite rightly our funders expected honesty and trust from us and by the same token we deserved and expected the same in return. It took many years to establish relationships with funders. Bankers make a note of every conversation. We always did what we promised. When times became tough this track record surely helped. When Key was sold we had facilities of £125 million. So how did such a small company raise so much money? Firstly, it took at least ten years to establish a track record that would stand the scrutiny of our lenders. After auditing our business they could see that the quality of our loan book really was AAA. We became an expert in our field and our funders were always looking for high quality business. There is no shortcut to building a track record so that business partners trust you implicitly. My own personal integrity meant that we would walk away from a deal if our funders might be at risk. Long term profit has more value than short term profit. We developed unrivalled market knowledge and our funders loved us because our business was extremely low risk. Only one of these banks had a bad debt in eighteen years and as the director told me, "David, we have made well over £1 million profit from your business in the last four years. This is one of those occurrences in the scheme of things".

Sale of Key

When Key was sold, it was like handing over a young adult that had been lovingly nurtured from birth. When the deal was signed, it was a poignant moment, yet there was no real elation or excitement from me. I felt detached and balanced. I had strived for many years with the ultimate aim to sell the business yet when the moment of glory came, in that moment I felt strangely cool, calm and collected. I wondered if the experience I had was similar to the moment of Self-realisation or enlightenment in spiritual terms. We shed blood, sweat and tears to reach our goal yet when it happens we may wonder what all of the fuss was about. Perhaps in my case it is because success did not come overnight and I had enjoyed the benefits along the way. It had taken years to find the right buyer at the right price. The eventual buyers of Key knew us and understood the value of the company. We had come close to doing a deal with another prospective buyer and we had also considered selling to a venture capitalist. When I asked Smiling Swami for his advice he told me to avoid the vulture capitalists!

So how did we find the buyer?

I had always been reluctant to go to competitors who were the most likely buyers of the business because I was concerned they would copy our finance packages that were not well known or in the public domain. As profits increased year on year, we finally located a discreet West End firm of corporate finance brokers to find a buyer. The brokers showed enthusiasm and quickly understood the uniqueness and value of the business. They were confident enough in their own abilities to accept a very small advance fee to cover their initial work with an agreed success fee when the business was sold. This approach differed to other brokers who wanted substantial advances not based on success. After quite a few false starts with interested parties, I received "the call" from George at the corporate finance broker. He had located an interested party for me to meet. Apparently they knew us. I was intrigued. Who could it be? It transpired that their CEO, Charles, used to run a bank that gave us funding facilities and he knew my father also. This was a good start. We did not have to justify our business and reputation. Negotiations took place at a steady pace. I presented the projected growth figures and they started to talk turkey. I had already begun the preparation of the due diligence report, which is the information that a buyer wants to see before they buy a business. I brought in a trusted friend to help me collate and copy the paperwork outside of business hours. It was not in my interest to tell my staff until the very last minute in case the deal fell through. I did not want to destabilise a steady ship. At this stage, my work days increased from the normal twelve hours to fourteen or sixteen hours, six days per week. Burning of the midnight oil had begun. In the last week of the transaction I was working twenty hours per day. My meditation was really helping me stay awake and alert.

MESSAGE FROM THE GREAT MASTER

When the deal was agreed, we had already appointed lawyers to act for us. I had been recommended a firm who knew our business and who were big enough not to be pushed around by the City firm representing the buyer. We agreed a fixed fee with our lawyers. They were business-like and humble yet to my surprise the buyer's lawyers who were a large City firm were quite the opposite: pompous and arrogant from the start. Wholly different to the gentlemanly, fair approach of Charles, the CEO of the buyer. Their lawyer wanted to call all of the shots. This was interesting to me as I would have thought that the advisers would reflect the personality of the client, but not in this case. Our lawyer, Colin told me not to worry. He had seen it all before. He just told me to stay focussed on what we wanted and to ignore the rhetoric. Written negotiations progressed smoothly. Then, as in every transaction, the sticking points arose, some expected and others unexpected.

I was sitting on a bench in the City of London, suited and booted, waiting to go into an important meeting with the buyer to tackle the points. Had the meeting gone badly the deal could have fallen through. I had already met with our lawyers earlier to go through the issues outstanding. It was a fine spring day. I was reading a newspaper, alert but slightly nervous about what might happen. Out of nowhere an Indian man walked towards me. He was not wearing a suit or tie, which is most unusual in the City. He stopped in front of me and declared, "You have a very lucky forehead and you will receive good fortune in the next few months." I was so surprised to be approached by him that words did not come out of my mouth. I smiled and knew that it was a message from the Great Master who had died three years before. Everything was going to be all right! I relaxed. I watched the Indian man walk away from me. He did not stop to talk to anybody else. As I write about this pivotal moment, the hairs on my arms stand to attention and I receive an electric shock through my body! Another reminder that nothing can be done without grace. Being conscious of this grace is wonderful. After many late nights the sale proceeded and all parties were happy which is the perfect conclusion to any deal. From start to finish the deal had taken four months.

I enjoyed the process of negotiation and quite rightly, in a takeover both the buyer and the seller want to be winners which I believe was the outcome. Our advisers in the transaction really did a fine job. They acted efficiently and humbly throughout. A poor choice of lawyers would have ruined the deal. Destiny had reconnected us with Charles, one of those true gentlemen that are rare in the business world. Honest, ethical and practical.

Sadly two years after I left the business, in spite of being on course to write £200 million that year, Key was forced into administration due to the Icelandic parent going bust. The final payout to creditors was 95p in the pound which shows that it should never have gone into administration. That payout was after the deduction of the usual hefty legal and accounting fees that accompany administration. Due to its large and loyal client base the business has re-emerged and is now part of a UK building society and is successful once again.

After the sale I worked as hard if not harder than before for the new owners. When I left the business due to personal problems, Laid Back Cigar Man, the master of the one-liners, reminded me that, "We have never lost a good one yet and now that you have retired you have become a non-person!"

The day after my farewell lunch, I was shopping in my local supermarket close to the office. As I approached the vegetables section, I noticed an envelope lying on the floor with the Key logo on the back. I picked it up. One of the secretaries had obviously gone shopping on the way to the post office and dropped it. I went to the nearest post box and posted the envelope with a smile. That was my last act for Key. It was no longer my problem.

One year later, my life changed totally. Within a twelve-month period I had left London, was divorced and no longer working. A completely new chapter was beginning. It was as if I was starting a new life in the same body with the memory of all that I had learnt and experienced.

CHAPTER 12
INFLUENCES ON THE MIND

RAJASIC, TAMASIC, SATTVIC QUALITIES

According to the ancient scriptures of India, we all have three inherent qualities operating and governing our physical, emotional and mental behaviour. These are known as the three gunas: Rajasic, Tamasic and Sattvic. When I first heard about the gunas at a lecture I was curious why they were talking about the Gooners, the nickname for my football team, Arsenal!

Rajasic qualities give the energy and desire to carry out tasks and work. In the extreme form, a rajasic person is highly restless, angry and greedy. Rajasic energy is manifested through the breath which flows in and out of the right nostril. This is also referred to as *pingala*.

Tamasic qualities give the energy to relax. In the extreme form a tamasic person is lazy in attitude, interest and energy. Depression and anxiety may follow. Tamasic energy is manifested through the breath which flows in and out of the left nostril. This is also referred to as *ida*.

Meanwhile, a sattvic person enjoys a healthy balance of rajasic and tamasic qualities leading to calmness, joyfulness and contentment. The latter is achievable through meditation. Sattvic qualities are manifested when the breath flows evenly in and out of both nostrils. This is also referred to as *sushumna*.

Lahiri Mahasaya, one of the masters in the lineage of Kriya Yoga indicated that in order to have a successful balanced lifestyle, one should spend eight hours per day in each of the above qualities. Eight hours working; eight hours relaxing; eight hours centred towards the Divine through prayer, meditation or thought. By meditating using an authentic technique such as Kriya Yoga, in time any imbalances in the above qualities are rebalanced automatically.

Successful leaders and thriving spiritual aspirants are likely to be rajasic with more "doing energy". Tamasic leaders are less likely to inspire the people who work for them and a tamasic spiritual aspirant will find it hard to motivate themselves to meditate.

It is very easy to see in one's own nature which quality dominates the most. A rajasic person is someone who cannot keep still mentally or physically and who has difficulty relaxing. However, to carry out activities in the world and get things done in business and initially in spirituality, a rajasic nature is needed. It is required to advance spiritually, because if the rajasic nature is weak, equilibrium or sattva cannot be attained. Rajasic qualities produce effort.

If someone is tamasic they will need a lot of sleep, have difficulty in getting up in the morning and lack energy to be motivated. Many tamasic people I have come across eat a lot of spicy food or junk food as intuitively and subconsciously they want to inject more energy or warmth into their system.

WE ARE WHAT WE EAT

Food can also be categorised as being tamasic, rajasic or sattvic. What we eat therefore has a great influence on which quality is more prevalent, balanced or unbalanced within us. Adjusting what we eat makes a large difference to any imbalance in the system. We all need the three aspects in our diets and lives according to the activity we are carrying out and the climate we live in. Garlic, onions, chilli, asafoetida, caffeine, too much salt, too much sugar and spicy food are rajasic. They all make the mind restless. Insomniacs will find it helpful to reduce or totally stop eating these ingredients. Doctors say that garlic and onions are good for the body but yogis generally avoid them as it brings more restlessness to the mind. Some insomniacs that I know have benefited enormously by not eating garlic, onions or spicy food particularly at night. Smiling Swami also advises those who cannot sleep to drink warm milk before they go to bed. Even reading before going to bed keeps the mind active so it is not advised. It is beneficial to meditate when lying down before sleeping even if it is simply watching the breath while focussing on each *chakra*.

Milk, live dairy products, many fresh fruits and vegetables, seeds and nuts in sensible quantities can help promote the sattvic qualities within us. Some example of sattvic herbs and spices are ginger, turmeric, coriander, black pepper, basil, rosemary and fennel. Mung beans are sattvic. Some foods can be part sattvic and part rajasic or part tamasic so the above only gives some basic examples. In hot and humid climates more salt will be needed to keep the body balanced or in some climates more spice required. Food that is overcooked, microwaved, preserved or frozen is tamasic. Fermented cheese, red and orange lentils and sour food are generally tamasic. By changing our diet we can help alter the extreme qualities within us. Overindulgence in alcohol or tobacco can also accentuate the prevalent nature within us.

As the above examples show, by taking more care on the food we eat and how we prepare it, we automatically take care of our minds and our health.

BREATH

I have observed that my breath changes sides from the right to left nostril normally every one and a half to two hours. It then comes out of both nostrils for some time before switching again. When it is coming out of both nostrils equally, I feel more equanimity. If calmness is felt then this is described as sattva. By placing your hand flat, palm down, under your nostrils and exhaling you can feel on which side the breath is operating. As explained above, rajasic nature manifests through the right nostril and tamasic nature through the left nostril. By being in tune with the universe, there are certain activities that are better to carry out when either breath is prevalent. I have observed that when I am in tune with the universe, the correct breath coming out of the nostril matches the activity at its commencement. Amazingly, even the success or otherwise of the day can be influenced by which breath is prevalent when awakening and which foot is put on the floor first. This "real" yoga is hidden and known by very few in the world but practised by some masters in India. What seems like fate in life can often be governed and influenced by the breath even down to winning an argument, investing money, eating food or taking medicine to cure a disease. In many ways this knowledge does not need to be known for those who meditate, as an authentic meditation technique or a realised guru will bring about more balance and equilibrium inside and around an individual. Successful individuals who are naturally in tune with the universe through good karma or good destiny who do not meditate will unconsciously be in tune with these teachings. I will expand later in the book on these practices which I have tested on myself and my friends to good effect.

EVERY BREATH JUST WATCH

The Great Master taught his students to be aware of our breath in every moment. Watching the breath is quite different to controlling or forcing the breath to change. By observing the breath flowing in and out of the nostrils it has a soothing effect which anybody can practice. I have noticed in recent years that my breath brings my attention to it rather than me bringing my attention to the breath consciously. This is a result of my *sadhana*. Watching the breath is a starting point of being aware of the correlation between breath and mind. I would recommend it for those who want to relax and gain more tranquillity.

If I am about to relax or meditate it is better for the breath to be balanced and coming out of both nostrils. If I am carrying out something which requires action then it is better to wait for the breath to start coming out of the right nostril at the start of that activity. If I want to relax then it is better for the breath to be coming out of the left nostril. Those who are meditating may notice as I have that the breath will move of its own accord to match the activity. For instance when eating it is better if the breath is on the right rather than the left as digestion is stronger. I have observed the breath on the left when starting to eat but after a few minutes it changes to the right and when I have finished it returns to the left nostril.

As mentioned before, I have also discovered that during the state of deep meditation the breath almost goes into a state of non-movement. It is as if it is moving in the space inside the head behind the forehead where the pituitary gland is located. This has happened of its own accord without any effort on my part but is certainly connected to the amount that I meditate and the techniques that I have been taught. When the breath slows, the mind and pulse slow down automatically. Smiling Swami tells me that in deep meditation everything slows including time and space. When time and space disappear there is no creation. However sometimes my breath becomes restless in spite of my practice. Regardless of any restlessness I endeavour not to pay too much attention or give it too much power over me. Many give up meditation because they are impatient to have more spiritual experiences or they do not experience calmness quickly. Giving up too easily and expecting everything to be automatic is unrealistic in any activity, spiritual or otherwise. On receiving Kriya Yoga initiation I was not just given a technique but also the opportunity to see the example and grace of some great masters who have helped me in all areas of my life. A basic yogic technique is to breathe in and out of our nostrils instead of the mouth. One of the main benefits of closing the mouth is to suppress a loose tongue! Another advantage is that the hairs in the nostrils act as a filter meaning that we inhale fewer bacteria from the atmosphere into our bodies. When breathing in and out of the nostrils it may seem unnatural and uncomfortable to start with but it brings inner change. Try it and see for yourself. At the beginning, you may feel the need to use the mouth sometimes or hold the breath. This habit will soon pass. It can even be practised when reading or watching television. It is relaxing.

BREATH CONTROL

Some gurus teach that we can control the breath. The Great Master said that, "Breath control is self-control; breath mastery is self-mastery; breathlessness is deathlessness."

If we control the breath or the breath controls itself then we can stack the odds to live a fruitful and happy life in our favour. By practising Kriya Yoga my breath has found a new rhythm which is slower and more relaxed. This was happening towards the end of my career more noticeably but it is also undoubtedly linked to retiring seven years ago. You might think that anybody who retires is calm but many retired people are restless. It is worth analysing the word "control" in the context of breath. The Great Master refers to the natural control of breath through practice. This control emanates from watching the breath rather than through mental control. It is enhanced by special breathing techniques which help regulate the breath taught by gurus such as the Great Master. I am sure that it is better to learn any technique from a realised master or his or her authorised teachers. As reiterated in this book, through the Kriya Yoga techniques my breath has become slow and rhythmic which reduces agitation and restlessness. Something so simple as watching the breath consciously can change people's lives.

There are many meditation techniques so which one works the best? I cannot say as I did not try any other techniques. Luckily I found the "spiritual food" that has worked for me so I have no interest to try another practice. The Great Master reminded us that spiritual growth is banked and never lost but anything material can be taken away at any moment especially as we will all die at some stage and leave everything behind. I feel extremely fortunate that I have been given a healthy body and mind yet sometimes I think negatively even if the result turns out favourably for me. I now question whether I can control my destiny yet if I can regulate my breath I am sure that the outcome, physically, mentally and emotionally will be far better than if I do nothing.

THE DIVINE JEWELS

So if the real wealth is inside of me, then surely it is inside everyone else also. Peace of mind and tranquillity make me feel complete and lacking in nothing. If I am given the strength to do good this helps my journey in life be joyful. The characteristics associated with carrying out good deeds are love, devotion and humility. I have a long way to go, but slowly these qualities are developing within me.

THE DIVINE THIEVES

Smiling Swami teaches that the six main thieves that steal our peace from us are within us. They are Desire; Anger; Passion; Infatuation; Vanity and Jealousy.

He encourages us to contemplate in a reflective way without criticism to judge which of the above apply to us. This is how the real guru teaches. The masters want us to look at ourselves inside. They encourage reflection and gentle inner change. I am watchful of my negatives but also remember my positive qualities. To live in the world some desire is needed. But too much desire steals our peace.

Anger certainly steals peace. Passion comes from extreme and needy love which is destructive through attachment. Infatuation with someone or something brings imbalance. Vanity with how one looks or how someone sees us can only bring disharmony. Jealousy speaks for itself. All the above lead to unhappiness. The way to keep these "thieves" at bay is to control the senses and the mind, knowing when to say yes and when to say no but to remain lovingly and compassionately detached.

In relation to the past, good or bad, there is an expression:

"The past is dead; bury the dead. Use your two eyes to look ahead."

MENTAL CONDITIONING

Many spiritual teachers suggest that while the seeker perceives separation from the Divine, he or she should use the faculties and skills that they have been given by God to help themselves and others in the world. This is good advice as it is impractical to expect a spiritual aspirant to accept conceptually and practically that they are ultimately not the doer. Without having direct perception of not being the doer, this becomes a theory which is of little use to most of us unless our faith is rock solid or our mind is conducive to such teachings. No matter how true this teaching, it is meaningless and unhelpful to the recipient because of lack of practical knowledge and experience. As a person becomes more sattvic, more awareness through experience comes and concepts become reality. I have been fortunate to have been found by two extremely humble gurus. Mentally I am relaxed to accept that I am not the ultimate doer and that I cannot do anything without the help of the Invisible Hand operating invisibly or through the help of others.

Everybody I meet is my guru. Every observation and interaction has purpose. I learn from the behaviour of others – good and bad. Whether we believe or not that we are the doer is almost irrelevant. Dan used to challenge me when I told him that I followed the edict that I am not the doer. He argued that we are given the grace of the gurus and as a result we act as the doer which requires effort.

He gave the example of a field that needed to be ploughed. He argued that it requires self-effort to plough the field. My reply was that if God wants me to plough a field he will give me the desire to do it. If I am not given the desire, then it will be given to someone else. I witnessed on many occasions how business increased not only because of my own agenda or efforts. Such is the beauty and variety of creation, success can come through either standpoint and neither view is more correct than the other.

I am always prepared to drop a belief if I find a replacement that fits more comfortably. If something "better" comes along then, if interested, I investigate but do not drop everything at the first sign of a new piece of knowledge. However since meeting the Great Master I have not felt the need to search for the meaning of life. I am content to "practise" the remembrance that I am not the doer. Perhaps one day it will no longer be a philosophy with the occasional glimpse of the extraordinary but full consciousness. Before my life-changing healing experience, I would have laughed at someone who spent their life contemplating and meditating on who the doer might be. If you are laughing I understand completely so I am happy to have made you laugh. The realisation of "doership" cannot be achieved through mental analysis.

So how do I calm my mind practically? Through a healthy diet, through meditation and less attachment to the world.

RESTLESSNESS

When I see the restlessness of others it reminds me how far I have come on my journey. A few years after meeting the Great Master I asked him why I sometimes felt so restless and other times so calm. He replied that, "God is in the restlessness and God is in the calmness. Clear? There is nothing to worry about." This gave me comfort and hope.

Although I have been in relationships since the breakdown of my marriage, I live alone and am happy to eat in silence or enjoy the company of others. I benefit from being quiet and being sociable. This is a balance between being rajasic and tamasic. Being on my own does not make me unhappy when my mind is still. However when I am unhappy my mind feels agitated. But how easy is it to meditate and keep a job and family? The unusual story about Kriya Yoga is that, when it was reintroduced in 1861 by Babaji to Lahiri Mahasaya, the teachings were given to a family man rather than a monk. For India this was almost unheard of as many of these practices are hidden from the outside world and only practised by monks. The message was that Kriya Yoga is for everybody including those with jobs and families. So many who practise are parents with busy lives yet they manage to incorporate meditation into their daily routine. Even setting aside a fraction of the day to meditate will help to establish some inner quietness. It is important for me to reiterate that nothing needs to be given up to meditate. It is just a question of time management and using a fraction of time that we normally waste. Taking the attitude that it is not that easy and not that difficult is helpful. The potential benefits surely outweigh any mental discomfort. Only fifteen minutes meditation per day brings benefits. Thirty minutes per day brings twice as much. Meditation can also be practised on the way to work or home so building it into our daily lives is easily achievable.

BOREDOM AND DISCOMFORT

When I am restless or bored my new habit is to sit still and look at the cause. On almost all occasions it is my mind and not my body that is causing me agitation. Making the usual excuse that someone else has caused my discomfort is not a mature approach on a spiritual level. If someone behaves badly towards me I can choose not to react and then my mind remains unruffled. This I am practising, sometimes with success and other times less so.

Most people are afraid to stop running to look at themselves. I cannot now consider a life without contemplating the meaning of life at some stage each day. What about you?

BLESSINGS

With regard to spirituality, Adi Shankara, one of the greatest sages in Indian history who created the main monastic orders in India in 500 BC, said that the three greatest blessings are to be given human life, to have desire for God and to be surrounded by divine personalities. Even though many believe the guru is formless and everywhere, nothing replaces the physical presence of the master. Faith in the formless is good but experience is better otherwise why would we or the master have a human existence at all?

MANTRAS

Another way to calm the mind is through the use of a *mantra*. *Mantra* literally means "the mind becomes free upon reflection on itself". A *mantra* is a series of syllables and words infused with divine power which when passed on by a guru can help the recipient overcome difficulties in their life. Most *mantras* are given after the guru has looked at the astrological chart of a person, although a realised master will not need to see the chart to know which *mantra* will really help a person. There are an infinite number of *mantras* for different purposes. The more advanced the guru the more likely the correct *mantra* will be given. In Kriya Yoga the sacred *mantra* is the breath. Someone once described a *mantra* to me as a lifejacket. When her life is going badly, the *mantra* flows and, like magic, calms things down like a rescue remedy.

There is a story of a student who went to see a guru to receive a *mantra*. The guru told him that he must never tell anybody else the *mantra* as it was a special *mantra* to gain reality and truth. Terrible things would happen to him if he disobeyed. The student left. He then proceeded to climb up the wall of the town until he reached the top. He stood up and started shouting out the *mantra* again and again telling passers-by that if they chanted it they would obtain liberation. The devotees of the guru were shocked and they brought him back to the guru. The guru asked him why he did exactly the opposite of what he had been told. The student replied that he was prepared to take the negative consequences if it meant that others could gain reality and truth. The guru smiled.

It is common sense not to reveal a personal *mantra* to another person. This is because the *mantra* like a medicine has been given specifically to the recipient according to their need. It could therefore be detrimental to share with others who have different needs. The true master will infuse the *mantra* with his divinity and then give it in the same way a doctor prescribes a medicine for a patient. The more advanced the guru the more potent the *mantra*.

Sri Anandamayi Ma states in *Matri Vani* that it is better to repeat the name of God or a master or deity that you are attracted to as a *mantra* rather than choose one on your own. She also confirms that when a *mantra* is given by a guru it is properly infused with divinity to help the recipient. Through the *mantra* the guru is instantly connected to the recipient and even when not physically present helps them invisibly. She says also that if we choose a *mantra* ourselves out of a book it can lead to difficulties and even more obstacles, if not given by a guru. In conclusion a *mantra* should be prescribed by a "professional".

So how to choose a *mantra* and do we all need one? Everyone can follow the simplest *mantra* which is the breath. If later on your path a guru gives you a *mantra* then accept it humbly and practise it. When I met the Great Master he knew that I practised healing and he asked me which *mantras* I used. I told him the ones that I had learned. He told me to use one of them and not the other two. Later I received two *mantras* from Smiling Swami to help me advance spiritually. These *mantras* come spontaneously to my mind periodically rather than me disciplining myself to repeat them strictly.

Interestingly, the highest mantra mentioned in the Upanishads, the last part of the Vedas, which literally means "good advice", is the breath. Even the kabbalists, (kabbalah is the mystical side of Judaism) refer to the *ruach elohim* as the breath of God. With regard to watching the breath, really dedicated meditators watch their breath as much as they can during the day, even when working.

CLARITY

Clarity in mind leads to certainty in action and then achievement surely follows. Some people do not have clarity. A friend of mine uses a pendulum to find clarity, much to my amusement. When she has a difficult decision to make she consults the pendulum. If it spins a lot it is a yes. If it does not move it means no. I asked her how she can be sure that the pendulum spin means yes and not no. I have seen her go against the "advice" of the pendulum so why use it in the first place! It is unhelpful to rely on someone or something to make a decision as the danger is that it becomes a habit, so much so that the person consults the pendulum when they do not know which cereal to eat for breakfast.

If I do not have clarity I do not act hastily. It is not really a skill that I had to learn, as by nature I have always been cautious and it seems like the common sense approach to take. If a problem came in business I would find the solution eventually or know that I had to be patient even if I was feeling impatient. In spirituality, I am watching more without pushing all the time for a solution which goes against the grain of the "old" David.

How many people really know what they want whether it be on the spiritual or the business path? How many of us stop to ask the simple question: what do I want and what really makes me happy? If there is no target or goal to aim at, then energy will be directed aimlessly and wastefully without proper direction. If later the target changes then that does not matter. A target is better to have for the mind rather than having no target at all. Perhaps my mistaken conditioning is to think that there is a goal and something to achieve in life. The Great Master made it clear that the goal of life was Self-realisation. Those who are naturally relaxed may not need to be driven but the danger is they become over tamasic and lazy.

Often I find clarity by knowing what I do *not* want. This means I do not waste energy in a direction that I do not wish to go. Nowadays, my mind for the most part is calm which gives me clarity automatically. When I have a few restless, turbulent or bumpy days for no reason I really notice it. I endeavour to accept these days as just part of life rather than an event that needs over-fixing. As a logical person I cannot help thinking that absolutely everything has a purpose even if it is beyond my comprehension or knowledge. When I question whether I should accept a situation or not I generally do not experience a battle within my mind. What makes me advance or retreat from a situation? Sometimes I advance towards something knowing that it will cause me trouble yet I still do it. Why? I can only conclude that it is a habit and like all habits can eventually be broken.

To decide whether to be active or passive in decision-making be it in business or spirituality can make or break a situation and determine success or failure. When I worked, what invisible factor determined if I contacted one particular potential business client on a given day who urgently needed finance instead of a client that arranged its finance one day before? In conclusion, what I could do was increase my chances of success and decrease my chances of failure by contacting more clients.

NEGATIVE THOUGHTS

Worrying about what we do not have will not change what we have; however no longer worrying will change us.

So when do my thoughts become worries and why worry about being worried? Worry is a natural human trait and it comes normally when I do not have enough confidence or belief in myself. Of course when negative thoughts come, it is my choice whether to react or follow them. Worry solves nothing yet worry still comes and still I react to it. Perhaps worries come to make us think positively. Anything that makes me miserable and afraid is non-productive. Luckily I have not been afraid to fail. Failure is only temporary and a sign that I need to put in more effort or think laterally. There is always a solution even if the solution is to let time pass by before taking action.

Some people are so in touch with their feelings that when they think negatively they are unable to act rationally as emotions and pain associated with mental discomfort paralyses them. Half the battle is to accept that negative thoughts come rather than over-analysing them. Inner stillness comes with mental satisfaction. When I am hungry I eat and am satisfied but this is impermanent. How can I make satisfaction permanent? By having less desire. So how can I reduce my desire and why should I? If I want to be happy it is not possible if I have unfulfilled desires. Too much desire leads to discontentment. When I become agitated it is often because I have a desire which is not being satisfied. This desire can even be a non-desire. Desires come from thoughts so how can I calm my thoughts? As mentioned previously, sometimes when I meditate I can sit for several hours and I do not think or feel my body or remember where I am sitting. Suddenly I will regain some body consciousness and I may find my arms are crossed and numb or my head is down. When I forget my body and mind through meditation I have nothing to think about in the world. At that moment the world does not exist. There is a void. When I am in this state of meditation I am in the present. This is not escapism but the result of this process slows down the thoughts and in my daily life I begin to see what I really think, what I really desire, what is the true desire coming from deep inside of me.

In conclusion, meditation is the superfood for the mind. This superfood calms my mind and I worry less. The less worry I have in the world, the less opportunity my mind will find something to worry about. I believe that living in the present is impossible to achieve without a peaceful mind.

The more in tune I am with the Invisible Hand the more positive my thinking which enables me to do things effortlessly or to be able to give up habits without effort. As I grow more spiritually, I accept more and more consciously that life does not have to be a journey about achievement, yet success can still come.

CHAPTER 13

MEDITATION: CHANGES & PERCEPTION

GUERNSEY LIFE

WHERE AM I? WHO AM I? WHAT AM I DOING?

After I left London for a fresh start and change in lifestyle, the sixty to eighty hour weeks went to zero overnight. Those who did not know me so well thought that I would be bored within six months and start another business. I knew better. I wanted to concentrate more on the inner journey and my mind was obliging because it was exhausted. Guernsey is a beautiful island in the Channel islands that have the most sunshine in the British Isles. It is a British crown dependency that has been independent since 1204 with its own parliament. It is well known for its natural beauty, financial expertise, tourism and cows. Income tax rates are 20%. Victor Hugo lived and wrote *Les Misérables* here.

When I came over here for the first time I was mesmerised by the calm, blue sea and the smiling friendly people. It also helped that I found a Chinese restaurant that did lots of vegetarian food! Had there been stormy weather and awful food I would have left with a different impression. My God speaks to me in simple ways! The first house I saw I bought. The completion date was the birthday of one of my gurus. Another coincidence? I really feel and appreciate the blessings of the Invisible Hand for my fortunate position. Friends will say that I put in the work and deserved the reward but I do not accept that I did it on my own.

Although I worked hard there was no guarantee of a happy ending.

One of the differences I noticed in Guernsey compared to London was how relaxed everybody was including the "suits" with their shades on strolling down the high street during their lunch hours. It was a marked difference to the hustle and bustle and stress of London. It is no coincidence that monks meditated on some of the outer islands here many centuries ago. Guernsey has that community spirit without a feeling of being backward. It is also two and a half hours commute from Central London door to door so it suits me well.

So what is my change over the seven-year period since my retirement? Before addressing these questions, I must say that my body is much fitter than it has been for the last twenty years. My weight has decreased and I am as slim as I was in my early 20s. This is connected to my happiness as well as the effect of my *sadhana*. I let all of my business relationships lapse with the exception of a handful. I am no longer in the thick of it. My ambition and desires have diminished substantially. In fact I do not see that there is anything to achieve anymore. I am neither excited nor unexcited but this is subtly different to disinterest and apathy. Could this be the meaning of being balanced? I spend more time meditating, sometimes two to three hours in the morning and walk on the beautiful beaches or cliffs. On the whole I am equally comfortable being alone or with others. Although I feel less and less the need to over-socialise, I still go to restaurants and films and see friends and family. Let us not forget that one of the meanings of yoga is friendship, so in these activities I am practising yoga.

YOGA

Four particular types of people are attracted to yoga. Some people who practise yoga want to look great and keep fit. They have flexible bodies and look fantastic. They want to make their bodies look even better. There is nothing wrong with this approach. Another set of people are unsuccessful and generally unhappy with life. They come to yoga often dissatisfied with what their religion or the world has offered them. A third group of people are busy in the world yet are consciously or unconsciously aware that dissatisfaction and lack of fulfilment is present. A fourth group of people use yoga to enjoy themselves more in the world. Let us take tantric yoga as an example. What is it? You may as I used to think that it is about enhancing sexual performance and gratification. Tantra is a vast subject which I have never felt the need to research, however it is a series of rituals and practices. As time has passed the real meaning of Tantra was misunderstood. From a highly evolved spiritual science, Tantra was represented as a tool for magical power or sexual enhancement. Tantra is none of these. It is an ancient discipline that provides a vast learning, a deep understanding of life, and a way to attain the truth. In its highest form Tantra is like yoga – the path of meditation. Through Tantra and yoga the realisation comes of ceaseless union between body and soul where the soul is intertwined with the body (which is misinterpreted as sexual intercourse) maintaining its life through inhalation. Thus union with the Divine through the soul in every breath is the real act of love. Because the world is obsessed by sex, clever people find a way to tap into that energy and charge for the pleasure! Overactivity in the second chakra by using special breathing techniques for personal gratification cannot be good for mental, emotional or physical health. Regarding sex, as meditation purifies all of the chakras and relaxes the mind and body, then many benefits naturally arise in all departments.

For those put off by yoga because of their lack of flexibility, thankfully Kriya Yoga can also be practised by the unnatural yogis like myself. There is no need to be jealous of those who look magnificent and can stretch their bodies easily. I always remember my friend Lucy who sat with a perfect posture asking for my advice. She wanted to know how she could relax her mind during meditation as her thoughts were screaming at her. I was really surprised as her posture and demeanour during meditation gave the impression of someone in a state of stillness and serenity. I also found out, again to my surprise, that Lucy was a secret serial worrier. So for those who fidget and cannot sit still, which is natural for beginners, you are not alone. In spite of our thoughts, we must continue and not give up our spiritual practice to eventually experience stillness. That is all I have done and in time the thoughts have subsided. During meditation it is absolutely natural to have good and bad thoughts. Thoughts are the product of imagination involving various hypothetical situations. Yet most of these ramblings are probably without substance, so why waste time thinking about them? If the mind has crazy ideas, then just let them flow. Even after deep meditation sometimes the immediate thought is, *What am I going to have for lunch?* So what? It is natural. An advanced spiritual practitioner will perceive that every thought is from God. A less advanced spiritual practitioner may pompously tell others what they should or should not be thinking. In the same way, some meditators think that the ego and the mind are the enemy. Such an approach can create a barrier. This barrier then becomes a focus and a default excuse for failure. My answer to the spiritual person who explains everything negative as being the result of ego is simple. If the creator created everything, then that includes the ego and the mind and the thoughts that come and go. The mind has served me very well so I befriend it rather than make it an enemy. What is certain is that if I attach to negative thoughts or negative actions around me, I become restless and unhappy.

Smiling Swami says that *bhoga*, which is Sanskrit for enjoyment in the world, if overdone, can lead to *roga* which is disease. Hopefully before *roga* the person comes to real yoga.

YOGA: THE PATH OF MEDITATION

I heard a story about a king. This king was betrayed by his close advisers. Fearing for his life he fled into the forest to avoid being killed. He came across a hermitage and noticed that the people who lived there and even the wild animals seemed peaceful. He met a businessman on the path. The businessman had a family who had betrayed him and they had threatened his life. He also had fled to the forest. The sage in charge of the hermitage asked them both why they had come. The king spoke first and said that both of them had similar problems as both had been betrayed. The sage taught them how to meditate. During meditation, the Divine Mother appeared to each of them separately. She asked the king what he wanted. He said that he wanted to be rich and powerful again and to be king once more. The Divine Mother smiled and told him that his wish would be granted. The King's name was Suratha which literally means "having a beautiful body chariot". He was only concerned with the material world even though he would still experience restlessness and the never-ending cycle of happiness followed by misery. His pull to the world in spite of experiencing calmness through meditation was too strong. The businessman meanwhile had never felt so peaceful so when the Divine Mother asked him what he wanted he decided to ask for knowledge. He wanted to know what was behind this calmness that he was experiencing. He wanted the real knowledge. The world and its fruits were not enough anymore. His name was Samadhi. In this context *samadhi* means "balanced mind". With a balanced mind through meditation he attained enlightenment. The sage was called Medha. *Medha* means wisdom. *Medha* had given them a choice. This story comes from an important scripture known as *Devi Mahatmya* or *Chandi* meaning *The Glory to the Divine Mother*. Which would you choose?

SPIRITUAL & MATERIAL SUCCESS

Successful people continue down the path they are taking regardless of whether it is easy or difficult, because they have courage in their convictions. When the going gets tough or if the result they expect does not materialise automatically, they continue. My business training and experience is helpful on my spiritual journey as the same attributes are needed. I summarise these qualities later in the book.

In spirituality and business it is essential to continue even when a result is not apparent. Of 100 people who learn meditation over a weekend, (based on my experience of arranging programmes for eight years), I estimate that within one month 50% are barely practising at all. After one year, only 20% are practising. Of these maybe 10% practise each day. I doubt very much that this statistic varies regardless of the new activity or hobby pursued. Of the 100 that practise meditation, only 10% continue and of those 90% are crazy! Just kidding!

The master does not always attract angels, which is logical, in the same way that the doctor does not attract healthy people. So why continue to practise when nothing seems to be happening? When I first learnt Kriya Yoga I met a few people who had practised for twenty years or more. I could really see their radiance and calmness and I thought that these would be good attributes to gain so I continued. Meanwhile in business I observed the people who worked hard and enjoyed the fruits of their success, so I knew that constant application and effort were required to achieve anything. When I went to the office at the weekend many bosses and entrepreneurs in the same building were also working. My experience of working when I was too tired meant that everything took twice as long as when I was fresh and alert. I chose therefore to work early in the morning and found my productivity almost double at this time when the office was quiet. I achieved a huge amount between six and nine in the morning after meditation, much more than the evening hours of six to nine when I did not meditate. I was often too tired at night to meditate and while twice per day is recommended once is better than nothing.

Anyone I have met who practises *sadhana* sincerely or works hard admits that real effort is necessary to achieve their goals. In my own working life, I stuck to my career through thick and thin and did not jump ship when the going became tough. The same applies to Kriya Yoga. I found a technique that worked and stuck to it. By changing technique, the same barriers are likely to arise again under a different guise so continuing is often the best course of action.

So when is it necessary to look for a new guru, a new technique or a new job? That is a tricky question. I changed job in my early career when I realised that the career path offered to me did not match my ambitions. I never had difficulty in making a decision as to when to change jobs. Had I been unhappy with my guru because I did not feel that he had reached a level which could take me to my spiritual goal, I would have learnt what I could and then moved on. When a change is coming, good or bad, my conclusion is that I cannot avoid it but intuitively I can help myself by knowing when to act. However sometimes we might not find the business opportunity or person that we seek to help us progress, and this can be very frustrating. In such circumstances all I have ever done is kept going and kept belief in myself. I have to accept that destiny will bring what is good for me and not necessarily what I think is good for me.

In relation to destiny, I also have to accept that I cannot pre-empt every occurrence or influence or predict every outcome. There is a story about a Indian multi-millionaire who was told that he would die within one year and the cause of death would be an aeroplane crash. He had been given an indication of the time of his death and he immediately stopped flying anywhere. When the pre-destined day arrived he was on a train going to a meeting and an aeroplane crashed into the train! As much as he tried, he could not avoid his destiny no matter how clever he tried to be!

The best I can do is to be aware of my actions and reactions and act humbly in a sensible and balanced way regardless of what destiny brings. Yet I may not always be sensible or balanced.

Concentration, fortitude and obstinacy have all helped.

FIVE STAGES OF SPIRITUALITY

Once I went to a Kriya Yoga lecture. To explain doership, the speaker illustrated how our consciousness can oscillate between the following at any time of day:

I AM doing;

I AM doing because of God;

I AM doing the work of God;

GOD IS doing through me;

GOD IS doing.

The same stages apply to meditation:

I AM meditating;

I AM meditating because of God;

I AM doing the meditation of God;

GOD IS meditating through me;

GOD IS meditating.

When the latter stage in both examples is reached then free will and individuality dissolve. Spiritual advancement comes when the meditator realises that he or she is not the ultimate doer. When that state is permanent for 24 hours per day then enlightenment has arrived.

FIFTY TYPES OF BREATH

I have mentioned earlier the intricate link between the breath and the mind. I have also experienced occasions when the breath is calm and at the same time the mind is restless. This is contrary to what I have said in this book. It was an odd experience as if there was a decoupling or disassociation between the breath and the mind. In addition I became aware of two breaths operating simultaneously, one being calm and one causing restlessness. According to the Great Master this is because we have fifty types of breath operating in our bodies. Forty nine breaths for our evolution and one to find the truth. Apparently these individual breaths are linked to every activity we carry out. For example compassion, forgiveness, kindness and even ambition, greed and anger are influenced specifically by one of these forty nine breaths. The fiftieth breath residing in the *ajna chakra* can be described as the calm breath that gives rise to the ultimate sound of realisation. Although this may be interesting I do not walk around thinking which breath is operating. By focussing on the breath and concentrating on the *ajna* or the crown chakra, the calm breath or *udana* breath will eventually manifest bringing stillness. Some gurus teach about the Lower mind and the Higher mind. For me to think like this gives me a headache. I do not therefore contemplate such thoughts however truthful they may be.

Experience will lead me to knowledge. Humility and love will lead me to *the truth* and *the truth* will set me free.

Knowing or understanding

What do I really know and really understand? I am being careful in this book to filter out saying things that I have not experienced or quoting others too much apart from the masters who I believe are speaking from truth. Some say that a teacher or guru is not necessary. If I follow that teaching then the person that gave me the advice is effectively becoming my guru if I follow him or her! Once I find a teaching or theory that I like that sits comfortably with me, I stick to it. I am very lucky to have been given the experience and opportunity to receive direct teachings from living gurus. Reading the words of a master is just not enough for me. I want to know and experience rather than think I understand from what I read. If I know, then there is no need to understand. If I think I understand I still may not know as I may have misunderstood!

Pranayama, lifestyle and peace

Many spiritual teachers talk about the breath and give various breathing techniques which in yoga are commonly called *pranayama*. There are many different *pranayamas*. The Kriya Yoga *pranayama* and in fact the whole Kriya practice is based on constant breath awareness. My observation is that I cannot force my breath to change unless I hold my breath unnaturally which is not recommended. Kriya Yoga *pranayama* helps to develop a slow, rhythmic breath which brings calmness with practice. This determines the change in my breath so that I can have this peaceful experience. Yet many are practising and not experiencing this peace and are still restless. If I reflect on my past, I was 90% restless and 10% calm for much of my working day, and now I am 90% calm and 10% restless. If it has happened to me then this change can happen to anybody. If I am restless now I find the experience shocking whereas before it was normal.

I judge happiness simply as being in good physical and emotional condition along with a calm mind. People who are new to meditation are worried that calmness will make them boring. They are either boring or they are not – it is not meditation that makes them boring! Those who say this are for the most part mentally conditioned that having a good time is based on external pursuits or in a worse scenario losing control, normally through alcohol or drugs, and waking up the next morning with a huge hangover. I understand this attitude totally because I was no different. But when my healing experience came, this wake-up call made me realise that in the long term this lifestyle was not the path to happiness.

So when I am attached to someone or a desire, then trouble will be around the corner and heading my way. Copious desire is the cause of difficulty in life, yet the external world encourages more desire. What can I do to avoid the temptations of the world? I could consciously endeavour to reduce my desires but this does not always work effectively as a battle ensues which consumes the mind. Sometimes I change my thoughts or actions, but having stopped smoking, drinking and changing my diet naturally, I know that a desire finishes of its own volition. Therefore I recommend spiritual aspirants and people interested in meditation to just relax and not worry about what they may have to give up and focus instead on what they will gain from meditation. External activities can still be enjoyed but with more consciousness and joy. Bad habits will go naturally when they are ready.

Financial freedom was the treasure that I sought during my working life. This I have achieved but I am sure that this was just practice for the real freedom which is spiritual freedom.

LIBERATION

Spiritual freedom or liberation for me means having full knowledge of the mechanism behind every situation and having full consciousness of what is driving me and others. At this moment many masters say that the feeling of separation from others and God disappears. I am not making this a target to achieve as my main quest is to keep calm and see what comes from the stillness inside.

ARE ONLY SPIRITUAL SEEKERS LIBERATED?

Once there was a King whose son decided to give up his rights to the throne and worship God instead. The King was really angry. He demanded to know who this person called God was who had taken his son from him. He spent his whole life angrily searching for God around his kingdom. When he died, the saints and sages who had already departed Earth were surprised to find the King in heaven sitting next to them. They asked God if he had made a mistake. God replied, "There is no mistake. He spent his life thinking about me and searching for me!"

There is another story about Girish Chandra Ghosh who became a realised disciple of his master Ramakrishna

Paramahamsa. Girish was an eminent playwright, actor and director who enjoyed life to the full, womanising and drinking. He also scorned religion and those who believed in God and the role of gurus. He met Ramakrishna Paramahamsa several times and was unimpressed. He was even blind drunk in his presence and was quite happy to charge him to see his plays. He did not care for Ramakrishna Paramahamsa's reputation. However the master persisted and told him how divine he was inside and that transformation was coming. Girish was shocked by this and challenged him by asking how he could lead such an unprincipled life and love God at the same time. Slowly Girish became closer to Ramakrishna Paramahamsa but could not give up the alcohol or women. His master told him not to worry and only to love others. On one occasion he forgot his bottle of alcohol in a carriage and his master went to recover the bottle and gave it to Girish telling him to drink in front of him as there was no reason to be embarrassed or to hide his habits. The change came when his master told him that whatever Girish did he would take the karma and responsibility for Girish's actions so he did not even have to give up any habits! This brought consciousness to Girish who became uncomfortable womanising and drinking knowing that his master would be taking on this burden. Slowly his habits changed and Girish became one of Sri Ramakrishna's most loyal and advanced disciples.

Finally I particularly like the story of another master who took pity on two devotees and gave them Self-realisation. This momentous event happened to both of them when they were on a train! When they returned to the ashram the residents questioned the master's judgement. They told the master that they could understand why he had bestowed this gift on one of the devotees because he was humble, pious and studious. However the other was lazy, unworthy and unhelpful. The master smiled. He told them that he decided to liberate the latter before he got into even more trouble.

Great masters see the potential inside of us even if it is unapparent to ourselves and others. Perhaps if I misbehave enough my gurus will take pity on me also!

So is liberation really linked to what we do in the world or not? If we already arrive with credits and debits from previous lives we may not be able to avoid certain events through our destiny or karma because they have to manifest in the physical body. Earning promotion may well seem important to us, but our attitude and consciousness whilst doing our work is even more important. I like to think that I was brought up to have a good attitude towards work and people around me. My attitude was not always good at school, but bad attitude is often linked to boredom. Generally my attitude has been good and as my spiritual journey has unfolded, I really care about my conduct towards myself and others. As I have matured, this awareness has become more prominent but in the past I did not suffer fools gladly and could certainly have been more compassionate at times. That being said I have always recognised that every job has value to the world and all of us are as important or unimportant as the next person. Some may think that their qualifications or job title gives them social status above others. I have never thought this. In business, I just wanted to complete each task to the best of my ability, to earn a good wage and keep the client happy.

Smiling Swami tells me that there is a drink seller in Cuttack, India who is a realised master, married with a family and going about his day-to-day business in poverty, without others being aware of his spiritual status. It shows that we should never judge a book by its cover.

FOOD FOR THE MIND

The spiritual path is not a path to be followed by those seeking peer approval nor for that matter is the path of the entrepreneur. I am not able to discard the body or the mind so whatever assets or liabilities I have been given mentally, physically and emotionally, I have to accept and get on with life. I make the best of my talents and do not focus on the talents I have not been given.

The job of the mind is to be a monkey, jumping around from thought to thought. If people spent as much time looking after their minds as their bodies then they would be far happier. So how to slow down my mind when it is restless? Drink cold water. Take a cold shower. Do some physical exercise. Eat healthy food. Practise Kriya Yoga *pranayama*. All these are good and beneficial. Yet like cleaning a pan it will soon get dirty again. What do I feed my mind? Food is not just taken through the mouth. It is being eaten through my eyes and ears also. Staring at the internet all day or watching horror movies will not do me any good and will negatively affect my mind. So I can discriminate more carefully on what I choose to eat through my eyes and ears as well as my mouth. As much as I tell my mind to relax the thoughts keep coming. If I tell it to quieten down it can get louder. I can counter negative thoughts with positive thoughts as mentioned previously which could become a full time job and I may well do this instinctively but what else can I do? Firstly I have been given thoughts for a reason so why deny them as if they are a burden? They are not necessarily the enemy. So this is a positive thought but it is more than a thought. I come across many spiritual people who lecture about the mind and the ego. When I started to meditate and carry out healing, I found myself automatically going into the zone – like an empty space. This zone is a relaxed space in the mind.

I have a good friend who teaches mindfulness. Mindfulness derives from Buddhist teachings and introduces people to meditation through their minds and intellect. I joked with her that I was practising "mindlessness" and this is not far from the truth.

I have mentioned that food directly influences our state of mind. Secondly, environment will make a difference and thirdly exercise. I do not always enjoy the "thought" of carrying out a task but when it is done I feel good. The preliminary thought is often greater than the actual task.

DETACHMENT

Real detachment with love comes when the mind is at peace and expectations cease. I can really tell you that I have experienced such moments but they do not last. This type of loving detachment seems to be a state which cannot be practised. As detached as I may wish to be, I have found that I cannot control it. I have sometimes experienced the feeling that I am watching myself in a movie. It is as if I am the spectator and the actor both at the same time. It makes life feel surreal and a little unreal. This experience has certainly been apparent when writing this book.

The Great Master teaches us to carry out any task no matter how simple or small with love and without the expectation of any result. This is easier said than done. Try telling an athlete who trains four years for the Olympics who then becomes injured just before going to the games to be detached. All that sacrifice and hard work wasted. Yet what is the purpose of that experience? It is akin to meditation. When I practise and practise, a result or change does not seem to come for months or even years. Good preparation is never wasted even if the result does not turn out as I expect but it prepares me for another experience in the future. Ultimately if I am really detached to the outcome then the result will make no difference. Detachment leads to loving surrender. I am watching myself and focussing more on how I do things rather than the result but I cannot deny that I still hope for a positive outcome. This is wholly different to my experience in business where I worked tirelessly for a good outcome in spite of many barriers to achieve it.

EFFORT IS GIVEN AT THE RIGHT MOMENT

When something agitates me now I have total awareness of the internal conflict between calmness and restlessness instead of running around frenetically. One part of me tells myself that I cannot change anything so I may as well relax and let the thoughts be as they are. The other part tells me to do something about it. Yet if I really believe I am not the doer, I should not criticise any action or non-action. I asked Smiling Swami why when I believe 99% that I am not the doer these difficulties still occur. He replied that I need to believe that I am not the doer 101%. So only 2% to go!

TRANSFORMATION WITHOUT EFFORT

The main change I am experiencing is the feeling of being broken out of a mould. The "old" David is being destroyed gently and systematically. It is as though I am going through doors and as I go through them they turn into walls behind me. The past is really dying and I am going forward without looking back. There is no return to my previous life in the world. This does not mean to say that I know where I am going because I have no idea or imagination of what lies ahead. However, I am enjoying the process and am not afraid even if I have less and less in common with people some of whom I have known for many years. This destruction feels more like gentle reconstruction. I have the feeling of not being able to go back because there is nothing worth returning to. It is like I am walking across a bridge which is crumbling behind me. The ground on which I am now treading is unfamiliar. I feel as if I am being held to the earth by a thin strand. The past is like a gaping hole; a void without memory or importance. I am being engineered and reconstructed from the inside out. In some ways as this detachment continues it is like a bereavement, yet unusually there is no pain although the unfamiliarity can be uncomfortable. A veil has been lifted and a new pair of eyes are seeing the world from the same body and mind.

For the past seven years I have been undergoing a huge transformation. Whatever is happening, it is unusual from a rational viewpoint. It really helps to have a guru close when these experiences take place. Spiritual aspirants theorise about detachment and spiritual teachers preach about it. However, experiencing it is indescribable. My experience tells me that I cannot make it happen at all but the groundwork of meditation makes the ride less bumpy. It just happens of its own volition a bit like how this book has appeared.

A friend suggested to me that with the time I have invested in writing this book, I must have had a burning desire to tell my story. In fact I explained to him to his surprise that this was not the case at all. I have neither experienced a good or bad attitude in writing. It is an event that has happened almost through me and about me which I have witnessed often in the third person. Strangely it does not feel like "my book" at all.

BLESSINGS IN DISGUISE

On the rare occasion when my mind has been very still there is only joy inside. Everything stops. I am watching any karma burn away. For example recently I dropped a china soap dish which cut my foot and then I banged my head; a bloody day for sure! As the breath was still I reacted for once without swearing and smilingly observed the process. That's the last of the expensive china soap dishes so back to the plastic ones. I saw these events as blessings with the thought that a greater suffering was being avoided. I consciously adopt this attitude when something negative happens to me even though it is not easy to do so. Good karma can be beautifully described by the following story.

Another king had a close adviser who he trusted and respected. One day the king was hunting in the forest and cut his finger. The adviser said it was a good sign and the king should be grateful it was not something worse. The king was annoyed with the adviser because of his lack of sympathy and decided to banish him from the kingdom.

The adviser was left to perish deep in the forest. The adviser smiled and trusted in fate to take care of him. This agitated the king even more. Soon dusk came and the king was separated from his troops. Out of nowhere natives from the forest captured him and tied him up. They took the king back to their village. Unfortunately they were cannibals and he was the main course. Just as they were going to kill the king, the witch doctor saw that his finger was cut and stopped the ceremony. The cut had made him impure to eat so they let him go. The king was released. He did not know where he was going. After some time he saw someone moving in the forest near him. It was his adviser. The king embraced him and apologised for overreacting and could see that by cutting his finger it had indeed been for his own good. The adviser thanked the king for sending him away. The king was puzzled. The adviser explained that had the king kept him by his side as usual, then he would have been the sacrifice and not the king!

So the way I observe each experience, even the negative ones is quite different now. Although I have a little more consciousness, still I really know nothing about spirituality but am unfazed by this lack of knowing as I know it is coming. I now understand why the spiritual path is deemed to be a lonely path. Others carrying out their normal lives cannot comprehend what I am talking about and the "old David" would have dismissed such talk as nonsense. This is why the master in the physical form is so necessary from my viewpoint. Only the true master who knows the way up the mountain and back again will understand what is taking place. A good spiritual teacher will give the necessary guidance and teachings. So how does one find a good spiritual teacher? He or she will practise what they preach and exceed all of my ideas and expectations about love. I have been able in particular to spend a lot of time with Smiling Swami and have seen how he gives unconditional love to everybody. Spiritual teachers who think or behave like gurus can be great actors so it can take time to discover this. How do we judge greatness or authenticity of anybody in authority? Does it depend on how many books they have written, how they speak and how much popular opinion or press they receive? Is it because they spend their lives taking exams to obtain a list of qualifications? The real expert is successful through the understanding and practice of the fundamentals in his or her field or teachings from top to bottom.

ETERNAL HAPPINESS IS POSSIBLE

Before I meditated I wanted happiness, but did I really know what happiness was?

Every human being is seeking happiness. The craving for internal happiness will not be satisfied if it comes from outside. A life spent chasing unfulfilled desires can only lead to a life of unfulfillment and unhappiness. External satisfaction cannot give long-term internal satisfaction. Those who appear to be happy outside may be masking what is going on inside. How about you? Those who are happy inside have a glow about them which benefits everyone. When I am relaxed inside I tend to manifest this energy without effort externally. I do not want to be a miserable person hiding behind a false smile.

I remember an ex-bond trader who was not so popular. He was eventually sacked. He found it very hard to gain employment elsewhere. He lived in a block of apartments overlooking the Thames. Each morning he would leave for "work" at the same time wearing his suit just to keep up appearances with the neighbours. I found this very odd and thought how unhappy he must have been to put up such a charade for his neighbours who were virtually strangers.

TURNING UP LATE

Every week for eight years, we held a Kriya Yoga group meditation at our house. Two of the people in the group were unemployed. They always turned up late but the employed people would arrive on time. This agitated me. The unemployed people always had different excuses. I observed this week in and week out and then analysed why this might be happening. I concluded that they had lost their self-esteem and their respect for others and did not care whether they arrived late or not. The employed amongst us knew that we had to use our time efficiently while those out of work had forgotten the value and preciousness of time as they had so much of it.

In relation to punctuality, although I had a good attitude, I received a painful teaching from the FD of a substantial international company in my second job. I had arrived over an hour early. Rather than wait in the company car park I decided to leave and park elsewhere. To cut a long story short, I could not find my way back! When I did arrive I was twenty minutes late! The FD then kept me waiting the exact time I had kept him waiting. In spite of my apology and a cordial meeting he cut it short. He explained that I had lost twenty minutes of his time which he was not prepared to re-allocate. As someone who is and was always punctual it was a harsh lesson but one I have not forgotten. Other people's time is valuable.

Positives not Negatives

Once when I was sitting with the Great Master he started to give me compliments about my nose. "I have seen thousands of noses and yours is a great nose, even greater than Yoganandaji's!" I was somewhat embarrassed by this and other compliments he gave me. He never spoke about my negatives and only spoke about my positives.

This was a beautiful but simple teaching. I often find myself seeing the negatives in others rather than the positives. Such an approach to life was refreshing. I am working hard to bring this teaching into my life more. Negatives have the quality to bring out the positives in myself or others. Yet how do I convert negativity into positivity? Negativity should not be confused with caution and discernment. Negativity is like a disease. People go to the doctor looking for relief for a cold or a sore throat. Where can they go to ease the effects of negative thinking, which is far longer lasting and troublesome?

Every saint has a past

Every saint has a past and every sinner has a future. Why is it that there are things that I want to change about myself yet somehow I cannot bring myself to make that change?

Smiling Swami says that we should be detached in a loving way and change will come. To detach without love is far simpler to achieve yet the result is likely to be negative. So how does one depersonalise and detach from the world but remain loving, kind and humble?

Firstly one needs to disconnect from the influences of the mind. My true nature is inside of me yet if I have a busy mind I cannot perceive this. When I am in a passive state I can then become aware of my true nature to be kind and loving. When love manifests inside there is no sacrifice in anything that I do. It is just done with love and joy. Every thought given with love leads to every action being done with love. When I take in what is good for me and search for the gem inside, the bad and what is no use for me are automatically discarded. The more I discard the more I see who I am. In these circumstances the thought of sacrifice never crosses my mind. So what can I do when I do not feel this? Keep going regardless. Those who give up receive far less than those who continue.

MINI-REALISATIONS

Experiences in meditation as in life vary from the mundane to the exciting. When light, sound and vibration are experienced in meditation, it can be exhilarating. As I now have more thinking time, I sometimes reflect back on the daily routine of going to work each day and the constant effort required. Although my work was rewarding and for the most part enjoyable, overcoming tiredness, stress and difficulties in my personal life meant that focus and determination were necessary. I never let unhappiness defeat me and I rarely took a day off work even when I was ill. Boarding school certainly toughened me up although Smiling Swami told me once that when I was working flat out I was more like a coconut – tough on the outside and soft on the inside!

I feel often that I am making no spiritual progress at all. Sri Anandamayi Ma says in *Matri Vani* that when this feeling occurs, it is a crucial stage for the spiritual seeker.

She emphasises the need to continue and not give up even when it seems that no progress is being made. These "non event" stages can last for months and then my breath may change or some mini-realisation will arrive. In the same way these "non-event" stages can happen in daily life so even the non-spiritual seeker should take comfort from this teaching. Visiting the gurus mentioned in this book has helped me when I need a boost. So, when we need help for everyday problems we should seek a guru in the form of a friend or an adviser if we do not have access to a spiritual master.

Lately I have felt that what is going on in my thoughts is an actual event taking place on a different plane of existence to which I am connected but of which I am not fully conscious. It seems just as real and as important as what is happening in the physical world. It is like living in two worlds. My dreams are so real now that they are similar to everyday life. If I share a room with someone the type of dream I have will change. For instance, on a recent retreat I shared a room with a friend and dreamt of war and fighting which I never do. The same pattern repeated on the next night. Another time I had a beautiful dream of the Great Master and Smiling Swami. They beckoned me to come to the front of the room which was full of people to sit in between them. I reluctantly went up and the Great Master turned to me, smiling and said, "Everything is natural." I also dreamt of Hugging Mother and I was chanting a *mantra*. "Who is chanting the special *mantra* of the Divine Mother?" she asked. Then I woke up. These dreams may be meaningless but I enjoyed the message and memories from them.

Smiling Swami explained to me that the dream world is the world of the astral body which goes with us when we die as do all of our thoughts and knowledge both good and bad. If he is correct and the mind goes with us, perhaps we should spend more time taking care of it rather than so much time on our bodies which begin to decompose as soon as we die. Sleep is not enough to revitalise the mind. A stale lazy mind leads to an unfulfilling life and an unhealthy body. A fresh active mind leads to a fulfilling life and a healthy body.

CHAPTER 14

THE SPIRITUAL PATH: PEOPLE & EXPERIENCES

SPIRITUAL EGO

I met two monks. One was very humble and the other behaved more like a prince than a monk. They both attended a yoga programme. The "princely" monk was introduced by the organiser. The long introduction which he had written himself made him sound very impressive and learned. This "princely" monk had lots of ego and he tried to impress the audience with how great the humble monk was in his introduction. He then asked the humble monk to speak expecting him to give a long talk. The humble monk said, "Thank you very much. I do not know anything. Now I am going to meditate." He proceeded to close his eyes and the princely monk hastily retrieved the microphone looking rather foolish.

It is fair to say that, as in every profession, even a monk can be interested in their own grandeur and self-importance. This does not mean he does not care for others but his service to others may not be selfless. If the monk has a true guru, the guru will know this and give the monk an invisible rope. The good monk will use the rope to help others cross to shore; the egotistical monk will slowly hang himself as he will not be able to keep up the charade forever. However I am also acutely aware how easy it is to falsely accuse or bad-mouth others in the world no matter how much good they are doing. Take any saint or divine personality or the man who runs the corner shop. All will be accused in their lives of something negative, truthfully or falsely. The accuser is rarely without faults. In the world of spiritual seekers many have an opinion about someone else's spiritual teacher, often through what they have heard rather than experienced. One or two bad reports about a guru can lead to the guru being criticised or accused of wrongdoing. Throwing stones from a glasshouse is a dangerous game. If someone is unstable that is likely to be their inherent nature but it is easy to blame the guru rather than take responsibility for their own behaviour. I have found that a genuine guru will never criticise another teacher no matter what their flaws. No matter how sincere or great anybody is, there will be a wave of criticism directed towards him or her. If 99 million are content and one is not, the one who is not will have their story printed in the press as if it is representative of the whole truth.

I believe that those who do not behave spiritually are found out in time regardless of what clothes they are wearing. I took the attitude early on that those who chose monkhood were not necessarily spiritual using the analogy that a businessman wearing a suit is not necessarily a good businessman. I hasten to add that I have met many beautiful, humble monks. Instinctively I avoid certain people and have no fear in challenging them. I even have forthright discussions with Smiling Swami. We put our points of view across which are normally quite similar although he is less dogmatic and more godmatic than me. If we disagree, we agree to disagree, but this is rare. I am cautious of teachers or role models who dislike being challenged or who are stage-managed.

The "princely" monk mentioned above hid behind his intellectual ability and acquired knowledge. The humble monk just said nothing. I know which role model I have chosen to follow and I hope that you do not think I am going on an ego-trip by writing this book! A friend of mine recently described me as paradoxical. God willing, you can see from my story that I am telling it as it is and am just being me without attempting to present a false persona.

AM I READY?

When I attended the opening lecture of a Kriya Yoga retreat in the UK, the first words of Smiling Swami were, "Are your bags packed and are you ready to go?" We were all confused as we had just unpacked and as I had not known him for long I thought perhaps he was having trouble with the English language! It transpired that he was talking about leaving this life. Although death is inevitable, unless I am the first man in the world to live forever, when it appears it surprises us as soon as we or others depart. At the time of death, most people are afraid of losing their life because of identification with the body which will indeed perish. The spiritual person will keep in their consciousness that they came with nothing and will go with nothing. Fear of death is wholly illogical. Everyone dies. People from all religions and backgrounds are dying every day, from rich to poor, good and bad, old and young yet people remain afraid of death. Why? Fear can even come when giving up bad habits. By stopping drinking or smoking some will be afraid that they may not have a good time anymore, yet if illness comes through excess they will be unhappy and miserable. Fear is related to loss. When we know there is nothing to lose then fear dissipates.

On another occasion Smiling Swami told me that at the last moment before death, if the person is thinking about God or their breath or a divine personality then they will be liberated. When he told me, I playfully scolded him saying, "Why didn't you tell me this in my last life?" He smiled as usual and told me that it is not easy to think of the Divine in the last breath. When the Great Master passed away, one of the monks next to his bed observed that his last breath was an inhalation. Apparently if the last breath is an exhalation then the person will be coming back to the world, if it is an inhalation then that person will be liberated or is already. For the majority, the last breath is an exhalation. Of course if I do not know the exact moment I will die, it is hard to plan my last thought unless I am thinking of the Divine all the time. How often in the drama of allure and attachment to the world do I remember that I came as a visitor? All visitors have to leave. Hopefully in my case it will be with a big smile.

LETTERS FROM INDIA

On one of my visits to India I was travelling with Smiling Swami to a meditation programme which required us to take an overnight train from Puri. After a bumpy journey more akin to exercise than sleep, I was taken to a hotel by one of the organisers. The room in the hotel was £3 per night and had a black floor, matching dirty mattress, filthy sink and toilet. Boarding school memories seemed bright by comparison. After a couple of hours in the room I called my host Raj and asked him to find me another hotel. I could not stay there for three nights. He told me that no hotels were available as every one had been booked for an International

Rotary conference. I knew from experience that there is always a room available no matter how booked up hotels are as someone somewhere always cancels or does not turn up. I asked him to try some other hotels. Sure enough to his amazement and my good fortune, a room became available at a mid-range hotel. The hotel was clean and basic for £10 per night. So I had a clean room but my mistake was to go out for a Chinese meal where I contracted food poisoning and was then ill for the next week. This stopped me from travelling on to the next programme. I could not move my body for several days except to drag it frequently to and from the bathroom.

However, every cloud has a silver lining. When I felt a little better I spent time with Raj's father who turned out to be a modern day Gandhi. In spite of our age gap, almost immediately our relationship was close and very warm, like brothers. He was humble and quietly spoken. He told me about his life. Shortly after the Indian day of Independence on 15th August 1947, he was travelling by train from Pakistan to India with his parents and brother. During the journey the train was attacked. Only he and his mother survived.

We then spoke about corruption in India. I had previously been informed that corruption began under British rule when the Empire could not carry on paying the salaries of the people. The British in India therefore taught the Indian workers to take a small cut of the money that passed through their hands during their official duties to make ends meet. When I asked about various professions and the percentage of corrupt people in these professions he told me that many people were corrupt. He gave me an example. The family owned a shoe shop. Once when it was robbed, his son Raj, a chartered accountant went to report the robbery to the police. The policeman spent over an hour with him and then said that he was too busy to investigate the case. Raj returned home where his father and a friend were waiting for him. Raj relayed the story to them and that the policeman refused to help. His father's friend asked him if he had given the policeman a brown envelope. Raj and his father who were both honest men were shocked. Reluctantly Raj went back to the police station and gave the officer an envelope with some money. The officer scolded him for wasting his time at the first meeting and for not giving him the envelope sooner. He then promised to investigate.

He gave me some other examples. The family owned some vacant land. Once when driving past they discovered that someone had begun building on the land. They could not get the person to move. The police told them that they would need to take him to court. They started legal proceedings but it took ten years for the case to appear in front of a judge! When it finally reached court, the judge ruled that as the "intruder" was now living on the land that they had to accept another piece of land from him in place of their occupied land. They had no choice but to accept what the court said.

Finally he told me about his nephew who had rented out his apartment in Delhi to the president of a large corporation. After a few years the nephew wanted his apartment back to live in. The president told him that he was retiring and wanted to stay in the apartment and refused to move out. The nephew called on some friends who forcefully removed him and cut the telephone line so he could not call for help. This happened before the days of the mobile phone. The president was very angry and after his eviction, he threatened the lives of the nephew and his wife. The situation was getting out of hand. "Now my nephew was not without his contacts," the father told me. So the nephew called upon his senior contact at the police headquarters with a large brown envelope. The policeman brought in the president and his wife and sat them down in front of him. He looked at them both for over an hour without saying a word. They were both afraid. Then the police officer spoke about the seriousness of threatening people. They apologised profusely and the nephew was never contacted again by him.

To hear these stories first-hand was incredible to me, but perhaps I am naïve. I do not recount them to criticise India which I love to visit, as all countries have their own difficulties. Rather, when I heard these stories it made me more cautious and as a result I asked far more questions about the charitable work of our organisation in India. It made me realise that even if the charity I donate to is well run and has a good reputation, this counts for nothing if the people on the ground are corrupt. Fortunately I was satisfied with the answers I received about the charities I support. Sadly, I think that the larger the charitable organisation wherever they are in the world, the greater the risk that money will not find its way to the place or cause intended. Also, some charities sit on assets and still beg for money which is anathema to me. I prefer to obtain the financial accounts of a charity before donating money.

When I told Smiling Swami these stories he asked me to find a person that I could say was totally honest and a person who was totally dishonest. He argued that honesty and dishonesty all have degrees. As usual the master brings balance to the proceedings.

ADVICE FROM THE MASTER

My relationships with the Great Master and Smiling Swami have always been very informal. This does not always fit in with the expectation of others who are more formal with them. I have the highest respect for both yet my relationship is relaxed and similar as it is with any other friend. I have become aware of others who frown upon my informality with Smiling Swami. When I discussed this with him, as usual he smiled and then recounted a recent event that happened to him. He enjoyed a very informal relationship with an old monk. They spoke most days and joked a lot together. An old disciple of the Great Master who knew both of them well was shocked how informally Smiling Swami spoke to the elderly monk. He decided to tell him that he was being disrespectful to the elderly monk. Smiling Swami smiled and replied that, "Our relationship is our relationship." He said no more. The disciple, still dissatisfied, then approached the elderly monk who smiled and replied, "Our relationship is our relationship." The disciple went away realising he should mind his own business.

The Great Master said that, "Opportunity should not be neglected for it may never return." I am really grateful for my bond with these masters who have allowed me to have such an easy, enjoyable and fun relationship with them.

HELP FROM THE MASTER

Once there was a man who always complained that he was unlucky and had no money. Two gods were discussing his life. One god said that the man was lazy and did not take the opportunities given to him even if they were staring him in the face. The other god was more sympathetic and wanted to give the man another chance. So as an experiment, the benevolent god put a large gold nugget on the ground just ahead of where the man was going to walk. The two gods watched with interest. The man was walking along with his head down. Just before he reached the gold nugget he found himself walking alongside a blind man. For fun, the man decided to mimic the blind man by walking with his eyes closed. He stepped over the gold nugget!

I love this story because it really reflects those who complain about their lives. Opportunities are always presented to us but do we close our eyes to them through lack of awareness?

WE'RE ALL IN THE SAME BOAT

Once at a retreat, over lunch my companion said to me, "we are all in the same boat." My instant reply was that I hoped it was not the *Titanic*! I find it strange that some people feel the need to seek false comfort that they are not alone in what they are feeling when lacking self-belief. It is almost as if it is too scary to contemplate that they are the only person on the street who is ill or has a problem.

Also, I have met "spiritual" people who proclaim that, "we are all one." I tend to run for the exit at this point. Although truly admirable words, how many really experience this feeling of oneness? However I have felt on a small scale that when those around me are in pain and suffering, that this pain and suffering are somehow part of me. At this moment I send them love. This feeling of oneness is beyond the mind; it just is and I have not experienced it very often. When I do feel and see people as part of me, all negatives fall away and love takes over. I am also more conscious that it is the Invisible Hand that gives me these experiences.

WHEN IMAGINATION STOPS REALISATION STARTS

The Great Master often said, "When imagination stops realisation starts." After some years of practice, the Kriya Yoga student is given more advanced techniques to practise which will help deepen the experience of meditation. Some people make it a priority to gain more techniques. When I organised the programmes in London there was an Indian man who kept pestering me for more teachings. I asked how his meditation was progressing. He told me that the masters would wake him up early each morning and sit with him to meditate. I smiled inside. Although I did not say it at the time, the thought came to me that if he was sitting with the astral bodies of all these masters, then he should ask them for more techniques when he sees them the next day! For once I did not speak my mind.

AGITATION AND ANGER

Agitation used to come to me when I did not get what I wanted or when someone mistreated me. I would then find a way to relieve the agitation through finding a solution.

My staff laughed at me stomping around the office when a printer exploded on the busiest day of the year or when we ran out of letterheads or envelopes at the crucial moment. It was almost as if the Invisible Hand orchestrated events so that something new went wrong on the busiest day of the year. Worst of all was when the computer programmer went on holiday only for us to discover that the system would not work properly. I rarely disappointed with my reaction! A few expletives and then off to find a solution. No doubt a saint would not react that way, but I am no saint. Fortunately, I can only remember losing my temper temporarily a few times in my life.

Illogical rules or responses still agitate me but anger is not one of my friends. The good news is that even Smiling Swami admits to having been angry when he was younger so there is hope for me yet! In fact, when I analyse myself more, small problems bother me more than big problems. My reaction was greater when a lack of detail or laziness contributed to an error, especially if it was mine. Although I had been meditating for ten years whilst I worked, agitation still came. Meditation definitely helped me, but in hindsight I did not take a lunch break very often or get enough physical exercise. Laid Back Cigar Man was the same but he always managed to have a nap at his desk.

When Alexander the Great went to India he came across a sadhu. A sadhu is a holy man. Alexander the Great stood in front of the sadhu and blocked the sunlight. The sadhu asked him who he thought he was to be blocking the sunlight. Alexander was not used to being questioned by anybody. He told the sadhu angrily that he was a great emperor who had conquered many countries. The sadhu replied, "My child you may have conquered many countries but you are the slave of my slave." Alexander was insulted. The sadhu continued, "When my anger comes it will come when I want it to but you have no control of your anger so you are a slave to your anger." Alexander was speechless.

The Great Master asked his students often, "What is your change?"

FULL CIRCLE

There is a story of a mouse who met a guru. The guru wanted a daughter so he turned the mouse into a young girl. He brought her up and when she became a young woman she wanted to get married. She told him she wanted a great and powerful husband. The guru started to search for a husband. He approached the sun. "The sun is bright and powerful," he told her. She rejected the sun because it was too hot to get close to. "Who is greater than you?" the guru asked the sun. The sun replied, "The clouds because they can cover me up." The daughter rejected the clouds as they were cold and dark. He then asked the clouds who was more powerful than them. The clouds replied, "The wind, because it can blow us away." The daughter rejected the wind because the wind was too cold. He asked the wind who was more powerful than the wind. "The mountain is more powerful than me because I cannot move the mountain," replied the wind. The young woman rejected the mountain as it was too big and rough on the surface. "Who is more powerful than you?" he asked the mountain. "The mouse," came the reply from the mountain. "The mouse can make a hole in me!" The guru smiled. The girl was content to be a mouse to run around and be free. He turned her back into a mouse and she soon met another mouse to marry.

Sometimes accepting who we are leads to real peace and harmony.

THE POWER OF PRAYER

If I go to a holy place I usually experience a feeling of calm and perception of divine energy. Prayer is certainly powerful. Does every prayer have equal power? I believe that the answer is yes. Some prayers take longer to manifest than others and perhaps there is a difference in prayer power if the prayer is given by someone who is more spiritually advanced or humble. Sincerity may also play a part. Sometimes prayers do not appear to work quickly enough as the example below shows.

I have used homeopathy for many years and it really works like magic. In the UK official bodies criticise homeopathy, yet in India there are many positive scientific studies and support for homeopathy. When I was on a Himalaya trek, two of our group suffered from altitude sickness. One lady had been giving them "homeopathy" for days to no effect. I asked what dose she had given them. She told me 3M which is a huge dose. I could not believe nothing had happened. Then the punch line came. The lady had been unable to obtain the required remedy so instead she had bought sugar pills and had prayed to God to infuse them with the remedy! This is a good example to show that the placebo effect does not work! I intervened and gave the sick people 30c of coca. The next day they both felt better.

GOD TAKES CARE OF EVERYTHING

A man decided to test God to see if God would feed him wherever he was. Off he went, deep into the forest away from any paths and climbed a tree and sat on a branch. Some time passed. He then heard voices. Four pilgrims stopped under the tree. He watched with disbelief as they hung a bag of food on the branch below him and left. He could only speculate that they had left it there to keep it safe. He did not want to steal the food. If God wanted to give food to him then God should not tempt him to be a thief. Hours passed by. He was getting hungry. He heard more voices. Some thieves arrived. They set up camp and, looking up, saw the food. They thought it was a trap. As one of them climbed the tree, the man who was testing God was spotted. He had to come down. Now the man was worried. He asked himself why had he not eaten the food that God had brought him and just left? He explained to the thieves that it was not his food and that it had been left by some pilgrims. They did not believe him. The thieves thought the food must be poisoned so they forced him to eat the food. The man could not avoid God feeding him even through the hand of a thief!

INTUITION OR LUCK?

If there is a hidden force driving us, then why do we need intuition at all or is intuition coming from this hidden force? Is intuition just a form of consciousness or is it just being more in tune with our true nature?

When a friend came to visit in the early days of knowing her, I was unaware of the food she liked and disliked. I knew that she ate cheese and yoghurt so I bought vanilla yoghurt and goat's cheese without looking properly at the labels.

When she arrived, she asked how I knew that these were her favourites. Had it been luck or intuition?

Another time I was taken to a North Wales mountain range by a business client to meet a healer. My client felt that I would have a lot in common with the healer as I was interested in spirituality. We walked up the mountain under the full moon to discover that it was the Autumn Solstice day and some special anniversary of the mountain. I never knew this yet we were here on that special day. When I visited the Great Pyramid I discovered that immediately after our visit some of the chambers we visited were closed to the public for years thereafter. A similar event took place when I visited some holy sites in Israel. Three months later they became almost no-go areas due to the conflict there.

I also remember going to France with a friend when we were both sixteen. This was my first holiday travelling on my own. We found ourselves stranded at Chambord about 15 km from our hotel with no buses left running in the area. There were only two cars left in the car park. I approached one of them and the driver took us all of the way to our hotel. In the back of the car were two shot guns. By luck he was a hunter and not a murderer!

What determines that we avoid danger or walk straight into it? What determines whether the door of opportunity being opened and closed at a given moment is for me and not for others or vice versa? Surely it is more than luck or intuition.

IMAGINATION

An Irish friend's brother called her to tell her that he had dreamt that bank shares were a certain buy and recommended that she invest in them. She told him that he was mad and fortunately she trusted her own intuition and not his imagination. His dream was just before the credit crunch! He will not trust his dreams ever again.

So what is the difference between imagination and intuition? Intuition is foresight and imagination is imagined foresight. My experience of intuition can be described as making a decision instinctively which leads to a perceived outcome. Intuition occurs when my thoughts come to pass and imagination is when they do not. It is an ability to know something without being aware of how one knows it. Intuition develops with more meditation.

If our intuition is so good then why do we so often end up in the "wrong" job or with the "wrong" partner? Somehow I do not always choose what "seems" good for me. If I reflect in a more detached way, then maybe the phrases good and bad and right and wrong are just transitory experiences which last for pre-determined lengths of time.

My conclusion is that an event or a thought that is going to happen will happen anyway whether I am conscious or not of the reason why. Is it my thought or the thought of the Invisible Hand? Both or either are correct. Sometimes I believe that it is my thought or my success or my failure or due to grace or the Invisible Hand. Even this thought is given to me!

I do know that if my mind is positive then unpleasant or negative experiences will not be as bad. The only long-lasting and effective way to a good mind that I have come across is meditation. It is amazing that with so many scientists in the world they have not found a way for us to stay calm without being chemically induced. Perhaps more scientists need to meditate.

Calmness is achievable through meditation with no negative side affects.

CHAPTER 15

QUALITIES REQUIRED; KNOWLEDGE ACQUIRED

In this chapter I summarise some of the qualities required and knowledge acquired which have helped me in my life. I also recount more of the teachings I have received from my gurus. Some of these may help you also. Whatever I have been taught or practise, as I hope you have realised in this book, I certainly do not wish to preach to you in any way. I have always selected the rituals, diet or habits that feel right for me and suggest you do the same and find what is good for you.

Being an all-rounder has helped me to be successful. I was also lucky to have a good memory for detail which was especially important in business. By detail I refer not only to facts and figures but also to my clients and their personalities. However for those on the spiritual path and those of us who remember the negatives instead of the positives, Smiling Swami teaches that one of God's gifts is forgetfulness! He says, "The problem is we remember what we should forget and forget what we should remember." Forgetting bad memories and negatives about others is positive. To have constant memory of negatives is painful and makes it hard to forgive others.

I accepted and knew that I was not good at everything nor did I like doing everything. When I had no choice but to carry out tasks that I did not enjoy, my determination and concentration normally pulled me through.

In addition, I enjoyed taking responsibility but really thought nothing of it. It was usual for me to be in charge rather than receiving instructions from others. It did not seem like responsibility. I concentrated on my strengths but did not close my eyes to my weaknesses as it could have led to my downfall.

QUALITIES REQUIRED:

STRENGTH AND COURAGE

I have never followed the herd if my intuition told me otherwise. When others questioned how Key would be able to compete with huge banks in such a crowded market, I just knew intuitively that the banks did not understand the requirements of the legal profession or give an outstanding service. I saw this as an opportunity to build a niche company.

RARE SENSE

Otherwise known for some reason as common sense! Everything is possible especially when others say it is not.

SENSE OF HUMOUR

Running a finance house was a serious business but finding an outlet through laughter was vital even if this meant my staff laughed at me often!

ENDURANCE, TENACITY, PERSEVERANCE

It took ten years to build a solid business and another eight years to sell it. It took six years for meditation to become habitual and ten more years to experience more peace. It was not always easy but not always difficult either.

ENTHUSIASM & JOY

I am humbled when I see and meet people with such difficult lives who keep going with a smile on their face. Surely if my life has less hardship I can be enthusiastic and joyful.

ABSOLUTE DETERMINATION

I knew that with hard work a thriving profitable business would eventually be built. It just took longer and was harder than I ever imagined. This did not put me off. Single-pointed attention was required. Regarding my spiritual growth I am more relaxed to let the path unfold naturally but my inbuilt discipline helps me to persevere when others will stop.

SHARP MIND

The ability to think clearly and quickly has helped me time and time again.

FAST LEARNER

Finding out quickly where my abilities were helped me to progress. When starting the business it did not take me long to see I knew very little about running a finance house. My constant desire to learn brought me the knowledge and expertise required. As valuable as gaining knowledge, was the ability to learn quickly from my own mistakes and the mistakes or poor service of others and in particular from large bureaucratic companies. I was ever grateful to larger banks who would take a week to make a credit decision for a longstanding client whereas we would take a few hours. Regarding spirituality, I have learnt to follow the teachings that suit my mind and not the minds of others.

SINCERITY & TRUTHFULNESS

Dishonesty with oneself is the main barrier to prospering in life, business and spirituality. I really cared about our clients in business. This is not possible without sincerity. A lack of sincerity and honesty makes life difficult and spiritual progress slow. My progress is hindered when I do not follow what I know to be right in actions or thoughts. If I do a job I do it properly or I do not do it at all. I am as I am and cannot be anybody else but me.

When I make mistakes if I do not always learn from them I try again.

REACTING POSITIVELY TO DISAPPOINTMENT BUT WITH REALISM

I am still a work in progress on this one. However when bad news came in business, for instance when interest rates doubled overnight or a credit line was withdrawn without notice, I never gave up or thought that it was the end.

KNOWING HOW TO TRANSFORM DOOM AND GLOOM

When things have been tough at work or in my personal life or events do not go my way Kriya Yoga has helped me enormously. It has acted as a comfort and a deterrent to pursuing external excesses or habits which are bad for me. However, the occasional organic chocolate bar or dessert has also been soothing.

SEEING THE DETAIL AND THE OPPORTUNITIES THAT OTHERS CANNOT SEE

Having this asset has been an essential ingredient to any success. Developing financial products for clients that competitors had not created or perfected was the making of the business. In a similar way, recognising the rare opportunity to spend time on retreats and programmes and in particular with the Great Master and Smiling Swami has given me a distinct advantage to grow spiritually. Those who cannot recognise a good opportunity and miss the chance again and again may live to regret it.

At death, I want to be grateful for my life and not regretful.

MILITARY PRECISION REGARDING ADMINISTRATION AND DELIVERY TO CLIENTS

If an entrepreneur does not have this ability then he or she needs to employ someone that does. I had the foresight to see how much planning and preparation was involved in delivering the service I wanted to deliver. Good ideas are just not enough. Having management who were fastidious to the last, helped create a seamless service along with our other well-trained staff was essential. Knowing what I wanted helped this process also.

ALWAYS REMEMBERING THAT LIFE IS PRACTICAL AND NOT THEORETICAL

The Great Master repeated often for us to practise, practise, practise. He never said theorise, theorise, theorise.

NEVER BEING BULLIED INTO A DECISION THAT DID NOT FEEL RIGHT

Luckily I cannot remember so far having signed or agreed to something which made me feel uncomfortable or which I regretted later. There is a reason for discomfort. It is a warning sign but should not be confused with the feeling one experiences when something new and unfamiliar arrives. Of course I am open to gentle persuasion where others see benefits which I did not see myself – and I value good advice.

FAILURE IS DEFERRED SUCCESS

I have always recognised that failure is deferred success and that no is a deferred yes. If I keep searching the way will become apparent. If I cannot find the way, the Invisible Hand will send someone to help me.

AIM TO BE THE BEST WITHOUT HAVING TO BE THE BEST

Even if I was not the best I was not bothered. Someone else's success was positive encouragement and not a threat. I have always found role models who had skills that were of value to me even though I rarely searched for them. I admire people who can do things that I cannot. Great teachers like my masters want the student to be more successful than them. In business, there were always companies charging less but to this day I never saw a financial organisation give a better or more reliable service than Key. This gave us the confidence to quote and promote ourselves with sincerity without having any doubts.

THE BELIEF THAT I COULD ACHIEVE WHAT I WANTED

Whether this is based on naïvety or not does not matter. I was prepared to work hard and keep going.

EVERYTHING IS POSSIBLE

I believe everything is possible even if I do not know how to do it yet. My possibilities are someone else's impossibilities.

BEING REALISTIC AND ADJUSTING MY DREAMS

In my mind my expectations in life are realistic. If I want a dish specially prepared in an Italian restaurant because of my dietary restrictions, and I am told they cannot help me but they have the ingredients, I find that unreasonable. Others may take a different view by judging my tastes according to their own. My reality is not the reality of others. I have never been much of a dreamer; more of a creator, thinker and a doer. When I was young I thought I would retire at thirty. This naïvety soon left me when I saw the task ahead. Having such an aim may seem unrealistic but it had a purpose. Even if others thought my ambition was unrealistic I was not put off.

USING MY TIME EFFICIENTLY BUT NOT ALWAYS!

Smiling Swami is my teacher regarding time and efficiency. He writes at least two books each year as well as travelling around the world, leading programmes and dealing with people's problems. He never wastes a moment and is always joyful. Each day he writes and I have travelled with him when we have started the day at five in the morning and he has meetings to attend at midnight!

ATTEMPTING TO CONTROL BAD HABITS BUT NOT ALWAYS!

Ignoring my negatives but not always! By this I do not mean that I never bother to reflect on what I can change about myself to become a better person in my eyes. I just do not let the negatives consume me. Rather, by focussing on my positives, my negatives are swamped. In business, I would delegate to others where they were more efficient and skilled than me but I did not abrogate all responsibility. Where possible I matched the talents of the person with the job in hand. Particularly the jobs that required real patience. Giving up bad habits has helped me to cultivate more affinity with the Invisible Hand which has led to changes in negative patterns which could affect decision-making.

I RARELY COMPLAIN WITHOUT DOING SOMETHING ABOUT IT

Successful people have no time to complain constantly on how tough life is. Instead, they do something about it. I never envy the good fortune of others. Let everyone find happiness in their own way. Unsuccessful people use excuses as to why they have not succeeded. I have never understood this attitude as it is of no use whatsoever.

GOOD ROLE MODELS AND TEACHERS

In business, my father and Laid Back Cigar Man in particular were my confidants and teachers. In spirituality the Great Master, Smiling Swami, Hugging Mother and Silent Mother have helped me enormously. My friendship with Dan has lasted over 35 years. I was with Joy for 22 years. Both supported me through the good and the bad, as have my other close friends. Finding a great teacher whether it be a friend, a parent or a colleague is really helpful. Where possible I surround myself with positive role models. Negative role models or environments cause restlessness and unhappiness.

ASKING FOR WHAT I WANT

When I ask for what I want, I always believe that I will receive it. It is amazing what can be achieved with a little *chutzpah*, a smile or a laugh. Asking a question with a negative is sure to encourage a response in the negative.

Being happy and positive is key.

GOOD PERSUASIVE SKILLS

I love persuading someone that they can do something easily when their first reaction is negative. Persuasion needs to be supported by logic, clarity, charm and a smile.

VALUE OF OPINIONS

I do not underestimate my own ability or overestimate other people's abilities. If a professional gives me an opinion and the information does not "feel" quite right I verify the information elsewhere. Opinions differ and professional advice received is often right to follow but at other times it is not. If I keep receiving misleading or incorrect advice then I take it as a message from the Invisible Hand to change adviser. Undoing the effects of poor professional advice is costly and time-consuming. In business I found it important to trust my judgement and instincts after the advice was given but overall we had very good advisers. Sometimes spiritual seekers question their guru. If my guru was no good then I would have changed him or her. The more than likely option is that I was the one that needed to change myself.

UNDERSTANDING WHAT I AM DOING

In business or investments I never go into something that I do not fully understand. If I need to read something more than twice to understand the content then it is probably not for me. If more questions than answers arise then I pass on the opportunity.

KNOWING WHAT TO DO

If the business was not earning enough then either we were not charging enough or our overheads were too high. Ignoring problems rarely makes them disappear. If our product was no good then we scrapped or changed it. If a member of staff did not meet our needs then we let them go but as a small business it was not easy to find good replacements.

Regarding meditation it is easy to pretend to others that I am chilled out and spiritual. I aim to be aware and honest regarding how I am truly feeling, my difficulties and experiences to myself and others also.

Frustrations still come so why deny it?

SACRIFICE & COMMITMENT

Working long hours and getting up at the crack of dawn and even earlier to meditate was not easy. It was a strain, emotionally, physically and mentally. Those who think they can succeed without sacrifice will have a rude awakening. However sacrifice can be good if bad habits and time-wasting activities are left behind. I found it really difficult to keep a balance between life at home and work. Luckily my health was good but had I continued to work as hard it would have suffered in the long run. I applaud anyone who is successful and keeps balance in their life.

Regarding commitment, when the Great Master was asked by his teacher how much time he was prepared to devote to meditation, he replied, "The whole of my life." I have a long way to go before I can say the same with 100% sincerity.

COMPETITION

I did not worry too much about the competition in business but we had many "friends" who would keep us up to date with what was happening in the market place. Advanced knowledge is better than surprise.

PROMISES, PROMISES

I did not knowingly promise what could not be delivered. We gave realistic timescales to clients and always over-quoted the time it took to get something done. The client was always impressed when we came back earlier than promised. I was and remain grateful for the inefficiencies of our competitors or Key would not have existed. So many companies I come across in daily life fail to deliver even a quote let alone their product or service on time. So many spiritual aspirants promise themselves they will meditate each day and fail to do so even for five minutes.

How can we keep a promise to others if we cannot keep a promise to ourselves?

CULTIVATION

The best and easiest new business to obtain was to cultivate and maximise business opportunities with existing clients. In meditation, by attending more classes and listening to the sound advice of my gurus, my practice was cultivated to a greater effect.

KNOWING WHEN TO BE IMPATIENT OR PATIENT

I am still mastering this one. I am impatient when I know something can be done when someone else says that it cannot or if something takes much longer than it should. I am patient when I know I cannot do any more. This book has taken me four years to write full-time! Every time I think it is finished it is not! Luckily my realism keeps me in check.

INTERNET SALES ARE RARELY THE ANSWER
TO THE ENTREPRENEUR'S PRAYERS

Online sales work if the entrepreneur is marketing the business by meeting more and more people in the marketplace in which the business operates. This is the real way to learn and make contacts. Sitting back and staring at an expensively designed website will not be enough.

WHO DO I TRUST?

I consulted people whom I trusted and respected who had the expertise that I needed to help me make my own judgement. If the path ahead was clear to me I was not distracted by the doubt of others. If in doubt I contemplated further but then made decisions confidently. Indecisiveness is not the same as making a decision after a period of deliberation. Learning from my mistakes was crucial. Contemplation on repeated mistakes was also necessary. In conclusion, I trust in my own inner strength and judgement.

"If in doubt leave it out" worked well for me.

MODERATION

Moderation is only possible when there is calmness and mental balance.

BEING AT PEACE

Neti neti in Sanskrit means "Not this not that." It is one of the suggested paths to help find spiritual truth by eliminating all that is false. Such a seeker will look at the world and conclude that unnecessary pleasures and external activities are not the way to the truth. Illumination can come from elimination. Utilising such a practice is also helpful in daily life. By rejecting falsehood the truth will come. Being at peace with our philosophies and thoughts brings clear thinking in life.

I tend to prefer the opposite philosophy to *neti neti* – The Invisible Hand is everywhere and in every activity.

BEING PREPARED TO TEAR UP ALL THE KNOWLEDGE THAT I HAVE ACQUIRED

When I met the Great Master I had been giving healing sessions to people and guiding meditations. The moment that I met him I quickly realised that I knew nothing about spirituality. I felt no shame or loss of ego. I was happy to meet someone far more advanced who wanted to help me grow and who expected nothing back from me.

KNOWLEDGE OF THE BREATH
& DEVELOPING GOOD HABITS

There is a hidden yogic science which Smiling Swami has taught me related to breath which is beneficial to use in our daily activities. I have practised and incorporated these teachings into my daily life and they have helped me become more in tune with the Invisible Hand. They are simple but effective and complement the gentle reminder to keep introducing good new habits rather than focus continually on our bad habits. Additionally, we should never delay something that is good for us but delay indefinitely something which is bad for us. Like any science, what I mention is merely a basic introduction to illustrate what a difference the breath can make to our lives. The main teaching of my masters is to be aware of the breath as much as possible regardless of the activity. In addition:

1) Breathe in and out of the nostrils and not the mouth. Breathing through the nose allows the hairs and mucus to act as a filter to limit the amount of bacteria taken into the body from the air before it reaches the lungs.

2) When I wake up I observe which nostril the breath exhales from and when I get out of bed I put down the foot on the floor to match the side of the breath. This brings my body and mind immediately in tune with the rhythm of my breath. I always get out of bed on the right hand side. This is because the right side of the body represents activity and action. If the breath is coming out of both nostrils, then it is better to wait a little and meditate.

Apart from the above, when the breath is exhaling from the right nostril on waking up on a Tuesday, Thursday, Saturday and Sunday the outcome of the activities for the day will be more fruitful. The same principle of auspiciousness applies when the breath is exhaling from the left nostril on waking up on a Monday, Wednesday and a Friday. If my breath is not pertaining to the more "beneficial" side then I proceed with more caution on that day. It is like a weather warning.

I have really seen how it is harder to get things done when my breath starts the day on the least favourable side. The more one meditates and watches one's breath the more the breath will fall on the "auspicious" side. Observe and see for yourself. I have practised these techniques diligently every day for four years and have tested them out on non-believers who have vouched for their uncanny effectiveness. Also when the breath is coming out of both nostrils at any time it is auspicious to meditate or be still for a few minutes rather than carry out another activity as success will be less likely at this time.

3) If I become agitated, I drink more water and it is good to have a cold shower or do some exercise. I do not make important decisions that day.

4) To take care of good physical health and body-weight consider following the dictum of Lahiri Mahasaya, a great Kriya Yoga master who recommended that the stomach should be half full of food, a quarter full of water and a quarter full of air.

5) On the subject of health, when beginning medical treatment or curing a serious disease, it is beneficial to start the treatment when the breath is coming out of the right nostril. If a person has a fever, it is better to start treatment when the breath is exhaling from the left nostril.

6) I never read before going to bed. I meditate instead or find a more interesting loving bed companion!

7) I am always able to wake up early. If you have difficulty waking up early, drink water before going to bed. Nature will call you earlier than usual.

8) I smile as often as possible, even to strangers and I sing in the shower.

9) Instead of constantly focussing on weaknesses, a person may benefit from writing down the changes that they want to make in their life, how the changes will be made and when to begin the process. This approach can help overcome negative tendencies by looking at and dealing with them in a positive way. I follow the GID principle. "Get it done!"

10) If giving up a bad habit it is good to begin the process when the breath is exhaling from the left nostril. When learning something new it is good to begin when the breath is also exhaling from the left nostril.

11) I am less critical of myself than in the past. Criticising myself or others is unhelpful and harmful. Self-analysis is not the same as self-criticism. How can I love anybody if I do not love myself? Self-analysis can be achieved with practice without criticism.

12) I was not afraid to change my job if it did not match my desires. Moaning about a job is unproductive. Either change your job, your attitude or both.

13) Motivation comes from inside but is influenced from outside. Find something or someone to motivate you. A dance around the kitchen is always worthwhile!

14) Giving time to myself to reflect on my positives. A positive approach to life is possible in all circumstances even when tested to the extreme. A negative attitude will add to the stress but sometimes this is unavoidable.

HEALTH IS WEALTH

HEALTHY DRINKING AND EATING

It is better to drink when the breath is exhaling out of the left nostril. Spicy food stimulates restlessness in the mind as does oily food and too much salt or sugar which encourages insomnia. Practitioners of *ayurveda*, which means the "Science of life", teach that food should be eaten as soon as it is cooked or prepared and not after storage.

It is beneficial for digestion to eat when the breath is exhaling from the right nostril. I also thank God for the food on my plate. For those suffering from poor digestion or low energy, it is better to sleep on the left side of the body which will stimulate the breath to stay longer in the right nostril. For those who are restless it is better to lie on the right side of the body which will stimulate the breath to come out of the left nostril, bringing more relaxation. The Great Master also taught that we should chew our food 100 times for good digestion. Do not take this too literally but you get the point. Although it sounds obvious, we should eat the food that is good for us individually which is easy to digest. If digestion is poor then a main contributory factor is the diet. Being vegetarian is not necessary but it helps us to be more sattvic.

Regarding diet, cooking green unripe papaya as a vegetable is very soothing for poor digestion. Fresh ginger in hot water is good for circulation and also comforting for the stomach. Vegetarians should avoid tofu and spinach in the same meal as in the Far East it has been discovered that it can lead to stomach problems. Taking cold water with lemon or lime with honey increases immunity without weight loss. Having warm boiled water with lemon or lime and honey decreases weight and increases immunity. When a cold or flu arrives taking the latter as well as adding fresh ginger is helpful. It is good to take in the morning before breakfast.

It is beneficial to drink a glass of water around thirty minutes before each meal. This firstly limits how much food is eaten and secondly eradicates the need to drink afterwards. Smiling Swami told me that if water is drunk in quantity during the meal or within thirty minutes of a meal, the food ingested no matter how good turns to poison. He explained to me that the water firstly cleans the mouth and stops the flow of saliva. This in turn complicates and slows down the digestive process as we have different digestive juices for food and liquid. The digestive juices from the liver are reduced and are mixed with the water so that even though the food may have been good before the meal, it is ruined and is bad for our health. The different digestive juices do not function well together. It is also bad for the teeth. The same applies to washing the teeth straight after a meal. It is better to wait some time. A few sips of water during a meal is fine. Technically wine, tea or coffee counts as a food so we can keep some of our habits in moderation.

These simple tips can help all of us especially those who have digestive problems. I have followed this for some years. My weight is good as is my digestion. It is also advisable to sit down when eating or drinking. This is because the blood flows more to the feet when standing rather than to the stomach. If we stand we also have less awareness of how full our stomach is. If we sit we can feel how full our stomach is which reduces overeating. Eating fresh and non-processed food is also good for the mind.

It is beneficial to use a tongue cleaner after brushing our teeth. This removes toxins particularly in the morning after sleeping. A clear tongue also demonstrates the state of our health. Sometimes when I stay with friends I watch with horror when they have their first cup of tea without brushing their teeth! Every morning after brushing my teeth I drink a glass of water.

The Great Master taught me to massage the stomach in the morning when lying down. Use the forefinger and the middle finger of each hand and place just below the belly button. Press in three times gently. If you imagine the belly button to be the six o'clock position of a clock; then move the fingers three inches clockwise to nine o'clock and press in three times gently; then follow the process to twelve o'clock then three o'clock. If you feel pain then it is likely that your colon is not operating properly. You can repeat a few times and then give a gentle slap to the right side a couple of inches to the right of the belly button and then do the left side. The Great Master told me that this exercise carried out each day protects a person from bowel cancer. It can also help people with constipation as can a cup of warm boiled water especially in the morning. Aloe Vera is also beneficial. Regarding taking care of the gums one can gently press above and around the lips pressing gently on the gums. I have also maintained my tooth health by gently rubbing toothpaste directly on the gums after washing my teeth. I have one small filling otherwise a clean bill of health and surely diet has a role to play here although I ate plenty of chocolate at school. Drinking water at room temperature is also healthy.

Smiling Swami recommends that we eat something bitter each day. In India karela or neem leaves are eaten for bitterness. Neem is highly anti-bacterial and can combat diabetes. Although it is not easy to obtain fresh leaves outside of India, there are powders and pills available. I did try neem once. It was extremely powerful and I would advise going to an ayurvedic practitioner before taking. I tend to eat grapefruit regularly but do not always eat bitter food each day. I prefer to have a detox each spring with liver and kidney drops which include dandelion and artichoke. A few days after taking these drops I often feel agitated so I keep myself to myself when carrying out this dangerous internal mission! I normally take a good multi-vitamin at the same time. Otherwise I do not take vitamins each day.

All of us have the ability to make choices in life and the knowledge to make the choices that will help us. By constantly introducing good new habits there is less room for bad habits new and old. This chapter reflects the choices I have made and the disciplines that have assisted me.

CHAPTER 16

WHAT I HAVE LEARNT: I KNOW NOTHING!

THE MORE I THINK I KNOW THE LESS I REALLY KNOW!

The more I discover about love, human behaviour, grace and calmness, I realise that I know so little and have so much to learn. However, the little I know and the teachings of others can be put to good use to help myself. I need knowledge to advance but I realise that the need for humility is even greater.

There is an ancient scripture called Hitopadesh which states that, "Those who do not study the scriptures are plunged into darkness." The good news is, it then states that, "Those who study the scriptures are plunged into even more darkness!" This means that those who study should do so to intensify their *sadhana* and not to gain more theoretical knowledge to expand their ego.

WHO TAKES THE CREDIT?

Through increased consciousness of the Invisible Hand it is harder to take the credit for something that I have done. It does not feel quite right anymore. Can I really take credit when so much of my life and its events are so out of my control? Logic dictates that if I make a mistake or doubts arise, then if I ask for God or gurus to help me, it is no longer my problem and surely my behaviour will change with their assistance. If I feel it is "my doubt" or "my problem", then trouble comes. In business particularly but also in relationships a lack of confidence is off-putting. Clients want authenticity. If I was not able to present myself confidently and professionally, then the results would have been more mixed. People smell disingenuity even if it takes some time to come to the fore. Of course I needed experience and knowledge as without these I would have little to say.

But am I always true to myself and others? I am learning to say less about what I think especially if the person I am talking to has no intention of listening. Of course I want to share my positive experiences because I care about people but I know that I have no right to comment about anybody else's choices. This can be harder if people close to me are suffering. I have become better at expressing my feelings in personal relationships, shedding the boarding school mentality that showing emotion is a weakness. The softer part of me does not always want to be brutally honest if I know it may hurt someone. This is more difficult if I am in a relationship. However the fear of upsetting someone is unhealthier than upsetting someone with the truth. It is a fine balance between being honest without hurting people and not communicating feelings and emotions. I am working on it.

WHAT IS THE REAL PURPOSE OF MY LIFE?

As I have concluded that I am not fully in control of my life, then how do I change what makes me unhappy? Why is it so hard to give up bad habits and adopt good habits? Who or what gives me the courage or creates the catalyst for change? When I do things that I think will make me happy how long does that happiness last?

As described in the first chapter, the Great Master told me that the only purpose of life was to experience God-realisation. I believed him in the same way that I believed my father when he told me that I could have anything I wanted if I worked hard. It is easier to be successful if those around you are and if you find good role models. There is less effort to work hard when I am happy and when those around me are likeminded. The challenge is when they are not. Kriya Yoga helps promote this inner happiness regardless of circumstances although I do not always manage to stay in this peaceful state for long.

VALUE OF MONEY

From childhood I remember how my father would have different cars or vans to take us to school depending on what job he had. I also recall how early he got up and how hard he worked. He sacrificed a lot so that his children could have a good education. His incredible work ethic made a firm imprint on my life. If I wanted something I was going to have to work for it. The greater the ambition, the greater the effort required. Why do some seekers of spiritual or material growth expect to achieve results without putting in effort?

I am aware that whilst making money gives me more freedom and choice, it can tie me unnecessarily to the world. Financial trappings are fine as long as they do not trap me! Being a slave to money is quite different from money being my slave. Money is a form of freedom which I fully appreciate, so I hope that freedom manifests more on my spiritual journey. Gaining freedom externally is a reflection of what is taking place internally. Although the accumulation of money manifests in the material form, it is a spiritual manifestation. If I adopt some of the qualities gained from my life experience, particularly in business, towards my *sadhana* then I can only gain spiritually.

Material success has brought me external freedom; spiritual success has taken me along the path of inner freedom. Through effort so much is achievable but if desires are never satisfied then life can only be miserable. Every day I try to remember to be grateful for what I have been given.

THE MIDAS TOUCH

There are those rare people in the world for whom everything they touch turns to gold. Then there are people like me. In order to make something of myself I needed to fight, be prepared to confront others and put in real effort. There is no substitute for getting our hands dirty. What I have discovered is that material success counts for nothing unless I can benefit myself and others and turn this into something worthwhile. Having a material goal to achieve was necessary at the start of the journey, but when I reached my destination I knew that it would not be enough to fulfil me and make me happy. I have found that what really makes me happy can only last if it comes from inside. *Real* success can only be measured by inner contentment. This costs nothing yet is hard to obtain in a world of greed and desire. If we are going to be greedy perhaps we should be greedy for spiritual growth, calmness, positive thoughts and healthy unconditional love.

There are rare teachers who know the path to inner contentment.

SELF-LEADERSHIP AND MOTIVATION

As mentioned previously, staff will follow the leader only if they respect him or her. If the leader does not care or practise what he or she preaches, then why should the employees? An aspiring entrepreneur with a bad attitude should give up before leaving the starting block. Motivated people with a good attitude do twice as much work as others. Those with a good attitude do not ponder what they have done but remain focussed on the task ahead. Recognition and appreciation help to incentivise or motivate those around us but ultimately motivation has to come from inside. To be motivated in business with a pragmatic, ethical and spiritual attitude can only make the experience more pleasurable and rewarding. Those who take short cuts or cheat the system will always be found out. After working really long hours for quite a few years, there were times when I had to overcome tiredness and make an extra effort to push myself to do more. One rule that I always stuck to was not to take work home with me. Busy, successful people know how to use their time and how to get things done. Having a "cannot do" attitude is a common disease to catch and very hard to cure. Being the boss has its benefits and its pitfalls. Internal discomfort and difficulties come with the territory. Building a business or for that matter pursuing the spiritual path is not always a peaceful process. To be an entrepreneur one needs to be a fighter. Fighting inner negative thoughts and habits as well as external negative influences was essential so as not to be blown off course. Those who have more inbuilt discipline find it easier to overcome difficulties. Spiritual seekers can also fight, however as I have meditated more I realise that it is more effective to let the mind be and that there is nothing to fight but everything to love. Everyone should find a job and a home environment that generates good thoughts and habits but changing the external environment will not be enough if the internal environment is left untouched.

Enthusiasm is all well and good, but those who think that setting up a business is just a great idea and will be fun may have a rude awakening. Some who follow the spiritual path expect it to be easy and do not see the need to practise. Those who continue and invest in their spiritual practice reap the results of their efforts. Once mastery in spirituality comes, then peace and success follow in other areas of life. Real peace emanates from the breath to the mind. A balanced mind helps bring this peace. If the mind is unbalanced then problems will occur regardless of the activity.

In conclusion the main obstacles for the entrepreneur and those who want spiritual achievement are internal. Once any lack of decision-making, naïvety, poor confidence and fear have been eliminated, success follows.

WOMEN HAVE AN ADVANTAGE OVER MEN

Women who are good mothers have the potential to become great entrepreneurs because they already understand the necessity of commitment, sacrifice, nurturing and overcoming personal discomfort. Many women work, as well as juggling household and child responsibilities. From my viewpoint, gender or race made no difference to me in business. Performance, ability and results were the key, regardless of gender or even professional qualifications. Mistreatment of any member of staff male or female is unacceptable in any environment. Not treating women or indeed anyone according to their performance and achievements is first and foremost stupid, as well as archaic and inexcusable. The good news for women is that according to Chanakya, a great philosopher and politician who lived 2300 years ago in India, women have a great advantage over men. He said that compared to men, women have four times the intelligence, six times the business and bargaining mentality and eight times the desire and passion. There is also good news from Smiling Swami's perspective about the role of women in the world. He predicted to me in the late 1990s that the 21st century would be the century for women. Since then I have observed how many more female leaders are emerging in business and politics.

ENTREPRENEURS AND SPIRITUAL SEEKERS

Tony was a typical entrepreneur and a successful vineyard-owner in the Napa Valley. We met when I was on holiday. He had always been motivated to reach his goals without being too interested in the journey. In common with many entrepreneurs, he knew what he wanted and pursued it regardless of the difficulties. The pot of gold at the end of the rainbow was far more alluring for him than the rainbow itself. Our discussion centred on whether we were in control of our lives and destiny or not. After two hours, he sighed and admitted with a smile that he knew he was not in control really but liked to think that he was!

Tony's great desire and "can-do" attitude reminded me of how motivated I was to succeed in the world. Even at thirteen I had the desire to succeed materially. When I started Key I was hugely ambitious and had the attitude that I was responsible for driving the metaphorical train. After I met the Great Master I watched how the business grew more rapidly. As mentioned previously, a few years later I realised that I was no longer the driver but was hanging on to the back of the train for dear life! In one way this was comforting as I enjoyed the knowledge that I was receiving help from the Invisible Hand and the Great Master.

Spiritual seekers or non-achievers may disapprove of or criticise those who have material desire. However, a conscious spiritual seeker will appreciate the value of everybody in the world. The person earning money is contributing as much to the world as the spiritual seeker. We all have our part to play. If nobody paid taxes there would be no social services. Entrepreneurs employ people and some of the greatest philanthropic gestures come from wealthy people.

SPIRITUAL MASTERY

Material success which gives contentment is an expression of spiritual mastery over the lower *chakras*. Such mastery enhances love, generosity and courage. Satisfaction cannot follow if greed or fear is present. Greed and fear lead to unhappiness and restlessness. Therefore any experience of freedom in the world is spiritual. The crux is how long this new found freedom lasts. How many people retire and then complicate their lives quickly after retirement? Simplicity comes when we are free from the vicissitudes of the mind. A joyful mind leads to relaxation. No matter how unhappy a person is, they can do something positive to help change their situation.

Compared with Tony, I am now enjoying the journey more without a set worldly aspiration or target to achieve.

However, Tony's characteristics to reach the target give valuable lessons to the spiritual aspirant. The spiritual aspirant who constantly changes guru, ashram or technique, unlike Tony, will soon forget the goal and not go far. This is illustrated by the story of a fox and a cat who were friends. They had not seen each other for a while and the fox proudly told the cat that he had discovered many new ways to escape wild dogs. He proudly showed the cat all of the techniques in his notebook. At that moment they both heard the wild dogs coming. The cat ran to the top of the tree. The fox started to flip through his notepad. In spite of his friend calling him to run he became confused and could not decide which technique to follow. The wild dogs seized the moment and the cat never saw his friend again.

Both material and spiritual seekers need inspiration. Good teachers inspire. False teachers cheat their students and colleagues. Tony was inspired, but where does the inspiration come from? Writing this book has been a good example of inspiration arriving *ex nihilis*. It is unexpected and unannounced. It is intangible and yet is a vital ingredient of success which may arrive in different ways often through a series of events or meetings. My "impact" moment of inspiration regarding spirituality came after having a healing experience on my back. An unpleasant physical experience led to a pleasant spiritual experience and opened up a new world to me. During my childhood my defining moment was going to boarding school. On the one hand I was leaving an unhappy home and on the other hand I was inspired to grow up quickly through necessity.

Smiling Swami has a great saying: "Life is a little sweet and sour, we are to taste it." My boarding school experience became the foundation for self-reliance and independence, qualities which have been very important to my development. This of course is nothing compared with those children who have to shoulder adult responsibility early in their lives through tragedy or some other misfortune. There are defining moments in all of our lives that will occur whether we see them or not.

The true spiritual seeker will proceed regardless of their awareness of transformational experiences. In fact the true seeker is intent on avoiding distraction from spiritual experiences which may hinder his or her path. Distraction can be the downfall and attraction can make one fall further. With steadfast commitment problems dissolve. When fear comes, problems take over. Yet being intent on achieving something is not easy when temptations arrive, especially those that make us lazy like watching too much TV or spending too long on the internet. The path to material success seems more attainable than the path to spiritual success. This is because there are fewer role models who have achieved spiritual realisation than material success. Material success, not to be confused with people who own assets but with the loans to match, can be seen by the external demonstration of wealth, but spiritual success is hidden from view. This means there are very few realised spiritual teachers to guide us. What is common for seekers of material or spiritual success is that both need to take a leap of faith into the unknown. The consequence is that their peers or families may not understand what is taking place to their loved one because quite naturally they cannot relate to them, especially when it is a spiritual transformation. This is why the guru appears and in my case I feel fully understood and accepted unconditionally by my masters because they know what I am going through. They have taught me subtly how to remove my negative qualities and continuously emphasise my positive qualities. As I know only too well, to understand and accept others unconditionally is not easy and I have no right to expect others to do what I find hard to achieve myself. I really want to love others unconditionally and follow the example of my masters even if I fail miserably time and time again.

DIFFERENT SPIRITUAL ATTITUDES AND LESSONS

There are umpteen teachings, religions and interpretations. We also appear to have an infinite number of choices or possibilities in our lives yet I find myself on a certain path that I could not have imagined or planned. According to Smiling Swami, financial and material success were not in my astrological chart. Does that mean that my real destiny is hidden from the chart and is the result of divine grace? Is this by pure design or otherwise?

Many spiritual aspirants run after a guru yet if they find a true guru can they really follow the guru's teachings and example? It really is not so easy to do and many gurus are judged even by their disciples.

There is a story about loyalty to the guru. The guru had many disciples including a prince. The prince and the guru had a close relationship and this brought jealousy from the other students. Some thought he favoured the prince because of his position in the world. The guru knew about their jealousy so he decided to teach them all a lesson. He hid a mango under his clothes on his leg and complained to his disciples that he had an enormous infection which was very painful. They were shocked to see the size of the lump showing. He told his students that he needed a volunteer to suck out the pus as he was in so much pain. He asked who would come forward to help him. The prince immediately offered to help his "suffering" guru whilst the others shied away. The guru said that he did not want others to see his pain when the pus would be sucked out so he put a screen between him and the other students. The guru beckoned to the prince who was ready to suck out the pus only to find a mango. The guru signalled for him to eat the mango without saying anything. As the prince noisily enjoyed the mango the other students winced as they thought he was sucking out the pus instead. They thought how loyal and faithful the prince was to do this for his guru! They were no longer jealous of the prince but were filled with admiration.

SURRENDER AND EFFORT

I often discuss with Smiling Swami whether our effort really makes a difference or not. On certain levels it does but ultimately he says that if we have faith and trust in God, gurus or saints and raise our hand for help then they will lift us to the goal. Raising the hand for help is significant for me as it fits perfectly with the dictum "to do my best and God will do the rest". This is a beautiful description of surrender in the form of a helping hand. Surrender is often discussed by spiritual aspirants. As long as it remains a mental theory or process, surrender does not take place. Surrender to the Divine seems to come with knowledge and experience. Once the realisation comes that events take place for a purpose, then with understanding from experience comes direct knowledge and surrender follows naturally. Surrender and the recognition of grace seem closely connected. Not everybody needs a spiritual guru. Going direct with strong belief and faith in God is enough. Smiling Swami once observed that babies surrender to the mother in different ways. A human baby needs the mother to pick it up to feed it. The baby monkey holds onto the mother; the mother cat takes the kitten in its mouth to move it; whilst the baby kangaroo sits in the mother's pouch. These animals show us different ways of surrender. Hold on or be held. The lives of great gurus and saints often show how successful and versatile they are in their activities in the world. They act as examples of divine prototypes. Having spent time observing my masters, I have witnessed them devoting their lives day and night to others. They somehow manage to keep on top of their work without complaint and with laughter and joy.

Surrender is the final ingredient that is needed to really progress spiritually. The "bible of yoga" is called Patanjali's *Yoga Sutras*. Smiling Swami told me that the word yoga appears in it three times. The words for complete surrender are *ishwara pranidhana*. These appear four times. The only yoga mentioned in this "bible of yoga" is Kriya Yoga. Patanjali says that if we completely surrender, this is the simplest way to *samadhi*. *Samadhi* in this context is complete merger with the Divine.

Surrender can be a difficult concept to grasp. It does not mean that we have to give up everything in a material or relationship sense. As awareness increases, surrender develops naturally and realisation comes in glimpses. Surrender seems to be a by-product of spiritual maturity. As I find myself accepting more situations as they are, this openness leads to the realisation that everything will eventually pass.

Life comes and goes in perfect order even if this perfect order does not always suit my likes and dislikes.

To conclude, surrender comes through spiritual experience which leads to the realisation that I am not the doer. This should be obvious when I see how much around me I cannot influence. I now question more what the use is of being strongly attached to something which will not last. Those with no belief in God should have strong faith in themselves.

PAST LIVES

According to the scriptures known as *Garuda Purana* there are 8.4 million species on the earth and we have to experience existing as each one of them which takes place over one million years! If this is the case, what is the point of paying to see a psychic about a previous life? My change in lifestyle has shown me that time has become less important because time no longer runs my life. This does not mean that I value time less than before but I can now act more spontaneously without the need for rigid planning.

I asked Smiling Swami about previous lives as the thought came to me that they are all happening simultaneously. He told me that all lives past, present and future continue to exist and yes we even repeat them! This may explain why we sometimes have a *déjà vu* moment or meet someone who we have never met who seems familiar to us. I asked why we would want to repeat our lives again. He replied simply that we become curious and the cycle begins once more. However, he said that once we are realised we rarely go backwards. At realisation the three bodies, causal, astral and physical, are merged into the Divine. If it is the will of the Divine, a master returns with three "new" bodies with conscious memory of everything that the master has learnt or experienced previously. However they still may have physical suffering and they have all the human emotions. With regard to the guru and the disciple I questioned what happens also after realisation. He replied with a smile, "There is no guru and no disciple!"

WHEN THE MIND IS STILL
THERE IS NO FREE WILL

Smiling Swami also teaches that at the beginning of creation we have no choice or freedom and at realisation this lack of choice repeats again but "in full consciousness". I asked him whether God is really doing everything and we are really not the doer. He replied that for certain people with a similar mindset to me it was good to follow this approach but that it may not suit others. Luckily there are many religions, yogas and ways to realise our divinity, perfect for each one of us. For those of us who believe that God or some intelligence invisible to us created everything, then we should also honour and respect each other's different way to the truth. It is ironic that so many believe in God through their religion yet they refuse to accept other religions when all are praying to the same Creator. Those who do not believe in God should not be criticised because of their beliefs. True seekers and loving people give love and understanding to everyone regardless of their beliefs. My masters advocate that we can change our destiny with effort yet ultimately as the aspirant advances on the spiritual path he or she recognises that it is not his or her own destiny at all. At this stage personal ownership of karma becomes disowned even if the aspirant experiences the effects of that karma.

KEEP GOING

The path can seem very narrow, particularly for the entrepreneur and the spiritual seeker who are focussed on the goal. Nobody ever achieved anything by giving up. In *Matri Vani*, Sri Anandamayi Ma makes it clear that "endurance, endurance, endurance" are needed in life. She even uses the businessman as an example for spiritual aspirants to follow.

In the golden era of Kalinga in India in 265 BC, the respected businessman was highly revered and addressed accordingly as *Sadhava* on a par with a sadhu or a holy man of the highest esteem.

The entrepreneur has many difficulties, is constantly overloaded with problems yet he or she continues on the journey regardless of any temporary suffering. The spiritual aspirant needs the same qualities.

ACHIEVING THE GOAL

Accomplishing our goals and dreams can be very painful emotionally, physically and mentally. Knowing no limit helps, but how do we keep focussed on the goal? I managed to keep an eye on the goal of material success and remained motivated for most of the journey. However, for my spiritual journey the target is hidden with signposts appearing along the way. These pointers may appear as a spiritual experience or a meeting with somebody who has an impact on me. I have not needed to use the same work ethic or discipline to advance spiritually. It has been a natural unfolding but the effort to stay alert internally is just as important as it was in business. Although I know that calmness is the ideal state, I found it almost impossible to remain calm in the heat of battle for achievement. I channelled my restlessness to help me focus on what I wanted to achieve. I used the rajasic, "doing" energy to my advantage. When I was working, meditation became a rescue remedy which did not last all day, but every ounce of stillness helped. My life has changed totally now as my measure of a successful day is no longer how many deals have been won, but the ratio of calmness to restlessness. I am the same person, have the same body, same mind and same eyes, but with a totally different perception of life. I was used to feeling restless and on edge while working frenetically. Now I realise that peacefulness is the natural way.

DEATH OF DESIRE

I am beginning to experience the fading of desires. The seed of change is already planted and is growing inside me. I cannot stop it. When my attention is fixed on the top of my head as prescribed by the Great Master, then there is nothing to think or worry about. Everything in life becomes an event in which I am playing my role and being a neutral observer at the same time. I have noticed that as I become happier and more relaxed it highlights the restlessness of others, reminding me where I have come from.

TURNOVER

Every business needs a minimum turnover to cover the basic running costs. In order to make a profit a business needs to charge more than it takes to run it. This is a simple and basic concept, so why is it so hard to achieve?

Every spiritual seeker also needs turnover. This turnover can be defined as time spent in meditation or prayer.

Running costs, in the spiritual sense is making time available to pursue spiritual activities. This personal cost in terms of time and sacrifice is required to avoid the constant allure and distraction of the outside world. Some sincere seekers work just enough to give them time to meditate or to go on spiritual retreats. Spiritual turnover increases from investments in attending retreats or by spending time in the company of a realised master. More silence leads to greater spiritual turnover. When I worked I spared whatever time I could each day to maintain myself spiritually and invested holiday time to see the masters mentioned in this book.

As mentioned, both the entrepreneur and the spiritual seeker need to continue when it seems that nothing is happening or when no progress appears to be made. It is similar to the gardener who watches his vegetables grow. Sometimes vegetables hardly seem to grow or remain as seeds under the surface, but then a surge of growth occurs. Growth seems to be uneven from a human viewpoint, although I doubt that this is the case from a divine viewpoint. I feel that my growth is measured, uniform and perfect whatever my mind or others may tell me. Often growth happens without much apparent change but it must be nurtured. A strong will and a clear goal are essential. Proceeding towards a positive outcome will more than likely fail without these ingredients. Hard work in any field requires concentration and often bloody mindedness. If I believe that life is always tough then it will feel that way even if it is not. I follow the edict that everything is simple when you know how. I just need to know how.

On my business journey there was certainly pain. Too much work and pressure led to adrenal burnout, but like a trained soldier I transcended the pain, meeting different hurdles and challenges head on. Overcoming discomfort was crucial and somehow I managed to keep my focus and remember the goal. I have no doubt that my business life with its ups and downs has made me better prepared for my spiritual journey.

The reward of early retirement in exchange for hard work made the effort worthwhile. However, when I reached the goal of financial freedom, I did not feel ecstasy. I felt very level-headed and balanced. I was never interested in power, social position or self-glory. Material gain gives us the chance to enjoy the fruits of greater freedom although I am sure that the fruits of spiritual success will give us far more freedom. Internal liberation leads to real external liberation.

What about feelings?

Feelings and emotions at boarding school or at work often needed to be checked. In one way I was too busy to wallow in self-pity or to think about discomfort, but without meditation I would have sunk and failed. It acted as a support and anchor. Uncannily, it arrived at just the right moment as the business started growing and the stress levels increased. As various spiritual experiences occurred I saw that there was more to life than just making money. It gave me a balanced perspective even though I did not always feel balanced.

So what was the real purpose in making money? When I said goodbye to the Great Master after our first meeting, he told me that I needed money for my liberation. I did not know what he meant at the time but I can now see how the grace of making money has bought me the freedom to engage and focus more on the inner world. To live without asking the fundamental question as to why I am really here was alien to me before my spiritual experiences, however now I cannot imagine not asking that question. What about you?

FEAR OF DEATH

Fear of death must rank highest on the list of human fears. Many people are even afraid to make a will because they dare not think about their own death. I am not afraid of death. However, why should I believe masters or scriptures or religions that proclaim that I continue to live after the death of the physical body? People view death differently. I once went on a charity trek to the Sinai desert where I met another David who suffered throughout the whole trip with a prolapsed disc. He travelled by jeep and camel and was in intense pain but he managed to smile and joke through his suffering. I called him recently after years of not speaking to him only to discover that he was dying of untreatable cancer from asbestos-poisoning. He passed away shortly after our conversation. In spite of his suffering his attitude was still upbeat and down to earth. He told me he had enjoyed a good life, a successful career and a beautiful wife and family. He was not unhappy and he was ready to go. I was humbled by his attitude.

I admire any person like David who, close to death, keeps smiling with their dignity intact. If we adopt an attitude of living in the present does that attitude continue when death comes? Smiling Swami once observed that when we are born the baby cries and others are filled with joy. He asks whether at death we will be smiling when others are crying? So what is my attitude to death? When the time of my death arrives, if I have warning I hope that I can be peaceful and joyful calm. I am interested to see how it will be. There is no need to be afraid of a process which is natural. I am more afraid of scientists who want to genetically modify my food or spray a cocktail of chemicals on the fruit and vegetables that I am eating. Something tells me that cannot be good for me.

WHO AM I?

Being conscious of the soul helps me to realise that I am more than just a physical body with a mind and feelings. The key is for the mind and body to be still in order to feel this unity. I am optimistic that real knowledge will come before my death. I am reassured by this consciousness of Soul or God within me and it seems quite logical also. As I sense this more, my feeling of separation from God is less. When I lose myself in true consciousness the real change and inspiration comes.

I once heard the expression that, "The mind will set you free." It is easy to misunderstand what is meant here. A more appropriate saying would be, "No mind will set you free." This does not mean stupidity or lack of intellect, but rather leaving our conditioning behind. Meditation has taken me to a place where "someone" which is "me" is witnessing events as if "I" am in a movie. I do not identify with David the individual in meditation. Sometimes I lose consciousness and hours pass by but it seems like seconds. The reason I know it is not sleep is because I am also practising techniques before losing awareness, and I am not snoring! When I regain awareness my first thought is to resume the techniques. In that state I lose sense of my identity, surroundings and time. Afterwards I sometimes have a spacey feeling of being drugged but it is different because I feel light, refreshed and lucid. At other times I am restless and cannot meditate for long but this occurs less and less.

Returning to the topic of destiny, I can be relaxed and happy for months on end and then suddenly I feel agitated without any obvious cause. For example, restlessness often occurs just before a full moon or a new moon when there is no moon visible in the sky. I have observed to my surprise that this does actually happen. This is due to the moon affecting us because of the large water content in the body and brain in the same way the moon affects the tides in the ocean. In Sanskrit there is a saying: *saha asti anya iti* which means "the moon is the Lord of the Mind". I could argue that I will only meditate if it is my destiny to do so. If this is the case then I am happy with my destiny. I am also more aware of the grace of God when things are difficult or things are going well. The Great Master gave me the Kriya Yoga meditation technique which I consider to be grace. I also thank God when I bang my head now which for some reason seems to take place at key moments when I visit holy places! A subtle or not so subtle wake-up call perhaps. Meditation helps when things are going smoothly and I thank the universe with joy and gratitude for the provision of my good fortune. In contrast when things are not going so well it is better to lie low and to be as inactive and detached as possible. If I did not have this awareness then when things were going well I would take all the credit and when things were going badly I would conveniently blame someone else!

Reflections

When I worked I was able to overcome the stream of thoughts, and focus on the job at hand which was a form of controlled calmness as opposed to natural calmness. But I was never taught at school or by anybody else how to calm my mind. If parents or teachers could teach their children that peace and contentment are internal rather than external then I am sure the world would be a happier and more peaceful place. But do parents and teachers know how to achieve this state themselves? Agitated people are not calm inside and calm people are rarely agitated outside. Calm people stand out because of their rarity.

Working crazily whilst meditating for the last eleven years of my career, showed me the stark contrast between daily life at work and my spiritual practice. I am becoming more aware of the Great Master's teaching that everything is spiritual. There is no separation between materialism and spirituality. This teaching impacted on me and I am becoming more aware of this truth gradually. When I see two separate worlds, it is only due to my ignorance. Spiritual masters call this veil of ignorance or illusion, *maya*. *Maya* hides the truth. The Great Master would declare loudly, pointing his finger at me, "You are not you. You are the real You!" Many schools of thought purport that to realise our divinity, be enlightened or conscious we need to give up our desires and go beyond *maya*. Yet we need desire to desire this also.

Perhaps we are given desire to fulfil our destiny and nothing more. Desire may remain unfulfilled and restlessness will result unless the desire is fulfilled or drops away. On a human level the desire to push myself was inbuilt yet to proceed spiritually I am beginning to question the benefit of constantly manifesting all desires as one desire can lead to another. What is the path to eternal and nontransitory peace and love?

As I spend more time not working in a busy environment, I reflect on what really has value to me. Twenty years ago my first answer would have been money. Now my answer is love and kindness. I do not think I have developed a new trait but in the busyness of the world there is less time to consciously develop these qualities which are inherent in all of us. Love helps me proceed spiritually. It just might take a long time in my case. However this does not mean that I give myself a hard time when I slip up. I am on a spiritual trip so sometimes I will trip up! I met someone in New Zealand who was very unhappy. He told me that he was a victim of life and always had been. I was shocked. If I do not love and accept myself then how can I express this love to others and how can I expect others to love me? My mission is not to become a narcissist but to be happy inside. Those who crave happiness externally can never be satisfied so to continue to run after it just masks the unhappiness inside. One day either through old age, deteriorating health or death, everyone will have to slow down. At that moment the true inner state will reveal itself as misery or joy. The constant search for external happiness can only end in internal unhappiness.

UNDERSTANDING A MASTER

A master or a guru has a human body. They can experience disease, hunger and pain like anybody else. True masters do not sit on a pedestal even if their devotees through love put them on one. Smiling Swami says of the Great Master that he saw him in the "human" form doing what we do, but he was always aware of the Great Master's flow of divinity. Another monk once said to me that the longer he knew the Great Master, the less he understood him, the more he loved him.

GREAT MASTER STORIES

I heard many stories about the Great Master. One monk told me that in the days before email he received a letter from him. It had been sent six weeks earlier and the letter told him to contact his mother as she had been taken ill. On the evening of the letter's arrival, he had news that his mother was unwell. How could he have known? Another time the same monk picked the first mango from the tree at the ashram in India. He mentally offered it with thanks and devotion to the Great Master before eating it. A week later he received a letter from the Great Master telling him how much he had enjoyed the mango that had been offered to him.

LET'S TALK ABOUT LOVE

If I visited this planet for the first time and observed what type of love was demonstrated and projected in the world by the media and on the internet, what would I see?

LOVE of money;

LOVE of power;

LOVE of sex;

LOVE of assets: cars and houses;

LOVE of glamour: beauty, fame, vanity;

LOVE of alcohol, overeating, drugs;

LOVE of gambling;

LOVE of violence;

LOVE of disputes and disagreements;

LOVE of scandal, theft, dishonesty;

LOVE of anger, pride, cruelty and jealousy.

Can you disagree with me? If we look in the mirror and ask if we love what we have or what others have what would be our answer? If the above topics were removed from the news or media, what would be left? The poisoned love projected in the media is probably only 1% of the true love in the world. The 99% of real love in the world is manifested every moment by those who help others when they are in need, care for those who have disease or pain and suffering, act selflessly and bravely to save another person, show acts of kindness and generosity. True love is loving someone without condition or thought or criticism. Real love is unconditional and goodness is within all of us. Even the thief will kiss his wife and children before going to work. Surely some thieves change to a more honest profession. Our small acts of smiling at someone including when I look at myself in the mirror is a good start. Stroking an animal or giving up my seat for another person are all small acts of kindness. Small acts become big acts. So it is my choice which love I want to demonstrate that will bring myself and others more peace. Contentment is possible but not if I am intoxicated by the love that is portrayed in the media.

So what do the gurus teach? Give more love!!! This is refreshing compared to everyday love in the world which the Great Master referred to as the "kiss and kick" approach. So how to give more love when we do not always feel loving? Faking it is not the way. If we cannot give love, we can at least remain neutral and not cause pain to a fellow human being. Unconditional love will hopefully develop more within me. I am also learning to receive love from others more. What is clear to me is that the happier and calmer I am within myself, the easier it is to love others unconditionally. If I am happier, then I will also be more loving to myself and will treat my mind and body with more love and respect.

There are many ways to demonstrate unconditional love. For example, the world would be a far more beautiful place if we all smiled at strangers on public transport without them thinking the person smiling at them is deranged. It would also increase happiness in the world if when we felt anger instead of opening our mouths we stopped for a moment before reacting. Simple activities such as opening the door for a stranger or planting some flowers or herbs in a small pot might also bring more joy. These all may seem trivial "valueless" activities but the more we do them the more joy comes.

My masters demonstrate unconditional love and give help to others without expecting anything back even if they are criticised. They continue to give regardless of the result. It seems that I have a long way to go on the path of enlightenment.

This is how Smiling Swami describes love:

"Love is the state of completeness and calmness. Love is the state of contentment through a feeling of oneness. Love is complete surrender and ultimately the state of total absorption. Very few people know the art of loving in silence.

Love is patient. It does not take account of time. It is immersed in a state of timelessness. Love fortifies one with inner strength and patience to reach the goal of spiritual life. Only a person who is patient can reach the state of cosmic consciousness.

Love brings forth acceptance. In love there is no expectation. Love is based on faith and trust. Love increases as faith becomes stronger. Where there is love there is no doubt. Manifest love constantly while speaking, looking, listening and working. Nothing is impossible when we overflow with love. Life itself becomes complete.

Love is not attachment. Grow in detachment and understanding. There is no yardstick for measuring love.

Love is beyond all comparison and even comprehension. Love is infinite. Love is immeasurable. Let life be complete by merging in the ocean of love."

(An extract from *Kriya Yoga in the Flow of Omniscience*)

MY EXPERIENCE OF LOVE

A beautiful way to experience love is through relationships. These words once came to me:

LOVE is when you tell your partner what you have never told anyone before.

LOVE is when you hold your partner's hand behind your back in a special way.

LOVE is when you walk and talk together and look in your partner's eyes and you want to kiss them.

LOVE is when you can share intimate moments.

LOVE is when you can dance with your partner for hours on end.

LOVE is when you are in your partner's arms and feel safe.

LOVE is when you think of your partner and talk about them when they are not with you.

LOVE is when you tell your partner that you should be going with them when they leave you.

LOVE is when you can share the good and the bad without fear.

LOVE is when you can trust your partner with everything.

LOVE is when your partner makes you happy and laugh without you doing anything.

LOVE is when your partner tells you everything will be alright.

LOVE is when your partner surprises you and spoils you.

LOVE is when your partner is there for you rain or shine.

LOVE is when your partner understands and takes care of you and you can cry on their shoulder when life is tough.

LOVE flows unconditionally when nothing is expected in return.

LOVE ebbs and flows in its own way without thought.

LOVE makes everything possible.

LOVE overcomes all negatives.

LOVE like this is rare between two people.

LOVE is stronger than doubt and fear.

Never be afraid to LOVE or LOVE to be afraid.

What is a life without LOVE?

COMPASSIONATE LOVE

I remember being in Spain with a friend in her villa. I witnessed a beautiful episode of unconditional love. A young cat arrived that was hardly strong enough to stand. My friend started feeding the cat. I questioned the long-term wisdom of her actions as we were leaving in ten days time and the cat would be left again without food. I wondered whether it was selfish to befriend and feed the cat and then abandon it. She argued that if the cat had ten more good days in her life, then that was better than not having any at all. Her reply made me reflect. Her attitude was so loving and refreshing. The following week we went home and left the cat to its own devices. The next guests renting her villa fell in love with the cat so much so that they took it home with them. I learnt a humbling lesson that sincere love works in mysterious ways.

LOVE & JOY

If our purpose is to be loving and joyful, do we really know what that means? How often do our habits end in suffering, pain or disease? If balance can be found in our lives then surely a happier result will follow by sitting in that calm place inside. Meditation is the catalyst for this peace. Once this state of satisfaction is felt and becomes part of us then the need to seek happiness through overindulgence fades away. The outside search turns to the inside when the fruitlessness of searching and enjoying outside becomes unsatisfying and even mundane. We can fool ourselves that someone or something is making us unhappy, but ultimately nobody has that power. We cannot create permanent happiness by maxing out on rich food, sex, alcohol, drugs or spending money that we have not even earned. Yet this is the path or aspiration of many. Wallowing in sadness and self-pity and then seeking temporary respite through bad habits can never be the answer. Those who want to eradicate temporary happiness and replace it with more permanent happiness could meditate. After twelve months of sincere practice it will become impossible to give up, provided the seeker has an authentic technique and a loving teacher. In a similar vain, the search for love from someone else is futile when analysed properly. Changing ourselves and being good to ourselves attracts more love inside and attracts others to us. Telling others to change because we do not look at ourselves is not a recipe for happiness. Smiling Swami advises us "not to fall in love but to rise in love!" So long as I seek happiness over and over again outside of the "real" me, then the inside will continue to suffer.

Love is the real key to happiness, power and strength. If we can love others without expectation or the thought of reward then the real growth begins.

COURAGE

As our journey together in this book nears its end, I would like to leave you with a story I heard about courage. I am humbly praying that courage finds you when you need it the most. The story is about courage, fear, bravery and intelligence.

A hungry lion was walking through the forest. He spotted a goat. The goat saw the lion approaching and knew he was on the lion's lunch menu! The goat decided he had nothing to lose so he stood on his two back feet and growled as loudly as he could when the lion approached. The lion had seen many goats who were always afraid and on four legs, but became unsure what type of animal this was. This animal looked like a goat but was showing no fear. As the lion approached, in his loudest voice the goat asked the lion where he had been as he was hungry and wanted to eat the lion for lunch! The lion became afraid and ran away.

On his hasty retreat the lion came across a jackal who could see the lion was quivering with fear. The jackal had never seen a scared lion before, so he asked him what had happened. The lion told him that he had escaped from being eaten by a strange animal that he had never seen before. The jackal became curious as he knew every animal in the jungle. He calmed the lion down and persuaded him they should go back together so he could discover what type of animal could make a lion afraid. The lion said he would only agree if the jackal tied himself to his tail as he did not want the jackal to run away. They approached the goat. The goat thought his luck may have run out this time but decided to be brave again. Puffing out his chest, he stood up on his hind legs, looked straight into the lion's eyes and boldly declared, "Mr Jackal, I am glad to see you again. Thank you for bringing me a lion to eat for lunch yesterday and I see that you have brought me another one today." The lion did not stick around and ran off with the jackal hanging on for dear life!

Be a courageous warrior on your path to success.

EPILOGUE

In the final chapter of this book, I ended with a story about courage. The more faith we have in our own ability, the more courage and love arrives from the Invisible Hand to help us to face up to our troubles that look impossible to solve.

What happened in Egypt, the story of which I am about to finish, left me full of courage, faith and love for God. When you also come across a difficult moment in your life in whatever form that may take, I pray that something good comes to you and help from the Invisible Hand arrives just when you need it. Love, courage and faith are the antidote to fear, doubt and suffering.

THE GREAT PYRAMID AWAITS

Many tales have been written about the Great Pyramid. I do not for a moment profess to know which, if any, are true. Mainstream Egyptologists, historians and academics are adamant that thousands of slaves built it with pulleys and ropes, while some suggest that man possessed anti-gravity technology which we have yet to rediscover. The fact of the matter is that I needed only to go inside and around the Great Pyramid to know that I was witnessing and experiencing one of the great wonders and mystical places in the world.

During the trip, we were not only being spiritually prepared for our visit to the Great Pyramid, but we also learned a great deal of fascinating Egyptian history. Our guide, whom Dan had dreamt about and then contacted when we arrived, took us to the Cairo museum where we saw Tutankhamen and even a 3,000-year-old gearbox!

He told us that scientists had evidence that the pyramids and the Sphinx were more than 5,000 years older than is generally thought. I wondered whether to give these stories any credence. Then I thought about how often that I automatically believe events reported in the media which later are proved to be false. Many stories that seem bizarre, unlikely or impossible, turn out regardless of what others insist to be the case, to be true. It is possible to have an open mind without being credulous.

On the evening of our visit to the Great Pyramid, I had showered and changed and was ready for the off. I sat quietly on the balcony observing this huge pyramid looming over me ominously on the horizon. I was, as so many before me have been, awestruck by its huge and powerful presence. Our hotel was situated close by. It was a breath-taking sight. Once again, spontaneously, without any encouragement, I was conscious that the Light was flowing through me. Although I had no idea what lay ahead of me, I was being filled with light and courage. It was as if I was being activated by some higher power. How had I, a run of the mill business-man, ended up here? Joy who was generally not sensitive to different energies, was on edge. She told me she felt like "a cat on a hot tin roof". She could not put her finger on it but she had an uncanny feeling that something dramatic and power-ful was about to happen. Not wanting to intensify whatever anxiety she was feeling, I decided not to say anything to her about our group being infiltrated by the Acharnin.

Before setting off all of us, except for the Acharnin in the group, congregated in Dan's room. We all tried to relax and centre ourselves but there was a palpable, uncomfortable edge in the air. Dan was very quiet, looking focussed, intense and concentrated. He explained that he had been combating some unwelcome energies during the whole trip. We all meditated together. In the moments that followed we exchanged a few words and some of us talked of a shared feeling that a new and exciting experience was awaiting us, while others, without knowing why, expressed a certain nervousness.

Finally, it was time to leave for the Great Pyramid. It was two hours before midnight. Once on the bus, we all sat quietly. I closed my eyes and allowed my thoughts to flow silently inside my head. The bus suddenly jolted to a halt on the unlit road. Our guide stepped off to be welcomed by several armed guards. Ten minutes passed as he struggled to negotiate our entrance into the restricted area which he finally accomplished thanks to some forceful words and a briefcase stuffed with banknotes. As he got back onto the bus he shouted, "Yalla, yalla!" signalling the driver to move on to the Great Pyramid. I stared ahead in awe of the mighty edifice looming straight in front of us. We had reached our destination.

In the still of the night the full moon directed the way ahead as the shadow of the Great Pyramid engulfed us, drawing us into its dark, silent beauty. We clambered up the rocks to gain entrance to the pyramid where two more guards greeted us. The two main Acharnin who had infiltrated our group from the start of the trip hung back with the last few people off the bus. The rest of us filed slowly towards the narrow entrance in single file, our shadows apparent in the bright moonlight. We did not have long to prepare for the midnight hour.

The climb up through the centre of the Great Pyramid was arduous, and I felt my legs ache as I moved ever onwards and upwards. We had to crouch to avoid the low rock ceiling as we clambered up the steep wooden staircase. A few bare light bulbs helped us navigate our way. As we climbed, the passage grew ever shorter and narrower, slowing our pace as we edged step by step towards the top. The bitter taste of dust filled my mouth. All the time I felt the presence of the Invisible Hand – the atmosphere was smouldering with anticipation. The Light was purifying me, filling me with more strength. We finally reached the King's Chamber at the top of the Great Pyramid and squeezed through its narrow entrance. The chamber warmed up as we removed our shoes and surrounded the sarcophagus, a large open empty tomb. But something did not feel right. My stomach was gripped, tied up in a knot of anxiety. I felt out of sorts and the thought came to me whether I should be here in this chamber or somewhere else.

As we prepared for whatever was in store for us – in fact I had no idea what was going to take place – Dan, aware of what the Acharnin may be planning, asked if everybody was happy to stay in the chamber. No one spoke up. He asked again. Something tugged inside me. I was needed elsewhere. I stepped forward and was then followed by Elisha who felt the same uncanny sensation as me. Dan later told me that he would have gone himself if nobody had volunteered. We set out to find the Acharnin to check if our companions Françoise and Lionel were with them. We quickly slipped on our shoes and headed down the centre of the Great Pyramid not knowing where to go. We sped down the poorly lit staircase focussed only on the Light.

We had been descending for perhaps five minutes when we came to an opening on our right. We saw a dim light emanating from a passage that was deep underground.

We decided that they had to be down there. As we moved further down, the tunnel became narrow and we were forced to crawl on our knees as we headed towards the opening. As we were about to enter, Joanna, one of the Acharnin, appeared and asked for us to wait in the passage to let them finish their ceremony. We looked into the chamber and saw that Françoise and Lionel were standing there, motionless. Some type of dark ritual was taking place. The leader of the Acharnin, with her piercing blue eyes and curly blonde hair was speaking softly, summoning the forces of darkness while facing Françoise and Lionel, whose eyes were closed. They seemed to be in some kind of trance. Joanna, a quiet, intro-verted woman was sitting on the floor. Without exchanging a word, Elisha and I knew that we had to do something and quickly. They were taking part in a conversion ritual. We began to call quietly on the Invisible Hand to help combat the dark energies which had been summoned. The effect was instant. Joanna was now squirming on the floor, becoming increasingly uncomfortable as the Light began to confront her. She started to cry. The Light was penetrat-ing the Darkness. It was time to go into the chamber. We had no plan, guidelines or experience. It was a leap into the unknown, but a leap that we had to make.

As we entered, we could see the leader embracing Françoise and Lionel. Were we already too late? Had they been taken over to the dark side? We needed to intervene at once, to make them aware quickly that there was a choice between the paths of darkness and of light. The leader of the Acharnin turned towards us, glaring with menace and anger, but I felt fully protected and she knew it. She could not touch me. I was not afraid. Without hesitating, we brushed past her and she retreated. We faced Françoise and Lionel who were standing motionless in the middle of the room. Lionel stared straight ahead of me, his eyes vacant, seemingly unaware of my presence or even his own. He was clearly in some kind of unconscious state. He had been possessed. He was alive but almost lifeless – his energy had been drawn out of him. A dead look from his eyes passed through me. Elisha stood in front of Françoise who also appeared chillingly lifeless. All the time we continued to summon the Light, the calls increasing in volume, urgency and intensity. I felt an enormous heat building up in my chest. I felt no fear, only the intense urgency of purpose to bring them back into consciousness. Light was pouring through us towards them. Elisha told me later how she had been conscious at that time of invisible dark hands encircling Françoise's throat.

Joanna, the quieter of the Acharnin, began to writhe and scream on the floor, possessed, sobbing as the Light flowed around and through her. Her body was being moved erratically by some dark force holding onto her like a rag doll. Unable to stand the intensity of the light, the leader of the Acharnin fled from the room and stood just outside of the chamber entrance. Would Lionel and Françoise follow her? She called them to join her. Had they been initiated as instruments of the dark forces or had we intervened in time? For a moment Françoise seemed to edge a fraction forward and looked on the point of following the leader, but somehow her feet just would not carry her. Elisha began to move her hands around Françoise without touching her. Light was pouring through her into Françoise's motionless body. Lionel beckoned with his hand for me to be quiet but I was not about to be a silent spectator. My hands were near him vibrating with energy and light. His eyes were still glazed over with a dark, vacant, dead look, yet shining in the dimly lit chamber. He continued to look straight ahead and was clearly becoming agitated by my presence. But his feet could not move – it was as if he had been stuck firmly into the ground. He was possessed but the Light was mysteriously holding him there and I was not budging. If they wanted to leave they would have to make the conscious choice to walk around us. They were faced with the starkest of choices: the Darkness or the Light?

The leader of the Acharnin still remained in the tunnel unwilling and unable to enter inside the chamber which was filled with Light, and again called the three inside the chamber to follow her. Joanna's high-pitched screams increased to fever pitch. The Light was challenging her to stay also and despite her discomfort she did not have the will to move her limp body outside.

Time had stood still. My throat was burning dry, the dust mingling with the sweat on my skin. But nothing was going to upset my concentration. Discomfort meant nothing. It did not even exist. Eventually Françoise gestured for silence and we followed her wishes. The screams turned into whimpers. The air was electric and humming in the Light.

Then as if in a trance, Françoise began to speak, the pitch of her voice eerily low. She was in a dreamlike state and started to describe her vision, almost trying to take us with her. But every word she spoke with a positive she countered with a negative. A battle was underway within her between darkness and light. Her words were garbled, incomprehensible. I remained silent, but I knew that my focus on the Light was vital. Throughout this bizarre episode, I still felt no fear. Fear is too afraid to show itself where the Light shines!

Finally Françoise finished speaking, and as she and Lionel regained full consciousness the four of us hugged in the Light. The darkness had been forced out of them. At that point the leader finally summoned up the courage to re-enter the chamber. She came a few feet inside and, showing no trace of emotion, pulled the bedraggled Joanna off the floor. She looked at us contemptuously and sneered, "The Light is always victorious!" Perhaps with these words she was already leaving the door ajar for her own long journey back into the Light. Even those following the path of darkness could truly be forgiven – such is the true power of the Light.

Françoise and Lionel gradually regained their senses but even days later they could hardly recollect what had actually taken place. We rejoined the remainder of the group upstairs in the King's Chamber and all took part in a blessing and prayer for the planet. I felt a profound sense of relief and also an ecstasy that I had never previously experienced. Everyone was glowing in the freedom of the Light.

The Invisible Hand had been with me every step of the way. It always has been with me and always will be. I had been a witness but also somehow a participant in a series of incidents that were inexpressibly intense but were and remain all but incomprehensible. My business life would continue, but after returning home from Egypt it was clear that I had undergone a profound transformation. I might have seemed the same to my friends and colleagues, but I could never go back to how, to who I was before; my consciousness and outlook could never be the same again.

But I experienced no anxiety, no regret and still no fear. I felt liberated. My inner confidence expanded beyond anything I had ever known or thought possible. The Light was shining within me. I had been given a glimpse of something intangible, but very real and I wanted, needed to know more. There was no turning back.

THE LIGHT OF THE MASTER
IS NEVER EXTINGUISHED

In November 2002, I said goodbye to Baba, the Great Master for the last time before he passed away. "Baba" is an affectionate term used often in India literally meaning "father" commonly used when addressing distinguished men or elders. "You are alright," were the final words he said to me. I never saw him again.

I did not hear those words until five years later in Calcutta when I was sitting in front of a cheerful guru who wore glasses and spoke softly moving his hands just like Baba. Three of us had come to visit him. After a few hours we took our leave. He smiled at me knowingly. He held my hands, looked into my eyes and said "You are alright!" Perhaps all gurus are truly one.

I was lucky enough like many others to be given much time and attention by Baba in the four years leading up to his death. Whenever I came to Miami he would see me privately every day. If I missed a day he would ask me the next day why I had not come to him. He was so amusing and we joked and laughed a lot together. Everyone has their own special relationship with the master. However some were really afraid to approach or speak to him. He was quite strict with a few people and gentle as a lamb with others. Perhaps he reflected the way we were with him. I felt informal and relaxed but respectful at the same time.

One day an odd question came to me. I asked if he had been with me before I came here. "Yes," he said. Have you been with me since I was younger? "Yes!" he said a little louder. Have you been with me since birth? "Yeeesss!" Really I was amazed and yet unsurprised at the same time. My body shuddered involuntarily as he answered. Who was this Great Master and what was my connection with him?

I WOULD NEVER HEAR THE GREAT MASTER SAY "SPEAK" AGAIN.

On 3rd December 2002 we received the news that Baba had "left the body" to go into the state of *mahasamadhi*. *Mahasamadhi* is the description given in India of a realised yogi who leaves his physical body for the "Great Sleep". Only the physical body is asleep. The true formless guru is alive and everywhere.

After we heard the news I lay down on my bed and lit a candle in front of Baba's picture. I felt his invisible presence. It was midnight in London. Before I went to sleep I asked Baba mentally to keep the candle burning until I woke up. It was a small tea candle. When I awoke six hours later I had forgotten about this "inner" request. I looked up from the bedcovers and my eyes gazed towards the candle. The flame flickered and at that exact moment it went out.

ACKNOWLEDGEMENTS

So many have inspired me with their love, faith and encouragement, especially my father. I am also grateful to the lineage of Kriya Yoga masters and my master Baba who has lovingly steered me towards a spiritual life. I have been gently cajoled to write and share my story by Paramahamsa Prajnanananda Giri, the current master of Kriya Yoga who is the smartest, funniest and the most humble loving person I have ever met.

My real appreciation to my invaluable part time editors, in particular Michael Mannion, and to my professional editor Karl French – a firm agnostic on his first read of *The Invisible Hand* who now meditates. Living like yogis we worked fifteen hour days to polish the final version, laughing, meditating and teasing each other about our grasp or otherwise of the Queen's English. I also received great advice from Tony Booth, Margot Borden and lastly from Joan Watson, who saw the vision of the book even before I met her.

Finally my sincere thanks and gratitude to Prajna Publications and Prajnana Mission who have kindly given me permission to quote from their books and materials.

THE GURUS WHO HAVE HELPED ME GREATLY IN MY LIFE

The Great Master:	Paramahamsa Hariharananda Giri	www.kriya.org
Smiling Swami:	Paramahamsa Prajnanananda Giri	www.kriya.org
Hugging Mother:	Sri Mata Amritanandamayi	www.amma.org
Silent Mother:	Mother Meera	www.mothermeera.com

ABOUT THE AUTHOR

David Green went straight from school to work for one of the oldest merchant banks in the City of London. His career progressed quickly and he went on to work for other substantial financial organisations in asset finance and Eurobond trading. He started his own finance house at the age of 23 and built a niche company until it was sold. David retired in 2006 when he was 42 and now lives in Guernsey in the Channel Islands. He has practised meditation for eighteen years and is involved with charity work in India.

If you enjoyed reading *The Invisible Hand*, then please post a review with the bookseller where you purchased the book.

To keep in touch with David please visit
www.the-invisiblehand.com

CPSIA information can be obtained at www.ICGtesting.com
Printed in the USA
LVOW12s0328250414

383199LV00014B/393/P